DESIGNING
AND CONDUCTING
YOUR FIRST
INTERVIEW PROJECT

Bruce K. Friesen

JOSSEY-BASS
A Wiley Imprint
www.josseybass.com

Published by Jossey-Bass
A Wiley Imprint
989 Market Street, San Francisco, CA 94103-1741—www.josseybass.com

Jossey-Bass books and products are available through most bookstores. To contact Jossey-Bass directly call our Customer Care Department within the U.S. at 800-956-7739, outside the U.S. at 317-572-3986, or fax 317-572-4002.

Jossey-Bass also publishes its books in a variety of electronic formats. Some content that appears in print may not be available in electronic books.

Library of Congress Cataloging-in-Publication Data
Friesen, Bruce K., date.
  Designing and conducting your first interview project/Bruce K. Friesen.
    p. cm.
  Includes bibliographical references and index.
  ISBN 978-0-470-18351-9 (pbk.)
  1. Social sciences—Research.   2. Interviewing.   I. Title.
  H62.F745 2010
  300.72'3—dc22

                                                            2009054229

Printed in the United States of America
FIRST EDITION
PB Printing   10 9 8 7 6 5 4 3 2 1

CONTENTS

EXHIBITS, FIGURES, AND TABLES

For Brittany and Justin

PREFACE

This book aims, above all, to teach excitement through the joy of discovery. It is my contention that students *learn* more from doing than from listening or reading alone. Whether in a class of eight or eight hundred, students need to be given opportunities to kinetically explore the craft of sociology. Activity, accompanied by guided reflection and positive affect, stimulates engagement, internalization, inquisitiveness, and the search for answers. Through this semester-long project, students will taste what it feels like to *do* deductive social science. They'll search the peer-reviewed literature, form a class hypothesis, and develop the project from conceptualization to operationalization. They'll perform a handful of interviews, enter data into computers, and produce and analyze the results. They'll walk out of your class with a semester full of *experiences* on which to reflect.

This book is a part of the paradigmatic shift taking place in how college courses are being taught. A burgeoning interdisciplinary, empirically based literature on the science of college teaching has been revolutionizing the traditional college course (see, for example, Bain, 2004; Brookfield, 1995; Fink, 2003; Finkel, 2000; McKeachie, 2005; McKinney, 2007; and Weimar 2002). Lecture-based courses are being modified to include more group discussion, case studies, student presentations, peer-to-peer instruction, dialogue, and active learning projects. Radical new perspectives, defining teaching as a form of scholarship (Boyer, 1997), have been adopted by institutions of higher education and are being integrated into the institutional reward structures for the professoriate. Full- and part-time instructors are shifting focus from a science of *teaching* to a science of *learning*. There is good reason for this sea change: active learning strategies produce a more sustained, substantial, and positive impact on how students think, act, and feel. (I am indebted to Bain, 2004, for this definition of learning.)

DEVELOPMENT

This project has gone through several iterations, having been used consistently with Introduction to Sociology classes over the past twenty years. It's been refined though use with classes as small as twelve students and as large as 330. When executed well, the project teaches the joy of discovery through deductive social science. Students are presented with the notion that their perceptions of the social world are not always what they seem to be, which invokes a teachable moment that challenges students to ask themselves questions related to knowing. Asking questions is the first step in developing the mind of a scientist.

An enhanced version of this project has also been used with success in Research Methods classes for the past four years. Chapters Eleven and Twelve contain information specifically for use in upper-division classes. These chapters empower students to perform computer-assisted data analysis, thus familiarizing them with decisions affecting validity and reliability that must be made at every step of the process. Motivated to work through the problems in order to test their hypotheses and complete the project, students gain mastery in the logic and technique of computer data entry and analysis. That these are marketable skills goes without saying.

In addition to twenty years of use and revision, the development of the book form of this project was tested successfully with a group of Introductory to Sociology students in the summer of 2009. Five reviewers also gave invaluable input. The version you hold in your hands is much improved as a result.

ORGANIZATION

The book is organized according to the steps of the deductive scientific method. Essential to the success of this project are a few activities that take place during class after the appropriate chapter has been read. Further suggestions for course organization are available in the instructor's resources on the book's website. The first chapter introduces students to the process of choosing a topic, after which the class collectively decides on a topic to research. Chapter Two teaches students how to conduct a small literature review and how to distinguish empirical articles from others in peer-reviewed journals. Chapters Three and Four give students some practice in thinking about issues of conceptualization, theory development, and articulation of a hypothesis.

Chapters Five, Six, and Seven expose students to critical issues in research design, applying it to the class interview project yet to come. Chapters Eight and Nine are what amounts to interviewer training for the students, teaching them to be as systematic and as ethical as possible. Instructors will want to review these concepts in class the day they hand out the blank interview forms to students. It is the instructor who ultimately creates a brief, one-page, two-sided interview schedule to distribute to students. Students in turn interview enough of their peers so that the class as a whole completes at least two hundred interviews. Incidentally, many universities and colleges do not require full approval by an institutional review board for pedagogical projects of this nature. Be sure to check the policies at your own institution.

Chapter Ten instructs students on how to enter their interview data into a computer using SPSS. After cleaning the data, students submit their files in electronic form to the instructor, who in turn compiles all of the data into a master data file. Having students enter data greatly enhances their knowledge of the research process and decreases the amount of work an instructor would otherwise do. If desired, though, instructors can instead choose to enter the class interviews on their own and have students skip this chapter.

Chapters Eleven and Twelve are best used only with students enrolled in upper-division classes such as Research Methods. The chapters contain instructions on how to collapse variables, create simple composite variables using the Count or Compute command, and produce frequency and cross-tabulation tables using SPSS.

Chapter Thirteen informs students how to interpret a cross-tabulation table so they can decide whether or not the data support their class hypothesis. The chapter also covers the logic of controlling for a third variable and how to interpret tables produced through table elaboration. Included in the chapter are instructions on how to produce partial-order tables in SPSS for students in advanced courses. Introduction to Sociology students are fully capable of understanding the logic of controlling for a third variable, but only students in advanced courses should be expected to produce such output.

Chapter Fourteen is the final one; it includes the formal assignment and instructions on how to write about their experiences in a way that produces an excellent final paper. The assignment consists of a series of questions. Students demonstrate their knowledge of the research process by responding fully to all the questions.

In a concluding attempt to increase the quality of final papers, instructors are encouraged to have students perform peer reviews of one another's papers on the date they are due in class. This gives them specific feedback as to the grade they would receive if they were to hand in the paper in its present form. A detailed rubric created specifically for the peer review exercise is available on the companion website for this book. Students grade one another's papers on this day, using the prepared rubric. Instead of handing in the assignment, students are instead given an additional week to make further improvements, armed with the comments of a peer and the detailed rubric. This greatly improves the quality of the papers and, with the detailed rubric, makes grading simple.

FEATURES

Compared to other supplemental sociology texts, this book is unique. It assumes no prior knowledge of the scientific method or familiarity with SPSS on the part of the student or the instructor; all of this information is provided. It fosters an experiential-based learning opportunity that students build on over the semester. Instructors will find all they need in the instructor's resources online to familiarize themselves with the logic of the deductive method or with using SPSS.

Affect is as important a characteristic in classes as content, particularly in lower-division classes. Positive emotional states and contextualization of activities within the large questions of life give most students enough intrinsic motivation to be involved and aim for excellence (Bain, 2004). The text therefore includes examples and explanations designed to produce this affective relevance. Students who understand that their training has important implications for themselves and others are inclined to be motivated and happy.

The text also addresses the dearth of pedagogical materials needed to build quantitative literacy—a need formally identified by the American Sociological Association (ASA, 2006). To do this, the research project has been simplified to aid comprehension at the first-year level. Students need consult only three journal articles in their literature review. Tests of reliability are not conducted on indices or scales used, though individual instructors are welcome to do so on their own. Instructors have the choice of involving students in operationalizing variables, entering, analyzing, and producing tables. Opting out of these possibilities, this book leads students through the bare bones of a research project designed to teach one thing above all else: the joy of discovery.

The project is framed within the classic deductive method of social science, but this choice is in no way meant to suggest that deductive science is more valid or valuable than an inductive or qualitative approach to doing sociology. Development of a qualitative sociology has greatly strengthened the discipline and enriched our understanding of the complexity of human behavior. This project is simply an opportunity for students to become familiar with the deductive logic of science so they can knowledgeably evaluate for themselves its potential and its shortcomings. Sociology majors continue to graduate with an education deficit in quantitative sociology (ASA, 2006); once familiar with the process, students can be challenged to consider alternative ways of knowing, including a qualitative approach.

NOTE TO INSTRUCTORS

Instructors with varying levels of familiarity with quantitative sociology will feel comfortable adopting this text and course project. It assumes little prior knowledge of the process on the part of either the student or the instructor. Helpful resources are available on the companion website, for any instructor adopting the text. Concepts and procedures are clearly explained in the subsequent chapters. Instructors can modify the project to meet a variety of pedagogical goals. This assignment can be added to any existing course with minimal adaptation.

It is strongly advised, however, that instructors make use of the resources available on the companion website (www.josseybass.com/go/friesen). Important material describing the optimal way to integrate the project into a class is available, along with lecture materials, rubrics, and more. At a minimum, expect to dedicate approximately one hour of class time to select a research topic for the project, a second hour to review the interview schedule with students and conduct interviewer training, and a third hour for students to evaluate one another's papers. Demonstrating SPSS data entry in a class session is also helpful. Instructors of lower-division courses will want to produce and distribute tables for the class, to complete the final assignment.

If students are expected to enter the data from their own interviews, they will either need access to SPSS in computer labs or an opportunity to purchase the student version of SPSS to install on their own computers. Other options for course integration are shared on the website.

NOTE TO STUDENTS

Congratulations! You're embarking on a project that could change your life. This statement may sound like a bit of an exaggeration to you right now, but it's not meant as a joke. There are times in our lives when we discover something useful that applies to many parts of our lives. It's empowering. Some types of knowledge help us make better sense of our lives. Others help us gain control or make better decisions. You'll eventually decide on the kind of impact the knowledge contained in this book will have on you.

The new knowledge you'll gain through this class exercise is awareness of the methods by which people claim to "know" things. Think about it. How do you know that the world is round? Have you ever walked around the world, or otherwise circumnavigated the globe? Not many of us have. Have you ever seen the curvature of the earth? If not, how do you know it is round and not flat? You might suggest that you know it is round because you've seen pictures of earth that were taken from the moon or somewhere in space. But how do you know those photos were not fabricated? At some point many of us make a choice: to either *trust* or not trust the photos or information presented to us in books and online.

This is just the point: trust. In what ways of knowing do you put your trust? Suppose you read something in a textbook that contradicts something your parents told you. Which source is more trustworthy, in your eyes? Perhaps it depends in part on the question you are trying to answer. If you want to know whether you have, say, a brain aneurysm, you might trust a brain surgeon more than your parents for an accurate diagnosis. Which would you rather use to measure the speed of an automobile: a radar camera like those operated by the police, or a thermometer? "Don't be ridiculous!" you might exclaim. "You can't use a thermometer to measure speed!" This is, of course, precisely the point. Some ways of knowing are better than others, depending on what it is you want to find out.

Science is a way of knowing, a way to find things out about the world. When it comes to finding things out about the natural world, science has been an incredibly powerful tool in giving human beings the ability to control their environment. Today we can build massive dams (more than 60 percent of Holland would be under water if it were not for their expansive system of dikes), towering skyscrapers, and bridges. We know what it takes to increase human longevity and quality of life. Space travel has become so routine that even private companies now offer rides into space. We've also discovered incredible power in the form of nuclear fission that generates electricity for many homes and cities—but also has the ability to level entire cities in the form of a nuclear weapon.

How good is science as a way of knowing about our *social* world? That is the topic of this book. As you work your way through this project, you'll be exposed to the deductive logic of the scientific method and will use it to gather information about our social world. After the project is finished, you'll be in a better place to evaluate the use of science as a method to investigate the social world. Perhaps your respect for science will increase as you become more familiar with the logic and rigor inherent in the process. Who knows? It might even change your life.

ACKNOWLEDGMENTS

I'm grateful to a number of individuals who helped make this book a reality. Jossey-Bass Senior Editor Andrew Pasternack and Associate Editor Seth Schwartz were both simply invaluable. Their insight, patience, support, and commitment made completion of this project inevitable. Five reviewers offered comments on the entire manuscript, all offering suggestions that added clarity and sophistication to the final product. Their contributions are much appreciated. They are Dr. James Frideres of the University of Calgary, Dr. Howard Lune of Hunter College, Dr. Ryan Cragun and Dr. Jeff Skowronek of the University of Tampa, and Dr. Jessica Maguire, an applied sociologist in private practice in Austin, Texas.

I'd be remiss not to mention the hundreds of students who have enrolled in classes over the years in which this project was used. Their feedback and performance on the completed assignment yielded valuable information used to refine the project. I'm particularly indebted to the students in my summer 2009 Introduction to Sociology course at the University of Tampa, who were the first to use a draft of this text. The high class interest and extensive dialogue about the science of society, a result of the enriched material in the book chapters, actually surprised me. I appreciate their excitement for the book and helpful feedback.

Finally, this book was produced during a time of personal challenge. The ongoing encouragement and support of family and friends helped see this project through to completion. Particular thanks go to my partner, Cheryl Lucas; colleagues Dr. Jeff Skowronek, Dr. James Woodson, and Dr. Connie Rynder; extended family members Ruth Nickel, Dr. John W. Friesen, and Dr. Virginia Friesen; and my children, Brittany and Justin. There are others; you know who you are.

Though the content of this book has been enhanced by the contributions of many, I alone am responsible for its content. If it inspires others to imagine new possibilities as to how the world might be improved through sociology, my goal will have been achieved.

Bruce K. Friesen
April 2010
Tampa, Florida

THE AUTHOR

Bruce K. Friesen is associate professor of sociology at the University of Tampa in Florida. He received his Ph.D. in sociology from the University of Calgary (Canada) in 1993 and is the coauthor of *Perceptions of the Amish Way* and several articles and book chapters on topics ranging from heavy metal music to the quality of child day care. Friesen is the recipient of numerous teaching awards and commendations. Among his favorite courses to teach are Research Methods and Sociological Analysis. Friesen takes great pleasure in introducing students to the joy of discovery through social scientific inquiry.

1

Choosing a Topic

LEARNING OBJECTIVES

- Discover how social scientists go about choosing a topic to study.
- Be able to identify a sociological problem.
- Prepare for the discussion in which a topic of study will be selected by the class.

The first step in conducting a scientific study is to select a topic you would like to investigate. Your instructor will dedicate some class time for you and your fellow students to list possible topics for your research and agree together on one hypothesis that you will investigate as a class. The purpose of this chapter is to help prepare you for that discussion. First, we review how social scientists come to identify topics that they eventually do research on. Next, we help you think through some issues that will help your class choose a topic appropriate for this particular exercise.

HOW SOCIAL SCIENTISTS CHOOSE A TOPIC TO STUDY

Have you ever considered entering a vocation that involves discovering things people don't know? Many people who conduct research today do so, in part, because it is an essential part of their jobs. Social scientists who engage in research are often professors in colleges and universities around the world. For them, conducting research is a benefit of the job because a passion for the joy of discovery is what led many into their vocations in the first place. In some large research universities, one's ability to do quality research is even more important than the ability to teach. The ability to conduct research is, for many professors, the most important component by which they are evaluated.

Your own professor likely has job requirements that include conducting research and publishing the results. These expectations differ with the educational institution. Instructors in community colleges or technical institutes typically have a heavy teaching load and few requirements to conduct regular research. The same is true for part-time or adjunct faculty at large universities. They are hired primarily to teach. If adjunct faculty hope to get permanent positions as professors (rather than being hired year-to-year, often for low pay), they need to find time to do research and publish, in addition to spending many hours every week in the front of the classroom.

Faculty at private colleges are also rewarded by conducting research, though the expectations are usually somewhat less than for faculty in large public universities. This is because a primary mission of most private colleges is quality teaching. Still, few faculty get tenured without a reasonable record of publication. Articles published in peer-reviewed academic journals are still those that garner the greatest respect in science-based disciplines. Virtually all professors in the social sciences are expected to do research as a requirement of the job.

Other professionals paid to conduct research are people with a graduate degree (that is, a master's or Ph.D.) who are hired by government or research firms to investigate certain phenomena. Ph.D. graduates can secure a postdoctorate, a one- or two-year university position that involves doing research. For these and many other positions, conducting research and publishing the results are integral parts of the job. They do little or no teaching so they can focus almost exclusively on their research. Imagine what an opportunity it is to work full-time making new discoveries.

For professionals with a full-time research job, the topic they investigate is often predetermined by the company or expert they work for, the government department in which they are employed, or the client they are serving. Professionals employed at major polling firms, for example, typically enjoy a large salary and perquisites, not to mention many excellent resources to help collect good-quality data. For some, though, disadvantages of the job are having someone else dictate the research topic and having little time to more fully explore interesting relationships and patterns in the data than what was asked for by the client.

PURSUING YOUR OWN INTERESTS

A major joy of being a professor is that the selection of a research topic is often determined by one's *own* interests and passions. Think about it! What would you like to find out more about in life? What do you feel passionate about? Good-quality information is often a critical part of solving any social problem. If you want to reduce crime, for example, you first need to know what the crime rate is, what motivates people to engage in criminal activity, and whether or not there are patterns to certain types of crime. You'll also want to know whether any attempts to solve social problems are effective, or whether they're just wasting people's time and money. Collecting good-quality information on a topic about which you are passionately interested is one of the most rewarding aspects of a professor's job.

I'll share a personal example to illustrate. Growing up in the 1970s, I was keenly aware of controversy surrounding heavy metal music, which many deemed harmful or even evil. Many of my friends, though, closely identified with the music. For my master's thesis, I chose to conduct a qualitative investigation into the heavy metal subculture. At the time, heavy metal music was seen as the most deviant style of music around. I spent a year in the scene, with people who consumed and produced the music. I analyzed the lyrics of almost three hundred heavy metal songs. I even played in a hard rock band as a drummer for a few months to get a feel for what it's like to create the music.

Through this experience, I found that the values promulgated in the subculture weren't all that different from those of mainstream society, and especially other leisure-based subcultures. The symbols used to express these values, however, were different. For example, to express male dominance and aggression, male "headbangers" might wear a studded leather wristband or a leather dog collar around the neck, complete with eight-inch spikes. Mainstream society's negative reaction toward such symbols created most of the anger and animosity directed at those involved in the subculture (Friesen, 1990; Friesen and Epstein, 1994).

I concluded the study by suggesting that there exists a reciprocal relationship between society and subcultures labeled as deviant. Society benefits from this situation; for example, creators of and listeners to heavy metal music become identifiable groups that are easy to label as deviant, reinforcing the line between acceptable and unacceptable behavior and increasing the feeling of moral solidarity and superiority on the part of "normals." In return, heavy metal creators and listeners (overwhelmingly adolescent at the time) achieved a certain amount of power through fear. Others in society usually avoided eye contact or physical proximity in the streets and malls where headbangers would congregate. This type of personal power felt good to young people who were otherwise controlled by parents, schools, and societal constraints that restricted their freedom of movement, and even their voting and driving privileges.

It should be obvious that the selection of my research topic was something both deeply personal and intellectually interesting. I wanted to know what the heavy metal phenomenon was really all about. It was satisfying to thoroughly research the topic and come to an understanding of the phenomena in a way that made sense, both to me and to the broader academic community. Somewhat surprisingly, most of the heavy metal listeners I spoke with were also very pleased with my finished product. They felt that my research helped their voices be heard and added some reason and legitimacy to their activities. Giving otherwise disenfranchised people a voice is, incidentally, one of the goals of qualitative research (Ragin, 1994).

It should be noted that governments (federal, state, municipal) influence the research process by making research money (called "grants") available for people who investigate a subject about which government officials want more information. Government agencies advertise a grant competition and take applications from individuals or firms who design a study and offer to conduct the research. Over time, the various actors in this process compile a body of documented research literature on a specific topic, and what we know about a particular topic grows thereby. Most researchers end up specializing in a particular area of research and become well acquainted with other experts in the field and what questions remain unanswered through science.

THINGS TO CONSIDER AS YOUR CLASS CHOOSES A TOPIC

For the class project outlined in this book, your class has the luxury of choosing a topic in which everyone is potentially interested! This is your chance to think big. What questions about human behavior would you like to answer? Is there a topic about which you feel passionate, or curious? Perhaps you've recently engaged in an argument of sorts with friends or loved ones. What was the topic? Is it possible to gather information that would help resolve the dispute?

If you review the table of contents in a typical Introduction to Sociology textbook, you'll get an idea of what kinds of topics sociologists study. Those topics fit the aims of this particular course. The discussion at the end of this chapter helps ensure that the topic selected will be sociologically relevant and researchable in the context of your class.

THINKING SOCIOLOGICALLY

The topic you choose to research for this class will obviously be one that is *sociologically* interesting. This can be tricky. To choose such a topic, you first need to think like a sociologist. You don't necessarily have to choose sociology as a career or even a major, but getting practice in thinking sociologically exposes you to possible explanations of human behavior that you may not have thought of before. If you can think sociologically, it will make you more of an asset in almost any chosen profession, because you'll be able to add new perspectives when trying to solve problems.

In truth, thinking sociologically is something you already do. Do you hold opinions, for example, that attitudes or actions differ among groups according to age, or sex, or culture? Do you believe that children who are spanked will generally grow up to be different people from those who are not spanked? Perhaps you have an attitude on the impact of growing up in a wealthy home, compared to a middle-class or even an impoverished one. Human beings regularly form opinions on the impact that shared social experiences have on behaviors or beliefs. That's thinking sociologically.

Let me illustrate with a hypothetical example from the workplace. Let's say you've noticed that workers in your glass-blowing company are overly nervous and anxious at work. Work is interrupted or slowed down as a result, because the workers have to take time to manage their anxiety or cool down. If you poll most of the foremen and managers in the plant, they might suggest bringing in an expert who can teach the workers stress management techniques. This individual focus would have workers taken out of their work stations for a time to be trained in how to breathe or meditate, in an effort to keep their anxiety at a level that doesn't negatively affect their productivity.

With sociological training, one of the first things to focus on is the social environment in which these people are working. What rules govern how they work? Rules are part of the social environment because they are constructed by social actors to structure activity in a given situation. In this situation, you learn that the workers are expected to work ten hours a day, produce a large number of glass products, and have no breakage. If they do break an item, management insists on deducting the cost of the item from the pay of the worker responsible.

Thinking sociologically, might you suggest solutions to the employee stress problem other than stress management workshops? Can you think of things in the social environment that might be causing a higher stress level for the workers? A sociologist would likely recommend revising the rules of the workplace, such as decreeing shorter work days or longer breaks during the day. Changing the rules about who pays for broken glass would also decrease worker stress because they would not be as worried about breaking and paying for the products they are creating. Permitting a few broken items per week might reduce the stress level among the workers and increase their productivity.

The important point to take from this example is that the problem of productivity may not be something intrinsic to the employees. Employees are indeed experiencing stress, but not because of who they are. The problem is a consequence of their work environment; stress is experienced because the environment includes a variety of factors that induce stress. Understanding the influence of the social environment on the individual is part of the sociological perspective.

Social Problems and Sociological Problems

If you don't have much practice in thinking sociologically, you might first think of a topic that is considered by most to be a **social problem**. A social problem is something about society that we would like to change, something that causes people problems but whose roots are based in social, rather than individual, conditions. Poverty, for example, is something most people consider to be a social problem. Most members of society would like to see poverty completely eliminated, though people disagree as to how to go about it. Homelessness (a related problem) becomes a social problem if we as a society ask, "What can we do to eliminate homelessness in the United States?"

Can you think of other social problems that you could conduct research on in your class? Social problems are such that their causes or solutions are social in nature. Raising the legal minimum wage would have the effect of reducing the number of people living in poverty. Thus poverty is a social problem in that it can be reduced by changing the laws or rules of society. Racism, sexism, violence, terrorism, war, and the effects of social stratification are examples of other social problems addressed by sociologists.

As you think sociologically, you might think of a topic that is sociologically interesting but not exactly defined as a social problem. We call this group of topics **sociological problems**. All social problems are sociological problems, but not all sociological problems are social problems. For example, have you ever wondered what kinds of things influenced other students in your class to choose to attend your particular college or university? Was it conveniently located? Was it the lower tuition cost compared to other institutions? Perhaps it was the reputation of the school or of a particular program. Is your reason for attending this school similar to or different from those of your classmates?

This is a question that is sociologically interesting. That is, there are likely shared reasons students chose your particular school. We wouldn't call these reasons, or the decision to attend the school, a social "problem." Quite the opposite; we value people's decision to further their education. The question as to whether there are common reasons for people to choose a particular college or university is thus sociologically interesting. Answering this question is a sociological problem in that it is theoretically interesting to attempt to answer it. It is not a social problem in that it is not something we necessarily want to change.

Beliefs and Behavior

Whether you're formulating research questions that are sociological problems or social problems, thinking sociologically involves first considering social influences. Social influences are forces that exist *outside* of an individual that lead to changes in the individual. **Beliefs** are one *type* of social influence or social reality. Beliefs are attitudes held by individuals, but they can be social in being shared by others and reinforced through social interaction. It is generally the case that members of religious organizations hold common beliefs. Children raised in these organizations are taught the beliefs through a process known as *socialization.* Adults who decide to join these organizations are likewise taught the beliefs of the group, often in formal classes but sometimes in informal conversation or through sermons or other public lectures (also known as secondary socialization). These children or adult converts eventually *internalize* the beliefs of the organization; that is, they come to believe them for themselves. But where did the belief originate? It first existed in the social group that the individual joined. Thus shared beliefs are a component of the culture of a group.

Beliefs that are shared by many can be a major influence on behavior. People hold common attitudes or beliefs about almost everything in our everyday world: what people should wear, and how they should talk, walk, or even think. People hold attitudes regarding who should be president, or what should be done so that there is less poverty. People usually believe that one kind of family form is better than others, and they form beliefs dictating their positions regarding homosexuality (or heterosexuality) as a choice or innate disposition. Understanding what people believe is of interest to sociologists. Are there any beliefs, particularly those held by college students, that you would like to investigate? Perhaps you would like to choose one belief to study as a topic.

A second social facet that can be measured through social research is actions or **behavior**. That is, groups of people hold certain beliefs in common, but they may also exhibit similar behaviors. People acting in concert can wield great power. They can do great harm to others by way of violence, lynching, murder, or beatings. They can also give aid to others by helping them in times of trouble. Thousands of volunteers helped to clean up the devastation caused by Hurricane Katrina. Frequently attending church services or movie theatres would be other examples of behavior.

Are there specific behaviors you might like to focus on as the topic of your class study? In particular, do students engage in behaviors you would like to investigate? The amount of time spent studying, perhaps? how often people attend class? how many hours students spend at work outside of class? All of these are examples of researchable behavior.

ENSURING THE RESEARCHABILITY OF YOUR TOPIC

While you're deciding on the topic you would like to investigate at your college or university, it is important to note that some topics, though perfectly legitimate and sociologically interesting for other studies, are not appropriate for the purposes of this class exercise. In most studies, the topic selected determines the kinds of people from whom information should be collected. Not so for this project. Because the investigation is limited to using students who attend your school, a topic of relevance to this group needs to be chosen.

Collecting Information from Students

The decision to gather data only from your fellow students is made for several reasons. First, they are easily accessible to you. Trying to interview, say, a random sample of people in your town or city would require considerable resources and time in compiling a list of everyone who lives in the city, drawing a random sample, and then taking the time to contact these people (by phone or in person) and interviewing them. Second, applications for research projects carried out on human subjects at universities and colleges in the United States must first be submitted and approved by a human subjects review board at that institution. This too is time-consuming and effort-intensive. At many institutions this step can be avoided if (1) the research is for pedagogical or training purposes, (2) the data will not be published, and (3) the director or professor leading the research project uses common sense and does not design the project in such a way that would potentially harm or embarrass the people who take part in the project. (Your instructor will complete this review board application for the class if it is required at your institution.)

Your project will meet these criteria as long as it avoids questions that are overly revealing, embarrassing, or potentially harmful. Asking someone the number of sexual partners he or she has ever had, for example, or about involvement in illegal activities such as drug and alcohol use would be inappropriate. Asking about *attitudes* toward premarital sex or drug or alcohol use, however, may be acceptable for the project, depending on how the question is worded.

Ensuring Variation

Finally, the topic chosen for your class project must ensure that there is sufficient **variation** at your school to secure a variety of responses for each question asked during the interviews. Variation is important in social research because making comparisons is a crucial part of any science. For example, if your class chose to study the relationship of sex to drinking behavior but interviewed only males, no appraisal could be made of the drinking behavior of males *compared to* females. Variation is needed in every question that will eventually be included in the analysis.

Because of this, it is important to select a topic in which one can anticipate a variety of responses from the people from whom information will be collected. Let's say you are interested in studying the effects of a college education on voting behavior, for example. This would be an inappropriate topic for the purposes of our study. Why? If we were to use college education as a topic of study at your school, you would collect information only from people who are college-educated (or in the process of becoming so). Who would they be compared with? It would be essential to collect information from people who have not gone to college, but this is beyond the scope of our project; we already know that we will gather information only from people at your school.

Thus the topic you choose must support the possibility of variation—a variety of responses to every question. But a little variation only is not enough in small studies. For example, you might want to compare responses by the race or ethnicity of people at your school. Do you know the percentage of your school's population belonging to a group other than non-Hispanic Caucasian? It is ideal to have as much variation as possible for every topic of interest. If you identified only two categories for race (non-Hispanic whites, nonwhites), you would want 50 percent of the students to be in one category and 50 percent in the other. If you identified, say, four groups (non-Hispanic whites, Hispanic whites, Asians, and African Americans), it would be ideal to have 25 percent of all the students (or cases) in each category. This is maximum variation. Maximum variation is not as important in a study where information is collected from thousands of people in the general population, because it is likely that a critical number of responses will be gathered in each category of interest. It is essential, though, to anticipate a considerable degree of variation of responses when collecting information from a few hundred people, as is the case with this class project.

Therefore if the minority population at your school is quite small, selecting race or ethnicity as a topic would not be wise. This is because it is essentially a **constant** with little variation. When the data for this project are analyzed, responses for each question will be collapsed into two categories or attributes (for race or ethnicity, you would likely compare non-Hispanic whites to all others). The farther away the split in the two groups from 50–50, the less useful the question. This is especially true in studies like ours with a small sample size.

YOUR TURN: IDENTIFY SOME TOPICS!

With the previous discussion in mind, you're now ready to identify some topics you'd like to investigate further. This is the first step in the research project for this class. Once the class has selected a suitable topic to research, we'll develop it into a hypothesis and collect some data by performing interviews with other students who are enrolled at your school. Are you ready to put your own ideas to the test?

Keep the limitations of the study in mind in identifying topics that interest you. The topic your class chooses will need to be one that is not embarrassing or otherwise damaging to the students you interview. It should be an appropriate topic for college students, and one that we know will elicit a good deal of variation in your school population.

Have at least three appropriate topic suggestions ready for the day your research topic is discussed in class.

Write your topics here, and your explanation of why it is of interest to you:

Your Topic, and Why It Is of Interest to You

1. _____

_____

_____

2. _____

_____

_____

3. _____

_____

_____

SUMMARY

Choice of a topic to research is often driven by personal interest and experience, though some research-based organizations choose the topic for their employees to study. Choosing a sociologically relevant topic involves thinking sociologically. This is a process most people do throughout their lives anyway, so it is not difficult. Some sociological topics are social problems, but other topics are more conceptual and have to do with explaining one or more facets of human social behavior.

For this class project, it is important to select possible topics that are relatively impersonal and that are suited to investigation in one semester with college students and to expect variation in the responses to questions about the topic. This is your project! Regardless of the topic your class ultimately selects to investigate, you'll experience the joy of discovery as our activities move us from conceiving of a topic to collecting information that sheds light on it. It's an exercise that only a select few have the opportunity to engage in hands on. *You* are one of them.

REVIEW QUESTIONS

1. How do social scientists go about choosing a topic to study?
2. What occupations allow one's personal curiosity to guide the selection of topics for research?
3. What is a sociological problem? How is it related to a social problem? Is it important to understand the difference? Why or why not?
4. What is the difference between beliefs and behavior? Develop a survey question that would measure a belief. Develop a second question that would measure a behavior.
5. Why should your class choose a topic that is rather impersonal? What should be done first to get approval at your institution to investigate a topic that is more personal?
6. Identify a topic that it would not be suitable to investigate with college students. Explain.

KEY TERMS

Behaviors Actions exhibited by units under study. Behaviors can be carried out by individuals or larger social units such as organizations.

Beliefs Values or attitudes held by individuals that take on a social component when collectively shared and reinforced by a group.

Constant An aspect of social life that has no change or variation within a given context. For example, if everyone in a group is twenty years of age, then age is a constant in that it does not vary in the group.

Social problem A characteristic of society generally defined as something that should be reduced or eliminated because of its negative impact.

Sociological problem A puzzle regarding human social behavior needing to be solved. Answers to sociological problems are typically generalizable to more than one social situation.

Variation A feature of life that differs among individuals or groups. For example, if the ages of individuals in a group range widely between twenty and sixty years, the feature of age for that group exhibits variation.

2

Literature Review

LEARNING OBJECTIVES

- Understand why a literature review is essential for accessing the storehouse of scientific knowledge known to humankind.
- Improve your research skills by distinguishing types of articles published in peer-reviewed journals.
- Find new ways to search for quality research articles to become an expert on any subject.
- Learn the best way to collect articles for your own research paper for your class project.

In deductive science, selection of a topic or problem is always followed by a literature review. Before conducting an actual scientific study, it is important to investigate what other scientists have learned on the topic. Scientific knowledge is cumulative; that is, scientists working today try to discover new information about the world instead of reaffirming observations made long ago. Would you be impressed if someone said she had just discovered that the earth revolves around the sun? Probably not, since Copernicus illustrated this was the case in the sixteenth century. This is also the case with other kinds of scientific research. We want to add to the collective literature—the sum total of knowledge on a particular topic—so that human beings can move forward and improve their quality of life.

AN OPPORTUNITY FOR YOU TO HELP HUMANKIND

Discovering something new is an exciting endeavor. All of the scientific information humankind has collected on a particular topic is available to you as a citizen of a democratic industrialized country. This information is published in scientific journals found in your public library, and increasingly on your computer. A scientific journal usually focuses on a specific topic or discipline. Researchers around the world investigate problems at the forefront of their discipline, write up their findings in a research paper, and submit them to be published in a journal on that topic.

Over the years, the sum total of knowledge about a particular topic accumulates in the back issues. Academic, peer-reviewed journals are generally considered to be among the most authoritative sources of information on a given topic. Having access to this information is in itself a testament to the notion of a free and civil society.

As a budding researcher, your first goal is to find out what we know and don't know about a particular topic. Your second goal is to conduct a thorough enough literature review to make sure you identify all of the most important and most frequently cited studies on the topic. Aside from missing important information, it is embarrassing to have another researcher look at your literature review and criticize it for not mentioning a classic or well-known article in that field.

Say, for example, you choose to gather information on the effects of divorce on children. To find out what we already know, you would go to the library and start by looking for any published research articles on this topic. You might look for journals that publish papers on subjects related to your topic. For example, the *Journal of Marriage and Family* could be worth reviewing. By looking through the table of contents of past issues you could identify by title those articles reporting results of research on your topic or a similar one.

One could potentially accumulate hundreds of articles on this topic, depending on how far back the search goes and the number of journals consulted in a particular field and in various academic disciplines. Psychologists, social workers, and other experts obviously would be interested in the effect of divorce on children. Would you want to look at their research journals as well? It's a judgment call, but most experts primarily consult the literature in their discipline (sociology, anthropology) and only significant or influential studies outside of their field. To be sure, becoming familiar with the literature in your field is an essential part of this process.

SEARCHING FOR JOURNAL ARTICLES

The review process for these articles is fairly rigorous and follows high standards. A scholar submits a research article she or he has written to a journal, hoping it will be published. The editor first decides whether the article is good enough to send out for review. If it is, the editor will remove the author's name from the paper and send it to other researchers (usually about three) who serve on the journal's review board.

Those reviewers go over the article with a fine-tooth comb, looking for weaknesses in the method or the results. The reviewers then make a recommendation to the editor as to whether the article should be rejected, accepted, or returned to the author with a number of suggestions for changes. Once published, the article is made available to other experts in the field who read the journal. They in turn consider the article on its own merits. The review process usually takes a year or two from the time an article is submitted to a journal to when it is reviewed and finally published. It usually takes longer than that for a book to be published.

Peer-reviewed articles are made available to readers through libraries, and increasingly through online databases. Searching for research articles online today is rapidly replacing the hands-on method of paging through journals in the library or using reference helps such as the **Social Science Citation Index**. Libraries subscribe to databases of research articles that digitize content, making searching for articles easier and faster. It is important, though, to know there are serious limitations to conducting an online literature review. Each online research database is unique in its selection of journals. Many databases include journal articles from a variety of disciplines, requiring time to sift through to find articles with, say, a sociological focus only. All databases have to make decisions regarding which journals they will include and will exclude. Thus some excellent studies on your topic might be published in journals that are not included in any particular database. All databases furnish a list of their journals. Any responsible researcher would examine these lists for any important journals in his discipline not included in a database.

Because journal articles began appearing in digital form around 1995, online databases include few older articles. Unfortunately, there are excellent research articles published prior to this time available only to those who "hit the stacks," or go to the library and physically search through the hard copies of journals. This is changing as more journals digitize their older studies, but it is important to remember that not all journal articles are digitized. Some are available online only in abstract form.

TYPES OF JOURNAL ARTICLES APPROPRIATE
FOR A LITERATURE REVIEW

Conducting a good literature review is also complicated by the fact that *research articles* are not the only type of article that finds its way into a journal. Articles found in peer-reviewed journals can be divided into two major groups: empirical articles and nonempirical articles. **Empirical articles** report the results of research involving new data being collected about a topic. They could also produce new results by reanalyzing data collected previously by others, but doing it in a way that makes new discoveries. By contrast, **nonempirical** articles do not present new data or new analyses. Instead, they offer something else to the scientific enterprise, such as exploring or applying new theories.

When you conduct a literature review, it is important to distinguish these types of articles to be able to quickly identify the articles you want and make use of them. In embarking on a research project, you will probably find that empirical articles are of most interest to you because you want to identify what has already been published about the topic—what people already know. Our desire is to add *new* knowledge to the literature. To do that, we need to know what knowledge gaps exist in the literature as a whole. The next section discusses the differences between these two types of articles.

Nonempirical Articles

Recall that nonempirical articles do not report new findings brought about by the research process. Nonempirical articles often fall under one of the three categories: theoretical, conceptual, and review of literature. One other type of article, a meta-analysis, is empirical but likely too complex for you to consider adding to your own literature review for this project. Let's briefly discuss these categories in turn.

Theoretical Articles

Theoretical articles focus on exploring new ways of understanding social phenomena. Unlike empirical articles, they typically use logic as the sole method of determining what is true rather than testing ideas with data. These articles often discuss prominent approaches to understanding current problems in a particular field and attempt to deduce how useful a particular way of thinking about a topic might be. Theoretical articles usually explore ideas originally discussed by authors considered to be the founders of a particular field. By contrast, empirical articles attempt to test the validity of theories, but they allow *both* logic and data to inform their conclusions.

Box 2.1 show a sample of an abstract of a theoretical article. One can tell from the description that the article deals primarily with describing differences in perspectives, in this case between exchange theory and network analysis. It does not contain any reference to data that the authors might have collected. No new research-based knowledge is described in theoretical articles, making them inappropriate for the literature review component of your final assignment.

Conceptual Articles

Closely related to theoretical articles, *conceptual articles* discuss a topic, in part by referring to findings of earlier empirical studies or citing government information and statistics. Some attempt to analyze the impact of organizational or governmental policies, while others review previous studies and literature on the topic they are addressing.

BOX 2.1 SAMPLE OF AN ABSTRACT OF A THEORETICAL ARTICLE

Two Approaches to Social Structure: Exchange Theory and Network Analysis

Much convergence exists between exchange theory and network approaches to social structure. Starting with the work of Emerson, exchange theory increasingly has considered social structure explicitly, as both product and constraint. Exchange theory and network analysis both conceptualize social structure as a configuration of social relations and positions, i.e., as a set of actors diversely linked into networks. Exchange theory and most work in network analysis are based on similar conceptions of the actor. Where exchange theory and network analysis differ is in their view of the links between positions. Exchange theory stresses the exchange aspects of all ties and contends that the appropriate network in any analysis is one that contains all relevant exchange relations. Network analysis tends to be more catholic about the nature of the links.

K. S. Cook and J. M. Whitmeyer. Reprinted, with permission, from the *Annual Review of Sociology,* Volume 18:109–127. ©1992 by Annual Reviews. www.annualreviews.org.

At first glance, a conceptual article looks like an empirical article. However, the authors do not collect their own data and do not analyze other datasets in a way that adds *new* knowledge about the topic. It can be difficult to make this distinction since authors of conceptual articles often claim to be shedding new light on an issue. If they are, it is due more to their *synthesis* of a variety of materials and arguments than to their analysis of a particular dataset. Therefore they are not empirical in the sense in which we are using the word.

There are simple ways to tell whether an article is conceptual rather than empirical. All empirical articles include a specific section describing the methods used to collect data. Conceptual articles do not contain a separate methods section. Neither do the authors of conceptual articles attempt to review only scientific studies on their topic. Secondary sources such as news publications and popular magazines may also be consulted even though such sources do not usually engage in primary research. Third, conceptual articles may read like the kind of article you'd find in the popular press as opposed to a scientific-based journal. Empirical articles are generally more sophisticated in language, though not always.

The article abstract in Box 2.2 is an example of a conceptual article. Note how the author alludes to reviewing information on the topic but then proceeds to outline an article that focuses more on developing a perspective than it does on collecting and analyzing new data. Nor is there mention of the methods used to collect new data.

BOX 2.2 ABSTRACT OF A CONCEPTUAL ARTICLE

Sexuality and International Human Rights Law

This essay considers the extent to which international human rights now protect, or might protect, GLBT [gay, lesbian, bisexual, and transgendered] communities. The counterpoint between the potential width of application of international human rights instruments and their silence on sexuality has become the leitmotif of sexuality and gender identity within the international human rights framework. In addition, there is a symbiotic relationship between the international norms and domestic legal systems which directly affects the meaning of those norms. Domestic laws are not only needed to implement international norms, but are essential in overcoming the equivocations and silences of international human rights law as it has traditionally applied to GLBT communities. A fusion of the international norms with domestic legal systems through the principle of diversity, rather than the principle of equality, is needed.

Tahmindjis, Phillip. *Journal of Homosexuality.* Feb. 28, 2005, vol. 48, no. 3/4. ©2007. Used with permission. http://www.tandf.co.uk/journals.

You'll likely find conceptual articles published in journals dedicated more to a particular applied profession (education, business, criminal justice) than to a discipline commonly focused on using science as a primary way of knowing. Although conceptual articles are not appropriate for your literature review per se, they often make reference to empirical articles on the topic you are investigating. In this case, it is important to track down the original article and review it yourself instead of trusting someone else to describe the contents of the article.

Literature Reviews

Another type of article found in peer-reviewed journals is called a *review of literature, review article,* or *literature review.* In this type an author attempts to do just what you will do in your own literature review for this assignment: comb peer-reviewed journals looking for research-based articles on a particular topic and then summarize what is known about the subject and what has yet to be investigated. It is important to note that no new empirical findings are reported in a review of literature. Instead, the authors' "research" is library-based and the article is part of the secondary, rather than primary, literature on a topic. In social science, **primary sources** are those that report on an actual study. Such reports describe the data and the method in which they were collected. (In the humanities, primary sources are defined as actual historical artifacts from which original information is obtained, such as a letter or diary.) Primary sources are the source from which the information in question is ultimately derived.

By contrast, **secondary sources** are reports written to describe the material found in primary sources. For example, a newspaper journalist may read a primary source social science article that describes a study. The journalist then summarizes the results of the study in an article on the topic. The journalist's article is a secondary source because it simply relays the information found in the primary source.

Literature reviews are secondary sources. Authors summarize the findings of published studies on a given topic and form an opinion as to what is known and what remains to be investigated. Literature reviews do not involve collection of new primary data.

Box 2.3 contains an abstract for a literature review on the topic of dying. The author notes that most of the articles on this topic focus on biological processes resulting in death and pay scant attention to the effects of social processes. This is valuable information, brought about only because of a thorough review of the literature. Once researchers are aware of this deficit they can begin to focus research attention on the gaps in knowledge. Here, the author suggests that more information is needed regarding the manner in which social processes bring about or delay death or lead to particular definitions regarding the meaning of death. Note that the abstract does not describe a primary research methodology. It simply acknowledges that a review of the literature has been conducted.

BOX 2.3 ABSTRACT OF A LITERATURE REVIEW

Dying as a Social Relationship: A Sociological Review of Debates
on the Determination of Death

The research literature about "brain death" is largely characterized by biomedical, bioethical, and legal writing. This has led to overlooking wider but no less pertinent social, historical, and cultural understandings about death. By ignoring the work of other social and clinical colleagues in the study of dying, the literature on the determination of death has become unnecessarily abstract and socially disconnected from parallel concerns about death and dying. This has led, and continues to lead to, incomplete suggestions and narrow discussions about the nature of death as well as an ongoing misunderstanding of general public and health care staff responses to brain death criteria. This paper provides a sociological outline of these problems through a review of the key literature on the determination of death.

Allan Kellehear. Reprinted from *Social Science & Medicine*, vol. 66, No. 7, 1533–1544. ©2008, with permission from Elsevier.

Although published literature reviews do not report on new research findings, they could help you locate research-based articles relevant to your topic. They usually contain a thorough examination of the major works on a particular topic, attempt to make sense of the variety of findings, and offer suggestions for what kinds of research need to take place in the future. Literature reviews could be helpful to scientists for this reason, though they ultimately depend on how skilled the author is in finding influential articles, reporting them responsibly, and interpreting perceived gaps in knowledge yet to be answered by science.

As with conceptual articles, of course, you won't want to rely only on the interpretations of others for your own literature review. Literature reviews help in finding primary research articles, but conduct your own review of literature by finding and reading the articles yourself. It is always possible that the authors of a literature review did an incomplete job or arrived at conclusions different from those you would form if you examine the same group of empirical studies. For the purposes of your paper, a review of literature is a valuable resource, but it is not sufficient in and of itself. Be sure to look for other articles on your own as well.

Empirical Articles

In contrast to nonempirical articles, empirical articles are those whose authors *collect their own data* to investigate a particular question or hypothesis. In some instances the authors may analyze data that someone else has collected. However, the point of the analysis is to *discover something new or unique* that has not been previously investigated with the dataset they use. If the authors of an article report the findings of one or more studies but do not attempt their own unique analysis, the article is likely conceptual rather than empirical.

Empirical articles all contain one essential feature: a section describing the methods used to collect the data. Researchers want to give readers enough description of the data collection process to (1) critique the study according to scientific standards and (2) permit the possibility of *replication.* In replicating an empirical study, another researcher repeats the same study in another place and time to see whether comparable results are obtained. Empirical articles usually have a section of the paper formally identified by "Methods" or similar subtitle. Some empirical articles (such as qualitative articles, defined below) may label the methods section something less formal ("Getting to Know the Scene" or something similar) or include the description of their methods in a footnote.

The major types of empirical articles are *quantitative, comparative,* and *qualitative.* It is important to further distinguish empirical articles that are suitable from those that are not appropriate for your paper. *Needs assessments and methodological articles* (described below) *are best avoided. Meta-analyses or mixed-methods approaches* may be technically suitable for your review of literature but be too sophisticated for most undergraduates to easily comprehend. To assist you in your literature review, I describe unsuitable empirical articles before turning to a discussion of appropriate ones to use in your paper.

Unsuitable Empirical Articles

A *needs assessment* is an article that typically reports on the amount of assistance or need present in a particular group or area. The assessment seeks to measure the magnitude of some type of social need existing in a given population. Needs assessments are important empirical studies because they typically inform social workers, policy advocates, and politicians concerned about how much or how little social services are needed in a given area. However, assessments rarely examine *relationships* between concepts, or between two or more variables. As a result, they do not offer much useful information for a class project aiming to test a hypothesis.

Box 2.4 presents an abstract of a needs assessment. The researchers obviously went to a good deal of effort to obtain information from the Latino community in Virginia regarding health needs and need for services. The usefulness of the results, however, is limited to the immediate situation. There is little information gleaned from the study to answer broader questions about human behavior. The information is specific to the location and time, though the authors suggest the methods they use may be of interest to others collecting similar types of information in different social contexts.

BOX 2.4 ABSTRACT OF A NEEDS ASSESSMENT

Richmond Latino Needs Assessment: A Community-University Partnership
to Identify Health Concerns and Service Needs for Latino Youth

The presence of Latinos in Virginia is a new phenomenon and as a result, less is known about the health needs of these newest community members. We formed a community-university partnership to identify health concerns and service needs as they relate to Latino youth living in Richmond, Virginia, and the surrounding area. Using a mixed-method approach, survey data was obtained from 212 Latino adults, qualitative interviews were conducted with 15 community leaders and focus groups with 23 Latino parents (16 mothers, 7 fathers) and 6 Latino boys. Participants expressed concern about sexually transmitted infections/pregnancy among youth (76%), youth behavior problems at home/school (75%), and mental health problems (75%). Participants also expressed worry that youth would lose their connection to their Latin culture (83%). Qualitative data provided more information regarding these concerns by linking them with inter-ethnic tensions, and immigration and acculturation-related stressors. Survey participants also indicated a need for bilingual mental health services (88%) and after-school programs for youth (94%). This study provided the local community with information on the health concerns and service needs of a new group of community youth—Latino youth. Findings were presented to local community and city organizations that used the information to respond to the identified needs and/or concerns. The process in which the data was obtained may prove useful to other individuals interested in obtaining local level health information in emerging communities.

Corona, Rosalie; Gonzalez, Tanya; Cohen, Robert; Edwards, Charlene; Edmonds, Torey. *Journal of Community Health,* vol. 34, no. 3, pp. 195–201. ©June 2009, with permission from Springer.

Other empirical articles you encounter in your search may have a decidedly applied focus. In such articles, the results may not contain lessons beyond the immediate context under investigation. Program evaluations, for example, assess the effectiveness of certain programs or services and may be of limited relevance. In your review of the literature, you want to find articles teaching something about a particular hypothesis. Research designed in this way points to something potentially generalizable beyond the immediate situation.

Another type of empirical article to avoid is *methodological articles.* They seek to examine issues related more to valid and reliable collection or analysis of data than investigation of a hypothesis per se. The authors design and test new indices or scales to measure a specific behavioral or attitudinal feature of human life. Or such articles may compare the accuracy of measuring a concept (say, religiosity) using one kind of indicator (such as church attendance) versus another (perhaps a self-reported measure of religiosity). Still other methodological articles examine the utility of various statistical techniques in analyzing the same dataset. Psychological journals are rife with methodological articles. Methodological articles are empirical and are valuable in what they attempt to do. They do not furnish information about the nature of social life by examining relationships between two or more concepts. As a result, they won't be useful in your own review of literature.

Box 2.5 contains a description of a methodological article. The authors developed a scale that measures the extent to which a person is fearful of members of the Islamic faith, and they report on the testing involved that demonstrates the scale's reliability and validity. Though fascinating from a methodological perspective, the point of these types of articles has more to do with procedures and techniques of data collection and analysis than with hypothesis testing. Other articles will contain better information for your literature review.

A third type of empirical article is called a *meta-analysis.* This type of study is similar to a review of literature, but instead of merely reporting results from other studies investigators use statistical techniques to add together the subjects or units of analysis in discussing all of the articles. This produces a larger pool of data for researchers to analyze. It's as if the authors of the meta-analysis had access to every person in every article of the literature review and did one large study on all of them.

BOX 2.5 ABSTRACT OF A METHODOLOGICAL ARTICLE

The Islamophobia Scale: Instrument Development and Initial Validation

Opinion poll research suggests that a significant number of Westerners hold negative and fearful perceptions toward Muslims and their religion. Although evidence of Islamophobia has been documented in a number of poll studies, no psychometrically based, multifaceted measure that focuses exclusively on fear-related attitudes and is not confounded with a particular group currently exists in the scientific literature. The authors of this study describe the development and psychometric properties of the Islamophobia Scale, which measures cognitive and affective-behavioral facets of fear-related attitudes toward the religion of Islam and Muslims. The results of the study demonstrate a measure of Islamophobia that yielded acceptable psychometric properties of reliability and validity.

Lee, Sherman A., Jeffrey A. Gibbons, John M. Thompson, Hussam S. Timani. *International Journal for the Psychology of Religion;* Vol. 19, Issue 2, pp. 92–105. ©2009. Used by permission. http://www.tandf.co.uk/journals.

BOX 2.6 ABSTRACT OF A META-ANALYSIS

Intelligence and Socioeconomic Success: A Meta-Analytic Review of Longitudinal Research

The relationship between intelligence and socioeconomic success has been the source of numerous controversies. The present paper conducted a meta-analysis of the longitudinal studies that have investigated intelligence as a predictor of success (as measured by education, occupation, and income). In order to better evaluate the predictive power of intelligence, the paper also includes meta-analyses of parental socioeconomic status (SES) and academic performance (school grades) as predictors of success. The results demonstrate that intelligence is a powerful predictor of success but, on the whole, not an overwhelmingly better predictor than parental SES or grades. Moderator analyses showed that the relationship between intelligence and success is dependent on the age of the sample, but there is little evidence of any historical trend in the relationship.

Strenze, Tarmo. *Intelligence*, vol. 35, no. 5, pp. 401–426. ©2007, with permission from Elsevier.

Box 2.6 contains an example of a meta-analysis. Meta-analyses are usually easy to spot because they are identified in the abstract or title. In this article, the author combines several studies to determine whether intelligence, socioeconomic status, or grades best predict success in later life.

Meta-analyses are empirical and could be suitable for your review of literature. However, meta-analysis articles are sometimes difficult for undergraduates to understand, and their findings difficult to interpret. Don't think you have to include a meta-analysis in your review of literature if, after looking through it, you don't understand the conclusions.

Suitable Empirical Articles

Most empirical research articles engage in primary data collection. That is, the researchers design a study, go out and collect their own information, and analyze and report the results. Not all empirical articles of this sort are the same. They could be further broken down into at least three types: *quantitative, comparative,* and *qualitative.* Think about these three types of articles being located along a continuum ranging from *breadth* of information on one end to *depth* of information on the other. Quantitative articles typically collect small amounts of information from many people or units; they are located on the breadth end of the continuum. Qualitative articles collect a great deal of information from a relatively small number of cases; they are located on the depth end of the continuum. Comparative articles are in the middle; they usually collect information on a few cases, such that the researcher can know details about each case, but enough cases that they can start to identify patterns existing between cases (see Figure 2.1).

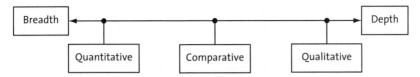

Figure 2.1. Types of Studies Emphasizing Breadth of Cases Versus Depth of Information.

Quantitative Articles In quantitative articles, information is collected and ultimately converted into numbers to facilitate statistical analysis. Articles such as these are usually designed in the spirit of the deductive logic of science. That is, a topic-relevant theory is discussed, a testable hypothesis generated, and data collected to see whether they support the hypothesis. Surveys, standardized interviews, and experimental methods are used most frequently in quantitative articles. These are often the most respected type of empirical article because the deductive method demands a considerable amount of control, standardization, and rigorous statistical analysis.

An example of a quantitative article is shown in Box 2.7. Note that the study analyzes the results of hundreds of students. Large samples are typical of quantitative studies. The abstract also describes a sophisticated statistical technique, in this case called a stepwise logistic regression model, and makes specific reference to variables. These too are typical characteristics of quantitative articles. Finally, the article notes that some variables are predictors of other variables. Much of quantitative research involves hypothesis testing in which one or more independent variables are identified as predictors of a change in the dependent variable.

BOX 2.7 ABSTRACT OF A QUANTITATIVE ARTICLE

Predictors of College Students' Binge Drinking: Experience of an Urban University in the Southwest

This study explores predictors of college student binge drinking. Eight hundred and seventy-two students were surveyed using the CORE questionnaire. A stepwise logistic regression model comprising 10 theoretically relevant variables was analyzed. Contrary to the belief of many people, our study found that variables of gender and perception of campus drinking norm were not significant predictors. Six variables survived the logistic regression model in predicting college student binge drinking: close friends' disapproval, perception of positive effects of alcohol, with whom they are living, precollege drinking history, marital status, and perception of risks of binge drinking. Implications for future research and campus substance abuse prevention and intervention are also discussed.

An-Pyng Sun; Maurer, Arlene Thomas; Ho, Chih-Hsiang. *Alcoholism Treatment Quarterly*, vol. 21, no. 4, pp. 17–36. ©2003, used with permission. http://www.tandf.co.uk/journals.

A variation of the quantitative article involves *secondary data analysis*. In these articles, researchers obtain data from other sources and analyze it on their own. Researchers are interested in looking at new relationships between variables in secondary analyses, though in an attempt to discover something different from what was found by those who originally collected the data. Like quantitative articles, secondary data analyses often use statistical techniques. These articles are also appropriate to include in your review of literature.

Comparative Articles Comparative studies often use numbers or statistics, so there is a kind of standard by which to make comparisons between the **units of analysis**. A unit of analysis is the entity or "thing" whose behavior the researcher is interested in studying. Instead of comparing the behavior of individuals, comparative studies often study larger units, such as organizations or even countries. Comparative studies sometimes appear to be quantitative, and indeed the differences between the two are not always great. Comparative studies are, however, unique in some ways (Ragin, 1994). The independent variable in these studies is usually measured at the nominal level and simply measured by the researcher rather than being introduced or manipulated as in some quantitative studies. Virtually all comparative studies are correlative; that is, their research design does not easily lend itself to establishing causality between the independent variables in the scientific sense. As a result, comparative researchers depend heavily on their theory to add legitimacy to any proposed causal statements.

The abstract in Box 2.8 describes a comparative study. Attitudes and a sense of well-being of Americans, Italians, and Iranians were compared in this study. Researchers measured individuals' sense of community and correlated it with their actual social participation. Although this study uses a fairly large number of individuals, the focus is on similarities *within* each group and the *differences* between the three groups of students.

Don't worry if you're unable to distinguish a comparative article from those that are quantitative or qualitative. For the purposes of your literature review, distinguishing a comparative study from a quantitative study is not as important as knowing that both are considered to be empirical and therefore worthy of being described in your literature review.

Qualitative Studies Qualitative studies often involve in-depth interviews or field research where the researcher spends months, or even years, in a particular social setting. Interviews are typically carried out with thirty or fewer subjects but often take two or more hours to complete. The focus is on getting richness of information and allowing subjects to speak for themselves, as opposed to the researcher following an agenda that is set before the data collection process.

Qualitative studies are frequently organized in the inductive style of science. That is, a researcher forms a broad research question and then collects in-depth information, usually from human subjects. This might include direct observation of and participation

BOX 2.8 ABSTRACT OF A COMPARATIVE ARTICLE

Social Participation, Sense of Community, and Social Well-Being: A Study on American, Italian, and Iranian University Students

Aim of the study was to assess the relationship between social participation and sense of community in a sample of university students and the impact of such variables on social well-being. A further aim was to assess the generality of the relationships between these constructs across different countries, specifically the USA, Italy, and Iran. The sample includes 200 Italian, 125 American, and 214 Iranian university students, male and female. Results show higher levels of social participation, sense of community, and social well-being among American students. Sense of community is positively correlated with social participation in all three samples; however, only among Italian students social participation positively predicts social well-being. Implications of results will be discussed.

Cicognani, Elvira; Pirini, Claudia; Keyes, Corey; Joshanloo, Mohsen; Rostami, Reza; Nosratabadi, Masoud. *Social Indicators Research*, vol. 89, no. 1, pp. 97–112. ©2008, used by permission from Springer.

in certain groups (for example, street gangs), time-consuming interviews with participants (called unstructured interviews), and a great deal of time spent in the setting where the people being studied feel most comfortable. Qualitative researchers often make elaborate field notes in which they try to write down all their observations. As they interact with their subjects, a theory is eventually generated to make sense of these observations.

Qualitative studies are particularly well suited for exploring new kinds of phenomena that have not yet been studied much, for generating theories regarding these new topics, and for securing richness or depth of information not found in other kinds of empirical studies. Some consider qualitative studies to be less rigorous or reliable than quantitative studies, but the former collect better, more accurate, or valid data because the researcher acquires a great deal of first-hand information generally lacking in quantitative studies.

Box 2.9 show an abstract of a study that used qualitative methods to investigate the kinds of individuals who attend raves—dances often organized spontaneously and depending on word of mouth for attendance. By conducting in-depth interviews with thirty-six ravers, researchers distinguished between types of people involved in raves, thereby challenging dominant social stereotypes as to the homogeneity of those who attend raves.

BOX 2.9 ABSTRACT OF A QUALITATIVE ARTICLE

From "Candy Kids" to "Chemi-Kids": A Typology of Young Adults Who Attend Raves in the Midwestern United States

Although young people attending raves have been most visibly associated with the use of ecstasy and other "club drugs" in the United States, there is reason to believe that they are not a homogeneous group in terms of their drug use practices. The purpose of this article is to begin developing a typology of young adult ecstasy users involved in the rave subculture—known as ravers or party kids. The study is based on focus groups and qualitative interviews conducted between November 2001 and September 2003 with 36 current and former ecstasy users, aged 19 to 31, in central Ohio, as well as participant observation conducted in raves, clubs, and bars where club drugs are often used. Findings suggest the existence of five main subgroups in attendance at raves: chemi-kids, candy kids, nonaffiliated party kids, junglists, and old school ravers. These groups differ in regard to musical taste, philosophy, style of clothing worn, amount of time in the rave subculture, and most importantly, patterns of drug use. For example, while the use of ecstasy appears most common among candy kids, junglists tend to be more involved with the use of ketamine and methamphetamine. The use of alcohol, cocaine, marijuana, and hallucinogens is also widespread in the rave subculture. The typology can aid in the development of communication strategies necessary for successful prevention activities among some categories of ecstasy users. "We are a culture, we have our own laws, we have our own, ya know, way of communicating."

Reproduced from McCaughan, Jill A.; Carlson, Robert G.; Falck, Russel S.; Siegal, Harvey A. *Substance Use & Misuse*, vol. 40, no. 9–10, pp. 1503–1523. ©2005. Adapted by permission from Informa Healthcare.

MONOGRAPHS, BOOK CHAPTERS, PROCEEDINGS

Aside from peer-reviewed journals, you might also find helpful primary research published in other forms. These include **research monographs**, thoroughly researched and carefully documented research-oriented books on a specific topic. The most useful type of monograph for a research literature review is one that reports on a particular research project. Studies that are reported in monographs are often large and carefully carried out, making them some of the more important studies in the field. Many monographs are subjected to some type of peer review in the publication process.

Similarly, some books are a collection of research studies by a number of authors carried out on a similar topic. Each chapter is a self-contained research report written by an author.

An editor, whose name appears on the cover, compiles the book. Although the editor will review most articles, some of these collections are peer-reviewed. As a result, the quality of some edited volumes may not be as good as others that have been subjected to blind review by two or three other researchers.

Researchers periodically organize conferences on a particular topic and publish articles presented at the conference in a collection called *proceedings.* Again, it's important to read the preface to these collections of articles and find out just how the articles were selected for inclusion. Some proceedings publish any of the articles presented at the conference, so they may not be peer-reviewed. Editors of other proceedings invite presenters to submit their papers for review and select only those that have been successfully scrutinized by others. Of course, there are proceedings of conferences that may contain articles that are not empirical. Pay close attention to these details when selecting articles to include in your literature review.

Searching for monographs or collected volumes such as edited books or proceedings can be done through your library's online catalog database. Conduct a search as you would for any book on a topic, but pay close attention to clues in the title or description indicating the reported research is actually empirical (and, ideally, peer-reviewed). You'll likely encounter most of the research reported in books or book chapters that is relevant to your topic of interest for the class project as you look for works cited in the bibliographies of journal articles you have found. I describe this technique below.

CONDUCTING YOUR LITERATURE REVIEW

From this discussion, you now know why researchers conduct a review of the literature. You also know the kinds of articles available to you in peer-reviewed journals, and you know that articles dealing with theoretical ideas but no data are inappropriate if you are looking for empirical articles (articles that examine data).

You are now ready to conduct your own literature review on the topic selected by your class. *Your task is to find several journal articles (three, unless your instructor tells you otherwise) that gather information related to your class topic, and to briefly explain what the research in each article tells you about the topic.* Find articles that are closely related to the topic you are planning to investigate.

First, investigate the kind of online databases your library subscribes to, and begin your search online. Your instructor may arrange a library tutorial on this topic if you haven't already had one in an orientation class. Librarians love to assist students genuinely involved in research; make use of them at your institution. They usually don't search for the articles for you, but they have excellent suggestions on consulting databases with useful information and making the most of them. Examples of databases sociologists find useful are Academic Search Premier, Proquest, SocIndex, Sociological Abstracts, JSTOR, and Google Scholar.

In addition to looking for appropriate journal articles on your topic, be aware that some databases include articles from sources that are not peer-reviewed. Databases may list articles from newspapers and news magazines. Remember, these are secondary sources that shouldn't be counted on for accurate information. News magazines and newspapers often discuss research findings, but you can't always trust those sources to accurately deliver the information to you. To have the most accurate information at your fingertips, always track down the actual article referred to by the journalist.

Pay attention to the year in which the data were collected, or at least the year in which the article was published (there's usually a time lag of a year or two). In a thorough literature review, you want to be sure that you have looked for the most recent, up-to-date studies on your topic (say, over the last ten years or so). Also be sure to identify any classic articles in the field that are a "must cite" source for information on your topic. These classic studies are typically the first record of research that is conducted in a particular area. Many such studies are classics not only because they were "first" to investigate a topic but because they set the precedent for the method or methods used in the investigation. Other researchers then use the same method in an attempt to see whether they can replicate the findings. Being aware of the common methods used to determine what scientists know about your topic could help you compare the results of other studies and possibly point out weaknesses in the literature. We know most about a topic if various researchers use a variety of research methods to study a topic and all reach more or less the same conclusion.

OTHER METHODS FOR SEARCHING

After accumulating a few studies on your topic, expand and enrich your collection of articles just by examining the bibliography of the articles. Researchers typically spend a good deal of time searching for articles on the topic they have chosen for precisely the reasons you are doing the same: to make sure they have a good grasp of the literature. The sources they consult will be listed in their bibliography. Review bibliography entries for titles of articles closely related to the topic or variables you want to learn more about. *Do not* rely on what the author says about a particular article in his text. Instead, track down the information and examine it for yourself. Empiricists always prefer to see the original information rather than depending on a description by another source.

Another reason to look over bibliographies is to identify any classic articles that you should include in your discussion. If some studies are listed in most or all of the bibliographies in the articles you have collected, they are likely classics in the field, especially if published earlier than most other listed articles. It is important to identify and examine these classic articles as well, because they usually included some of the first scientifically gathered information on the topic or were innovative in gathering information.

Librarians can often direct you to other reference sources that can make your search more extensive. For example, you're in luck if your college subscribes to (online or hard copy) the Social Science Citation Index (SSCI). The SSCI looks at all of the articles published in hundreds of peer-reviewed social science journals. They note the author of the article, the subject, and the authors of other studies cited in the bibliography of the published articles. You can use the SSCI to search for articles by subject and by author. Researchers usually become experts in one particular part of their field, for example, and publish more than one article on a given topic. If you find an excellent article on your topic by, say, a researcher named Mugabe, for example, you can search for his other published articles.

If Mugabe's research is important in that area, chances are other researchers in the same area have cited his earlier studies in the bibliography of their own articles. By searching for other articles citing Mugabe's research, you can also locate additional articles on your topic. This effort requires dedication, persistence, and attention to detail, but the fruit of your search can be a collection of high-quality research articles specifically on your topic.

LEARNING FROM YOUR LITERATURE REVIEW

Moving through your review of literature on your topic, you'll form impressions on a number of important issues. First, you'll come to a better understanding of what researchers have focused on so far in relation to your topic.

An Example

As I write this, for example, I am conducting a literature review on characteristics of college courses that influence how college students learn. Specifically, I am looking for studies examining the impact of course pacing on student learning. Some college instructors might try to cram too much information into their courses and present it quickly. Others might conceivably pace their courses way too slow for most students such that they grow bored.

My initial attempt to find articles on course pacing produced few results. I was surprised, because I know from my other literature reviews that there are thousands of studies examining the dynamics of college classrooms. Eventually I noticed that there was a difference between student or "self-pacing" (students having control over how fast or how slowly they cover material) and instructor pacing. Once I began using the phrase "instructor pacing," I found many more articles closer to my topic. I also looked for studies on comprehension, reasoning that courses going too fast might interfere with a student's ability to comprehend the information being presented. There is indeed a large literature on comprehension, but it deals almost exclusively with reading comprehension, not comprehension through lectures or other instructor-controlled course components that I want to learn more about.

So far, I'm learning that most studies on instructor pacing have focused on math courses and other natural science courses. I have yet to find meaningful articles on instructor-based course pacing regardless of discipline. I'm far from finished with my review of the literature, but if the same pattern continues I'll be able to claim that the study I'm conducting on this topic will add new information to what we know about course pacing. It's exciting to have an opportunity to investigate an issue with the potential for adding to the storehouse of knowledge human beings have created for themselves.

Things to Look For

In addition to learning from your literature review what researchers have (and have not) focused on in relation to your topic, familiarize yourself with the major *variables* examined in other studies on this topic. These variables are often discussed because they have been shown to be consistently related to your topic, as independent or dependent variables. Pay attention also to the most common *methods* used to investigate the topic. Of course, identifying what most of the research has *discovered* about those relationships is central to conducting a good literature review. Finally, pay attention to the *theories* most frequently used to explain the relationships between the variables.

Trust your initial impressions if you find that the literature is lacking or missing something in any of these areas. Think critically, because ideally the study your class will conduct should add some new information to the literature rather than just revealing what others have found out to be the case. In this way, the scientific enterprise remains cumulative and growing. In the paper you'll write for this assignment, you want to make a statement of how your study adds new information to the literature. To look for holes in the literature, ask yourself these questions:

1. *Do you like how other researchers have conceptualized or described the topic?*
   Nobel prize winner Muhammad Yunus (2003) from Bangladesh complains in his book that many charitable organizations from other countries define the "poor" in developing countries as small family farmers and then develop loan and grant programs to assist them as part of their efforts to eradicate global poverty. Actually, farmers are relatively rich as far as Bangalis are concerned, since farmers own land. There is another poorer layer of society: basically, indentured servants or slaves who work long hours for little pay and barely survive. Even as a lead economist, Yunus admits that he was initially somewhat oblivious to their plight. Once he realized the plight of the truly poor and what they were up against, he went on to form the Grameen Bank to offer small loans (about $100) to the very poor so they could start their own businesses and work toward financial independence. His efforts have been lauded and replicated around the globe. Yunus wasn't doing scientific research per se, but he did notice that one of the initial obstacles in solving the large poverty problem in Bangladesh was first changing the conceptualization of exactly who were the very poor. Even as chair of the Department of Economics at the University of Bangladesh, he saw that the literature with which he was familiar regarding poverty in his own country failed to identify and describe the plight of these desperately needy families. Once he gathered information regarding their collective conditions, he was able to conceive of a solution to their problems.

2. *Are there other factors associated with your topic that haven't been examined?* If so, you could design your class study around measurement of the new variable or variables to test if the factors are indeed related to the phenomenon you're studying. Stack and Gundlack (1992), for example, conducted a study on the relationship between types of music listened to and suicide. They found that the suicide rate of country music listeners was higher than for those who listened to other types of music. Few others before them thought to measure types of music preference when researching what factors might influence suicide.

3. *What types of methods have been used before to investigate your topic? Are they the only way to know about your topic?* Much of the literature on the effects of peer pressure, for example, is experimental. Asch's classic experiment (1956) put seven people in a room to answer test questions out loud. Only the last subject in a group of seven was unfamiliar with the experiment, but that last person didn't know that the other six (called "confederates") were really working for the experimenter. Each time they were asked a question, the first six confederates would give the same incorrect answer. In the experiment, approximately 75 percent of the last subjects also gave the same wrong answer at least once (even if they knew it to be incorrect). This demonstrates the power of peer pressure. Are people in the so-called real world as easily influenced by others as they are in an experimental laboratory? Using other methods to investigate this question can shed further light on the issue of peer pressure. Your class is limited to using interviews for this project. Nonetheless, thinking creatively about other methods can help point out weaknesses in the literature. Asking critical questions will help hone your ability to be a good consumer of empirical research.

4. *How strong are the results of the studies you are reviewing? Did the researchers take the right kind of sample so that we can trust that the results are representative of people other than those they took information from? Could a better study be designed?* We'll cover more of these issues in subsequent chapters in this book so you'll have a better idea how to look for these weaknesses in other studies. Suffice it to say that any research method has both strengths and weaknesses. You'll become more aware of the weaknesses inherent in each method, to be able to suggest that using an interview method for our particular course project might have strengths missing in other types of studies in the literature.

5. *Do the conclusions logically follow from the data?* You might read through a study and wonder how the researchers arrived at their conclusions. Sometimes our own egos or belief systems influence how we interpret trends in data. Tavris (1992), for example, notes myriad studies looking for differences between men and women. Most of them find no important differences, but instead of concluding that sex is not as important an influence as they thought many researchers conclude that they must have done something wrong in their study! Many of them so believed that there

were important differences between men and women that they found it difficult to accept the results even of studies they conducted themselves.

6. *Finally, do the explanations the researchers offer sound plausible? Might some other explanation better account for differences? Do they have concrete evidence in support of their theory, or are they mostly guessing?* When someone suggests an explanation of a relationship between variables after research has been conducted, it is referred to as *ex post facto hypothesizing* (guessing after the fact). But that's all it is: a guess. If the person has no specific evidence for the explanation and first presents it as a theory at the beginning of the research project and then tests to see whether relationships exist to support the theory, it has not been subjected to empirical scrutiny. This is an opportunity for you to think of alternative explanations that might be more meaningful, one of which you could test in your own research project for this class.

DESCRIBING YOUR LITERATURE REVIEW

In your final assignment, you'll need to write a summary of the articles you include in your literature review (see Chapter Fourteen). Write this section of your paper as soon as you have found your three articles, so that the results will still be fresh in your mind.

For this assignment, make sure you include in your literature review:

1. A one-or-two-paragraph description of each article you are describing. Each description should identify the major variables used in the study, the population and sampling method and sample size, the research methods used to investigate the topic, and the major conclusions.
2. Discussion of the articles in an order that makes sense. Usually, discussing the research in chronological order is best.
3. A brief summary at the end of the literature review that describes what is learned from the studies. That is, describe the major findings of the articles and then describe one or two areas that have either not been researched or not been researched adequately. This last statement can then be used as a segue to the next section of your paper.

SUMMARY

Scientists conduct literature reviews to determine where there are gaps in knowledge about a topic. Conducting a thorough review of literature is time-consuming and involved if done correctly, but the rewards are numerous. Now that you better know how to approach this task, you can become an expert on any field by rigorously searching for and consuming the scientific literature.

A review of literature involves looking for scientific articles in peer-reviewed journals, monographs, and research reports. This chapter has described several kinds of articles found in journals, so you are prepared to sort through the variety of information available in such sources. Empirical studies that are quantitative, comparative, or qualitative in nature are the most appropriate to include in your paper.

Now that you are aware of issues surrounding selection of sources for your literature review, find three appropriate sources and summarize them in abstract form. Then write a draft of the literature review section of your paper as described at the end of the chapter. Your professor may want to see a draft of your literature review. If not, keep it until it is time to complete the assignment described in the last chapter of this book.

REVIEW QUESTIONS

1. How does the body of knowledge human beings possess expand over time? How do scientists become aware of places where new knowledge is needed?
2. How would you feel if you conducted a study that added new knowledge to humanity's storehouse of information? How would you go about it?
3. What kinds of articles are appropriate to include in your literature review for this project? What sources are best to ignore?
4. What is the difference between a primary source and a secondary source? Which type should be consulted in your literature review, and why?
5. What things should be included in a write-up of a literature review?

KEY TERMS

Empirical articles Those reporting the results of research involving new data being collected about a topic.

Nonempirical articles Articles doing something other than reporting the findings from data collection. Such articles offer something else to the scientific enterprise, such as exploring or applying new theories.

Primary sources Articles reporting on the original collection or analysis of data. In the humanities, primary sources are actual historical artifacts such as a letter or journal.

Research monograph A book describing the results of an original research project.

Secondary sources Sources describing a primary source or attempting to make sense of it in some fashion.

Social Science Citation Index A resource combing through hundreds of social science journals and organizing them by subject, author, and cited references.

Unit of analysis The entity or "thing" whose behavior the researcher is interested in studying. Individuals, groups, organizations, and countries are examples of units of analysis.

3

Refining Your Study

Concepts and Relationships

LEARNING OBJECTIVES

- Expand your thinking by considering how concepts are related to each other.
- Understand the Western framework to understanding the world through the notion of the causal model.
- Learn how to develop hypotheses that enable you to test your ideas about how the world works.

Thus far you've learned how research topics are selected and how literature reviews are conducted. Once you've found articles on your topic, you'll quickly realize that social scientists almost always investigate a concept *in relation to* another topic or concept. This is what makes doing social science so interesting. In this chapter, you learn how to think causally and how to identify causal arguments in everyday ideas. This process is the key to eventually putting causal ideas to the test through science.

FROM CONCEPT TO RELATIONSHIP

Most of social science investigates the world by examining how a concept is related to something else. For example, one might choose to investigate the topic of juvenile delinquency. We could ask questions relating only to the phenomenon itself: "What is the rate of juvenile delinquency among the U.S. population?" "What are some forms of juvenile delinquency?" "How widespread is each type?" Questions like this are certainly informative, but they are also insufficient if one wishes to know what leads to juvenile delinquency. At some point, then, questions arise regarding a topic (such as juvenile delinquency) and its *causes* or *effects.*

Inquiring about the *causes* of juvenile delinquency is important. Society generally perceives juvenile delinquency to be a social problem, something to be reduced or avoided. To do that, causes of juvenile delinquency need to be identified so the conditions causing the problem can be changed, thereby yielding a reduction in the rate of juvenile delinquency. To be sure, there are many suspected causes; however, some explanations will have more empirical support than others.

What do *you* think causes juvenile delinquency? Some theorists suggest that single-parent families produce more delinquent children than two-parent families do. They hypothesize that children in one-parent families are supervised less often than those raised in two-parent families. If true, more children raised by a single parent would find themselves in trouble with the law. Family structure is a concept separate from, though possibly related to, the concept of juvenile delinquency.

You might come up with other potential influences that you believe might produce juvenile delinquency. What about friends? Is a young person who has friends engaged in criminal activities more likely to take part in those activities than someone who does not have friends who commit crimes? If so, the notion of "friends" is another concept or factor that might produce juvenile delinquency. Can you think of other potential influences?

Instead of asking, "What causes juvenile delinquency?" one might ask, "What does juvenile delinquency *cause*?" That is, if someone engages in juvenile delinquency, what might result from this behavior? A possible effect of juvenile delinquency could be greater likelihood to engage in criminal acts later in life. How does that experience, in turn, affect a young person's identity formation? How might the delinquent activities of a child affect family and other loved ones? Might engaging in juvenile delinquency allow the child to feel a closer bond with other criminals, or at least have more frequent contact? Might the child develop a disregard for rules established by authority figures? You can no doubt think of many consequences that engaging in delinquent acts as a juvenile might bring about; these we could call "effects" rather than causes of juvenile delinquency.

THE CAUSAL MODEL

Either way, science is generally interested in determining how concepts such as juvenile delinquency are related to other concepts in a cause-and-effect manner. This is a core assumption inherent in science: that the world (for our purposes, the social world) has a certain order to it, and this order takes the form of cause-and-effect relationships. Does the world really work this way? Ultimately, you can never prove absolutely that one thing *causes* another to change, but you can get very *close* to doing so by use of a combination of logic and science. The criteria for determining causality are that (1) the first concept must precede the second in time, (2) the two concepts must be correlated (a corresponding change in the second concept is observed as the first concept changes)), and (3) spuriousness has been ruled out. We discuss these criteria in more detail here, but for now it is important to note the assumption that the world is ordered by way of cause-and-effect.

EVERYDAY CAUSALITY

Why did you come to college? When I ask students this question, I inevitably hear many answers having to do with securing a better-paying or better-quality job when they graduate, or a promising future. I ask them if they really believe that college will do this for them, and almost all respond in the affirmative. What you have, then, is an excellent example of our belief in cause-and-effect: most college students are willing to pay thousands of dollars, forgo years of earnings, and do an incredible amount of academic work in the belief that they'll be further ahead in life with a college degree than without one. That's quite a bet—and one, by the way, that is consistently supported by data (U.S. Census, 2005).

This cause-and-effect way of looking at the world is called, appropriately, the **causal model**. It can be diagrammed as seen in Figure 3.1.

Figure 3.1. The Causal Model.

The causal model is a simple but effective way to visually depict relationships between two or more concepts. The way to "read" or think about the arrow is to say to yourself ". . . brings about a change in . . ." or ". . . influences . . ." or ". . . causes a change in. . . ." Thus, the model in Figure 3.1 would read "The Cause brings about a change in the Effect."

Let's apply this to an example. Thinking back to our example of *graduating from college* and *getting a good job*, can you identify one of these concepts as the cause and the other as the effect? In Figure 3.2, write "college degree" in the circle to which you feel it belongs, and "good job" in the other.

Figure 3.2. A Causal Model Exercise.

If you wrote "college degree" in the circle labeled "cause" and "good job" in the circle labeled "effect," you've got it right. This is because, according to the logic in our model, we believe that a college degree has the effect of getting a good job. It wouldn't make as much sense to suggest that getting a good job has the effect of getting a college degree. Reading the model from left to right, then, we would say, "A college degree influences getting a good job."

NOMOTHETIC VERSUS IDIOGRAPHIC EXPLANATIONS

You'll likely notice a difference in your college courses between those taught from a social science perspective (psychology, sociology, anthropology, economics) and those taught in the style of the humanities (English, philosophy, some history courses, art). The difference is subtle but can be important in helping you contrast those courses influenced directly by the scientific method.

A typical humanities approach to studying a particular topic is to examine it fully and completely, teasing out all the possible depth of meaning. For example, a historian might be interested in the topic of U.S. immigration. She or he will typically investigate the stories of immigrants, trying to identify *all* of the reasons or motivations that the many immigrants had for migrating to the United States. You can imagine how long the list might be. Even if the motivation of *one* person was to migrate simply because he found a neighbor in his home country to be annoying and wanted to get as far away from that neighbor as possible, historians would want to make note of the motivation.

Social scientists, however, are not so concerned with details that deal with only a few cases. In the spirit of science, we're interested in the most common or most frequently occurring *causes* bringing about certain *effects* (such as migration to the United States). In studying migration, then, we would ideally want to identify the *smallest* number of motivations of immigrants that explain the biggest amount of behavior (in this case, moving to the United States). We do this because we are ultimately interested in identifying relationships between concepts that are also likely to be relevant to cases other than just the one we are studying. If we find the most common reasons immigrants chose to move to the United States, those same reasons might also be the most common reasons immigrants choose to migrate to other countries in the world. This in turn allows us to develop a model of migration as it occurs around the world, wherein we could predict under what conditions many people might choose to migrate. This is valuable information in developing public policies or reacting to international crises.

These modes of explanation are called **idiographic** and **nomothetic**, respectively. Disciplines such as the humanities are more likely to use idiographic modes of explanation; they examine the rich detail in particular cases to thoroughly appreciate the diversity and nuances therein. Disciplines such as the social sciences are typically more interested in breadth than depth; the social sciences attempt to find those qualities about certain topics that one will also find in other, similar situations. Both approaches to studying human behavior are important, but it will be less confusing to you if you understand the difference. Of course, these typifications are not always true. There is in sociology a rich field of qualitative research that is more idiographic than quantitative sociology. The same holds true for humanities fields such as history, which is sometimes approached in a nomothetic manner.

Although beyond the scope of this project, social scientists are interested in developing models of human behavior that explain almost all of the variation in something else. To use this same example, what variables explain almost all of the reasons for immigrants migrating to other countries? A model that succeeds in doing this is called **parsimonious**; that is, almost all of the variation in something can be explained by only a few factors.

The reason is this: popular causes of something have a greater likelihood of being generalizable beyond the immediate situation. For example, if religious freedom is one of the biggest reasons immigrants came to the United States, then chances are good that religious freedom is a reason other countries have experienced immigration as well. Observations like this help us ultimately build models of human behavior applicable in many situations. This allows us to make predictions, and ultimately choices, about the kind of future we want for ourselves. If we know by way of social scientific research that religious freedom is an important predictor of migration trends, can you predict what will happen in a country that attempts to squelch religious freedom? All things being equal, one would expect oppressed people to migrate out of their home country. If world leaders consider this an undesirable outcome, they could encourage the leader of the nation in question to create a more tolerant society and reduce religious persecution. As a result, building generalizable models of human behavior can be a noble and potentially powerful endeavor.

BEING SPECIFIC: TURNING A RELATIONSHIP INTO A HYPOTHESIS

Once a scientist understands how to choose a topic, review the literature on the topic, and relate it to other concepts, the next task is to be more specific by turning each concept into a **variable**. Although related to a concept, a variable can be easily measured.

For example, psychologists often refer to the concept of intelligence, believing it varies considerably among individuals. Measuring intelligence, though, is a difficult undertaking. Psychologists and others have devised tests attempting to get at this important aspect of human life. The score a particular individual earns on one of these tests is called an **intelligence quotient**. Intelligence is the concept, and the intelligence quotient is the variable, or how researchers choose to measure the concept of intelligence. Scientists develop hypotheses using variables because they are measurable, whereas concepts cannot be measured.

To return to the causal model, in scientific nomenclature scientists often call the cause the **independent** or X variable, and the effect the **dependent** or Y variable. It is a good idea to memorize these terms because we will be using them for the remainder of this project. X, the independent variable, is perceived to change independently of any change in Y. Y, however, is *dependent* on X (it is the dependent variable). As X changes, it will have a corresponding impact on Y, causing a change in Y. Thus the causal model can be labeled using scientific notation (Figure 3.3).

Figure 3.3. The Causal Model Using the Language of Science.

Did you know that looking for causal models in things you read or listen to can improve your comprehension skills? Most people in Western societies lay out arguments for their positions in the form of *propositions*. These are, essentially, cause-and-effect statements. A good rule of thumb when you're not sure what an author is saying is, *"When in doubt, draw it out!"* That is, try to literally draw out the argument in the form of a causal model. Ask yourself what it is that the author suggests has changed or will change over time, and what brings about the effect. Once you understand the author's argument, you are in a position to consider and critique it.

Here's an example. See if you can identify the independent variable and dependent variable(s) in this text:

> The drug war has made war zones of some urban areas in much the same way Prohibition famously turned sections of Chicago into public shooting galleries. We've made millionaires of cocaine and heroin cartels in the same way temperance made wealthy men of Al Capone and George Remus. And we've made hardened criminals of small-time dope dealers the way alcohol Prohibition made felons of bartenders and distillers. The number of people behind bars in the United States for drug crimes alone now exceeds the number of people in prison in Europe for all crimes combined [Balko, 2004].

Can you identify the cause-and-effect statements in this paragraph? The author argues that America's war on drugs—the independent variable—has produced some outcomes that most would consider undesirable. According to Balko, the drug war has created war zones in some urban areas, enriched criminals, and turned minor offenders into hardened criminals by sending them to prison. These arguments could be drawn out in causal fashion (Figure 3.4).

Once you are able to clearly identify the cause-and-effect statements, you are in a better position to comprehend what is being said and critically evaluate the arguments.

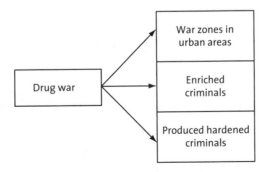

Figure 3.4. Causal Model Depicting Proposed Effects of Drug War.

TYING YOUR HYPOTHESIS BACK TO YOUR LITERATURE REVIEW

Now that you understand the idea of the causal model and the difference between concepts and variables, you are in a position to develop the next part of your paper. From your review of three articles in your review of literature, you learned what other variables researchers have associated with the topic or concept you identified at the end of Chapter One. You may think of other variables relevant to your topic but not identified by other researchers. With a more extensive review of literature, you might find articles that do deal with these left-out variables, but for the purposes of this project we are going to assume that your literature review represents *all* that we know about your topic.

With this in mind, write *three* hypotheses below that your class could test in the context of this project. As mentioned in Chapter One, remember to select relatively impersonal variables suitable to investigation in one semester with college students, and to expect variation in the responses to questions about the topic. Bring your hypotheses with you on the day your class selects one hypothesis to investigate for this project. Perhaps the class will choose one of yours.

1. _____

_____

2. _____

_____

3. _____

_____

SUMMARY

In this chapter, you have been challenged to expand your thinking by considering how concepts are related to each other in the real world. Social science is in the business of discovering these relationships, to help construct a better world for all. This is the essence of sociology—the science of society.

Embedded in the scientific method is the assumption that the world works in terms of cause and effect. This model is decidedly Western, but it is one that has already produced considerable results. For example, we are increasingly aware of the effect various government policies have on areas of social life. Choosing between possible futures involves making value choices about preferable outcomes. Finally, you're in a position where *you* can articulate hypotheses about the nature of social life. In the chapters to come, you'll test the hypothesis chosen by your class to see whether your educated guesses about how the world works are supported by the data you collect.

REVIEW QUESTIONS

1. What is the Western model for understanding how the world works? Can it be proved that the world works in this manner?
2. What is the difference between a concept and a variable? Why are variables used to construct a hypothesis, instead of concepts?
3. Do you believe that the world works in terms of cause and effect? Give an example from your own life of some activity you are involved in that you believe will produce a desirable outcome for you in the end. What does this say about your ideas on cause and effect?
4. Find an article on an Internet site that contains opinions about current topics. Identify the cause-and-effect statements embedded in the article. Does thinking causally help you better comprehend what is being said?

KEY TERMS

Causal model   A model inherent in the scientific method; the belief that the world is ordered in terms of cause and effect.

Dependent variable   The variable in a causal hypothesis believed to be affected by the influence of another variable identified as the independent variable.

Idiographic mode of explanation   An attempt to uncover all richness and detail of a particular situation to understand its uniqueness.

Independent variable   The variable in a causal hypothesis believed to exert an influence on another variable identified as the dependent variable.

Intelligence quotient   A score on a test by the same name, taken to be a valid and reliable indicator of an individual's overall intelligence.

Nomothetic mode of explanation   An attempt to identify the smallest number of predictors for a particular phenomenon that explains the greatest amount of the behavior.

Parsimonious   A state of a particular model of human behavior in which almost all the variation is accounted for or explained by the independent variables identified in the model.

Variable   A concept defined such that it can be measured and has various possible values.

4

Developing Your Theory

Thinking Made Explicit

LEARNING OBJECTIVES

- Recognize and gain practice in thinking sociologically, looking for sociological explanations of human behavior.
- Understand how logic is used in sociological theorizing to rise above the errors in thinking commonly found in everyday life.
- Hone your logical thinking skills by developing your own sociological theory for why a supposed relationship exists between your class's independent and dependent variables.

Completing this class project may well increase the time you spend thinking nomothetically in other areas of your life. As you consider the relationships between concepts that might exist among the student population at your school, you'll be stimulated to think about other relationships between concepts that are also true for noncollege students, and why. It's the kind of thinking that leads to answering the question, "Why do people behave the way they do?" Rather than merely getting caught up in the details of a particular situation, nomothetical thinking can help us learn from specific situations to reveal truths, or what sociologist Emile Durkheim (1982) called "social facts."

THINKING SOCIOLOGICALLY

The next step in preparing to think in this way (not just for excellence in this project but also to improve your skills) is to *think sociologically*. That is, when they're looking for explanations of why two concepts are related, sociologists often think first of social influences on our behavior. This comes easily to some people but is difficult for others. Recall an earlier example in which a factory owner is concerned about low productivity among the workers. Suppose the owner hires a consultant to devise ways to motivate employees to increase their productivity. Depending on her training, the consultant will immediately think of some possible changes but not others.

If trained in psychology, the consultant might look for changing attitudinal conditions in the minds of the workers. Are workers feeling stressed while on the job? If so, she might suggest some stress reduction training workshops, believing that workers who feel less stressed will be more productive. Another consultant trained in psychology might be interested in the personalities of the workers. Are some personality types better suited for this type of work than others? Employees might be subjected to a battery of personality tests to identify those who would be most productive in this work environment.

Consultants with sociological training would more often start by looking at factors *outside* the individual rather than inside. This is because sociological thinking trains you first to think of these characteristics before others. How is the work organized in the factory? Is the job that workers are expected to do reasonable? Is it humane? Do workers find the demands unreasonable or degrading? Are there rewards in place for people if they produce more products? Examining the structure of the social context in which work is done can reveal important factors that affect productivity. *To think in this way usually requires some practice or training—such as the type you're getting through this assignment.*

C. Wright Mills (1959) described this way of thinking as the **sociological imagination.** There are times in our lives when we encounter struggle. In our individualized culture, we often conceptualize the problem privately (that is, by believing I am the only one experiencing this problem, I conclude the solution ultimately resides with me alone). Mills suggested that some of the problems we experience personally are not ones we have brought on ourselves. Instead, they are a result of how society is structured. The social order—consisting of rules, laws, norms, and cultural conventions—also creates situations where some people experience certain types of problems. What people perceive to be a personal problem is often really a sociological issue.

AN EXAMPLE

When I was in graduate school, I worked for a nonprofit organization in an area of town where people didn't make much money. In my job, I heard firsthand accounts of people suffering from a variety of problems: alcohol abuse, domestic violence, abandonment by a parent or spouse, neglect, juvenile delinquency, drug use, trouble with the law, and the like. At first it was striking to see so many people seemingly making poor choices in their lives, and I struggled to understand their choices. Over a period of time, hearing the same stories again and again from different faces, I began to see that *poverty* was the common theme in people's lives. Many hadn't finished high school. As a result they worked long hours for little pay. Because parents were at work for so long and couldn't afford day care or a babysitter, their kids often remained unsupervised or looked after by older siblings.

These kids, in turn, felt abandoned by their parents. As they matured, they also realized that many others in society didn't respect their family; they felt they were on the bottom. Without supervision and much hope, some kids began taking part in delinquent activities as a way of acting out. Given the constant stress of insufficient money, parents too would sometimes seek escape in alcohol or drugs, or suddenly run away with another person who appeared to offer the hope of a wealthier, less-stressed life. In time I came to see the people I worked with as victims of the social order more than victims of their own behavior. Changes in government policies could drastically reduce the percentage of people living in poverty, which would in turn take away the stress brought on by financial hardship.

Less family stress would mean less frustration, less acting out, and less escapism through substance or alcohol abuse. What at first appeared to be the result of personal problems I later viewed as a sociological issue.

Thinking sociologically means looking first for explanations of behavior outside the individual, or of things that exist within the social context (Goldenberg, 1987). This includes considering the culture of a group, or the social structure (the rules) people in society are expected to live by. Expectations are a part of this social context, and they include stereotypes and perceptions most members of society have regarding categories of people. Gender, race, social class, and age groupings are examples of these categories.

Sociological thinking leads us to expect that these definitions of people will influence how they behave—a phenomenon known as a **self-fulfilling prophecy**. A sociological perspective lends itself to the belief that these social expectations are often more powerful in shaping behavior than any "real" or innate differences. This may not always be the case, but there is utility in thinking sociologically; it prevents one from automatically assuming that differences between human beings are "natural" or "biological." This in turn helps guard against racist and sexist stereotyping, which can damage real lives—values that are contrary to the democratic spirit of treating all people equally and granting them the right to pursue their own destinies. To test the validity of such sociological concepts as the self-fulfilling prophecy, one must first gain practice in thinking logically.

LOGIC: A TOOL OF THE TRADE

A hallmark of scientific thinking is carefully using logic in determining what is, or can be, "true" and what is not. Both natural and social scientists carefully weigh the evidence they collect with the theories they develop to help interpret what they've seen. Most people use logic to some extent in their everyday lives, but being logical all of the time eludes even the best of human beings. This is because, as human beings, we're likely to have "bad" days when our ego, emotions, selfishness, ethnocentrism, or other **nonrational** characteristics influence our thinking (Collins, 1992). Nonrational parts of our lives are those we have not (or will not) let logic govern. Because humans are not always logical, scientists (who are human) use the peer-review process. Inviting other experts to double-check one's logic is a control for one's inability to always be logical, because others can help identify logical errors in thinking.

COMMON HUMAN LOGICAL ERRORS

At the end of this section you will be challenged to develop a simple sociological theory explaining why you would think the two concepts or variables your class chooses to investigate are causally related. Using impeccable logic to explain your theory will prevent others from being able to criticize your ideas even before you begin. Therefore, it is desirable to avoid common logical errors when describing your theory.

Virtually all members of a society think sociologically from time to time. That is, we notice patterns of group behavior as we go about our lives and form opinions about people based on their group characteristics and affiliations. Do you have an opinion on why some people belong to religious groups but others are not religious? Do you believe that men and women differ in some ways, whether in attitude or behavior? Do you have an explanation for those perceived differences? Most of us form opinions on topics such as these, which are based on our own personal observations and experiences. Sometimes the conclusions we adopt are based on only a few observations, and the conclusions we come to may be misguided or downright wrong.

It's difficult for most humans to admit their favorite theories or beliefs *might* be wrong, let alone admit they *are* wrong when presented with good evidence to the contrary. According to social psychologists, this is because our theories, or **constructs**, form the basis of our understanding of how the world works. To change one of these beliefs can be personally threatening; it entails rethinking our assumptions about how the world is ordered. To protect our favorite beliefs and ideas from being disproven, we humans develop ultimately flawed ways of thinking.

Error One: Circular Thinking

One of the most common errors in logic is creating statements about the world or people that are simply true by definition; they can never be disproved or falsified. Circular statements like this are called **tautologies**. For example, consider the statement, "Real men are insensitive." Is this statement true? How do we test it? Let's say we develop a test of male sensitivity and administer this test to thousands of men, some of whom turn out to be quite sensitive in the way we've measured it. How might I, for instance, try to defend the statement despite evidence to the contrary? Simple: I would argue that the men who were shown to be sensitive were not *real* men. Thus my idea that real men are insensitive stands as being true despite evidence to the contrary. There is no way to disprove the statement as it stands. Developing tautologies helps us protect those beliefs or ideas that are near and dear to us, but this doesn't necessarily assist us in trying to discern truth from falsehood.

Error Two: Illogical Reasoning

Illogical reasoning is another fairly common logical error. Illogical reasoning is simply the result of deducing something such that one thought or idea does not meaningfully follow from another; it doesn't make sense. The question, "Would you rather go to Chicago, or by bus?" is, I trust, clearly illogical to you. The word *rather* implies two mutually exclusive choices, but what follows is not two exclusive choices. Going to Chicago and traveling by bus could both happen at the same time, and one could travel by bus to somewhere other than Chicago. Thus using *rather* when there are not mutually exclusive alternatives is illogical.

A few years ago a television commercial for a government lottery depicted people running to the store to buy a lottery ticket and then proudly exclaiming, "It's my turn!" This argument, of course, is illogical. Every lottery winner is chosen through a random process of number selection, and every drawing is completely independent of all the others. No one organizes lottery winners to stand in line, each getting "a turn" to win the lottery. In fact, the probability of ever winning a lottery is infinitesimally small, so much so that it makes more sense to *not* buy a ticket than to buy one, if having as much money as you can is your goal.

Here's another example of illogical reasoning. A young man went to the doctor and said, "I have a problem. I think I'm dead." The doctor asked the young man quizzically, "Why do you think you're dead?" "I don't know," the young man responded; "it's just a belief I've always had. My friends tell me this is a problem that I need to fix. Can you help me?" "I think I can," said the doctor. "Here is your prescription: for the next two weeks I want you to look at yourself in the mirror every morning and every evening. Each time, look yourself in the eye and say, 'Dead men do not bleed.' Repeat these words to yourself ten times each morning and ten times each evening for the next two weeks."

The young man returned two weeks later at his scheduled appointment. "Did you follow my prescription?" asked the doctor. "Yes, I did," responded the young man. "Every morning and every evening I looked myself in the eye and told myself, 'Dead men do not bleed.'" "Fine," said the doctor, "Now give me your hand." The young man extended his hand. As he did, the doctor took a small pin and pricked the young man's fingertip, causing it to bleed. The young man was silent for a moment, and then exclaimed, "Well what do you know! Dead men *do* bleed!"

Obviously, the assumptions that the young man held were so important to him that he was willing to reinterpret the evidence before him rather than change his belief to that suggested by his doctor.

Error Three: Positivistic Logic

Throughout life, we are exposed to perspectives and beliefs about a variety of subjects. Some of these we internalize, and they become part of us; others we reject. We are more likely to internalize ideas from sources we consider trustworthy, such as parents and good friends (Cantor, Alfonso, and Zillman, 1976). **Positivistic logic** is a system of inquiry in which a belief or theory is first adopted by an individual or group. Evidence supporting the belief is then gathered, while evidence to the contrary is systematically ignored or minimized. Social psychologists call this confirmation bias, because people often pay attention to information supporting their favorite beliefs. In fact, many also prefer to limit their exposure to information that contradicts their favorite beliefs, choosing instead to expose themselves only to sources that share their beliefs (McFarland, 1996).

It can be threatening to think that an idea or belief one has internalized might be incorrect, since beliefs can become part of our identity. As a result, information supporting our views is welcomed because it is not personally threatening, even if sketchy or tenuous. At the same time, we're less likely to pay attention to or take seriously information that contradicts or invalidates personal beliefs. In a biased fashion, then, we develop or embrace ideas and look for information that reinforces those ideas.

This method of information collection has its strengths, but its weaknesses should be obvious. People sometimes internalize beliefs and ideas that are simply false. Once part of our identity, they become difficult to dislodge or disprove. Further, information that is fairly tenuous is sometimes too readily accepted. In the pursuit of knowledge, one can see how using positivistic logic can cause problems over the long run. By contrast, science adopts a **negativistic logic**. In this process, all beliefs and ideas are assumed to be false until convincing evidence is offered to the contrary. This requirement of external sensory validation is known as **empiricism** and is a key assumption of science. I discuss this in more detail in the next major section.

Error Four: Mystification

A final way in which human beings protect their pet beliefs from being falsified is simply to hide or keep them from the scrutiny of logic or of others. They do this by creating a veil of vagueness around the subject. One cannot criticize something that has not been made explicit. For example, making the claim "You'll never understand" to someone else implies that what you believe is true, but that it is beyond the comprehension of the other and therefore will always remain true. People often make this claim about love: "It's a beautiful, wonderful thing that you'll never understand. It just is."

Can you think of other defense mechanisms that aid in mystifying, rather than clarifying, the beliefs of others? "I know what I mean but I can't explain it" is a claim with the same effect of suggesting an idea is true but not knowable by others. Other times, people just shut down the conversation about certain topics. "I don't talk about it" aids in mystification. In fact, a norm of politeness suggests that religion, sex, or politics should not be discussed with strangers. Because beliefs in these areas are personal, some feel threatened when their personal beliefs are subjected to criticism by others.

THE USE OF LOGIC IN SCIENCE

Up to this point, we've examined how causal theorizing and the informal way in which logic is used in everyday life are subject to error. Science tries to rise above these errors by building systematic controls into the process of inquiry. Researchers must first make explicit the theory or theories they use. Mystification or vagueness is not tolerated.

To control for tautological thinking and avoid vagaries, science embraces the principle of **falsification**. That is, once a researcher identifies concepts that she believes are related and describes the theoretical reasoning by which this relationship is made explicit, the researcher then constructs a research design allowing collection of data that could falsify her theory. Concepts and measures are carefully described so others can critically examine the logic inherent in the design. Researchers state at the outset the kind of information they will take as evidence that their theory is true and the evidence they will gather that indicates lack of support for the theory. Unless falsifiable, a statement is not a valid scientific theory.

For example, a theorist might suggest that children from single-parent homes are more likely to be arrested for juvenile delinquency, because (and here is the theory) they might have fewer hours of direct supervision—one parent cannot watch a child as often as two parents. The researcher would then decide how to measure family structure (one parent or two parents) and juvenile delinquency (perhaps he or she would ask the parent or parents in a survey if their child has ever been charged with a crime). The researcher would commit to saying that if more children from single-parent homes were found to be in trouble with the law than children from two-parent homes, it would be evidence supporting their theory. If the rate of juvenile delinquency were the same as or higher among children from two-parent families, however, researchers would accept this as lack of evidence for the theory. The theory would therefore be falsified, requiring that it be either modified or discarded.

By making explicit beforehand what kinds of information will be interpreted as supporting or not supporting ideas, tautology is avoided by allowing the theory to be falsified. Note how this falsifiability is more rigorous than tautological thinking and vagueness, where ideas can never be falsified. By allowing evidence to determine which ideas are accepted and which are rejected, scientific knowledge can accumulate.

Illogical reasoning is likewise minimized in science through the use of peer review. A researcher completes a study, writes it up in the form of an article, and submits it for publication in a scientific or academic journal, hoping for publication. The editor of the journal receives the article, removes the author's name and other identifying information from the title page, and sends it out to other experts (usually two or three) in that field of study. This is called blind peer review because the experts reviewing the paper do not know the identity of the author. The experts go through the article with a fine-tooth comb, looking for logical errors in the theory, methods, or interpretation of the data. They send written comments and criticisms back to the editor, who then chooses to (1) publish the article, (2) ask the author to make changes based on the opinion of the experts, or (3) reject the article outright.

Once the article is accepted and published in the journal, other researchers working in the same field also have an opportunity to consider the evidence in the article, critique it, try to replicate it, or accept the evidence therein. Through this process of scrutiny and replication, logical fallacies are minimized and scientific knowledge in a given field is allowed to progress. This objective examination of logic and evidence by other peers controls for bias and personal subjectivity on the part of the individual scientist. In fact, this process is the best and most rigorous test of knowledge known to humankind. Peer review and replication ultimately allow us to test the information that is eventually accepted as knowledge.

Finally, as mentioned previously, the logic inherent in the scientific method is rigorous because of using negativistic logic and requiring empirical support. By accepting this rigorous criteria, scientists are less subject to being swayed by cultural beliefs and values, religious doctrines, superstitions, emotional highs and lows, and other attributes of the human experience that often allow us to accept untested or unproven ideas. If errors are made in science, they are in the direction of not accepting some things that are true (because they have not been replicated in scientific studies) rather than accepting false ideas as truth. This standard of knowledge is obviously higher than the more positivistic standard we use in everyday life. Knowledge gained through science is typically more enduring than what is assumed to be true on the basis of other ways of knowing.

ASSUMPTIONS OF SCIENCE

Although scientists adopt a skeptical approach to acquiring knowledge, it should be noted that certain untestable assumptions are also a part of scientific inquiry. One cannot ultimately know whether these assumptions are correct, but trusting information collected through the scientific method first requires adopting certain propositions as articles of faith. Among the most important are that:

1. There is a real world.
2. The real world is knowable through sensory impressions.
3. The real world is ordered, by means of cause and effect.
4. Knowledge is superior to ignorance (adapted from Sjoberg and Nett, 1968, pp. 23–24).

If you think these are reasonable propositions, you may have a future in social (or natural) science! Ultimately, all knowledge accumulated through science is predicated on accepting these assumptions.

COMBINING SOCIOLOGICAL THINKING WITH LOGIC: THEORIZING

By now you should have a deeper appreciation for the difference between everyday, informal use of logic and the more rigorous ways in which scientists use logic. You're also becoming more familiar with how sociologists think. Combining these two enterprises to create more enduring and insightful perspectives on human behavior is one of the joys of being a sociologist.

When sociology was first developing, rapid social changes resulting from industrialization were causing many people to ponder the long-term effects of these changes on society and social stability. Would the changes be good or bad? Would they create societies that would ultimately worsen the quality of life for most citizens or bring about a utopian style of life that people before could scarcely imagine? Would exploitation become common, or would individual citizens become empowered?

At the same time, science as a way of knowing was also being developed. The publication of Charles Darwin's *The Origin of Species* in 1859 brought to public consciousness radical new theories about human evolution resulting from stringent use of logic combined with carefully documented observation and experimentation (constructive empiricism). It wasn't long before some people were thinking about applying the scientific method to the study of society. Why not? If general historical trends and principles existed, and some societies brought about a better quality of life than others, why not strategically think about studying and designing societies that would purposely create better societies?

Auguste Comte (1988) was one of the first theorists to formally make this suggestion. The new science of society, he argued, would be called *sociology*. By carefully documenting social causes and the effects they elicit, sociologists could begin advising politicians and rulers on how to create societies that would be veritable utopias on earth. Comte said that sociology would be the queen of the social sciences. Because of its broad approach, all other studies of collective human behavior would be subordinated to this large enterprise of scientifically designing society.

What a grand idea! Indeed, it is this exciting possibility that still attracts many people to major in sociology. The hope of uncovering the principles of human social life and using that knowledge to help create a better way of life for people across the world is to some an irresistible attraction. Alas, the enterprise has been fraught with pitfalls and disappointments. To design a better way of life, sociologists first had to uncover the nature of social life as it is so they could work on improving it.

MAJOR SOCIOLOGICAL THEORIES

The trouble started when social theorists began formalizing their ideas in grand theories that sought to uncover principles common to all societies and groups. In other words, what is the nature of social life? If, say, one thousand people were placed on an island with no memory of the way they previously lived, what would happen over time on that island? You surely have your own opinion of what would happen. As theorists articulated their views using formal logic, major disagreements were found at even this most elementary level. What is the nature of social life? That is, if left to themselves, what "typical" patterns of group behavior would emerge? Theorists attempting to answer this question fall into many camps. We'll cover three of them here as examples.

Functionalism

Emile Durkheim (1982) was one of the first social theorists concerned with how to achieve social solidarity. How is it that members of society come to see themselves as having something in common with each other and identify with one another? Durkheim noted that societies were historically held together by a kind of understanding known as **mechanical solidarity**. Prior to industrialization, traditional (not industrialized) societies were cohesive because they were relatively small. Many people in traditional societies know one another through face-to-face relationships and develop feelings for each other. Traditions develop that people find meaningful. As these traditions are reenacted, social solidarity is achieved. Society therefore functions as a smooth-running machine. Members are interested in working together toward common goals such as safety and well-being. When conflict occurs (as it is sure to do), people identify it as a problem needing to be solved. Through collective dialogue, solutions to problems are eventually agreed on through a process of consensus building. Ultimately, societies function because essential human needs are met.

Industrialization, however, changes this essential nature of cohesion. Durkheim was fascinated to see that societies still maintained some semblance of social order and social control even during times of rapid social change. To account for this, Durkheim suggested that **organic solidarity** replaced mechanical solidarity in developed societies. Compared to traditional societies, modern industrial societies are much larger, containing potentially millions of people. Engaging in face-to-face relations with everyone is impossible, as is dialogue resulting in consensual development of collective norms and values. Durkheim suggested that organic solidarity develops in the absence of functional, or mechanical, solidarity. Organic solidarity implies a sense of social cohesion based primarily on instrumental reasoning brought about by a sense of interdependence. As a member of society, one might not develop positive feelings for most others, but one begins to realize that quality of life depends on others, thanks mostly to a highly specialized division of labor.

For example, a teacher is hired to assist others in learning more about the world and preparing them for life in the society in which they live. Teachers do not typically grow their own food; farmers living in rural areas do this job. Farmers are not expected to know about all aspects of the world and therefore cannot be expected to give their children formal education. They depend on teachers for this service. Teachers and farmers alike realize that they depend on each other for survival and well-being, and as a result they feel some sense of community with one another. Multiplied many times, relationships like these lead to a sense of organic solidarity among people in industrialized societies.

Durkheim's ideas illustrate what has become known as the functionalist perspective in sociology. Extrapolating to all societies, functionalists believe that, all things being equal, social groups tend to develop a sense of solidarity or equilibrium. This solidarity motivates individual members to work together in developing a social system serving the greatest good. Through a variety of mechanisms, citizens supply input to the development and refinement of social institutions, which are regularized patterns of interacting. Through developing consensus, social groups seek to minimize problems and maintain stability over time.

Conflict Theory

A very different approach to understanding societies is the conflict tradition. Rather than believing that social life is developed through a shared process of consensus, conflict theorists see the essence of social life as conflict between competing groups. In a given group, say conflict theorists, smaller groups develop as they compete for scarce resources, be they tangible (land, trees, minerals) or intangible (power, prestige, influence). Eventually, one group gains a leg up on the others and secures more of these resources for itself. In turn, they use their control of these resources to control others in society.

Many of Karl Marx's writings formed the basis for what today is recognized as conflict theory. Marx (1992) believed that all conflict in societies is essentially the result of one's relationship to the means of production, which leads to social stratification, or class-based exploitation and animosity. In any society, elites gain access to such resources as political power and money, and then they use their superior position to control masses of other people. This gives them the ability to continue accruing more wealth, power, and prestige for themselves.

Theorists writing in this tradition since Marx's time have broadened the number of causes of conflict in society. It's true that class-based conflict exists in virtually all societies, but social groups stratify themselves over factors other than social class. Other types of conflict, for example, are rooted in racism, the belief that some people are inherently superior to others. Additional stratification systems are formed on the basis of sex, the most typical being patriarchy, or rule by men over women.

Conflict theorists also pay a good deal of attention to the ideological mechanisms that groups in control develop to legitimize their superior status in society. If people with fewer resources realized they have less because of what those in control have done, then physical conflict, riots, and other forms of violence may become frequent. Elites, though, develop ways of convincing the disadvantaged that the system exists for reasons other than that it works for the benefit of the elites. Because social elites usually have greater access to cultural industries (such as book and magazine publishing companies, television stations, popular Websites, and the like), they use these industries to send out messages validating the current state of affairs. For example, these messages include stories of people who went from rags to riches, implying that anyone in the society could be successful by just trying. Other messages deny that any real differences exist, or that members of the disadvantaged who get more for themselves find they aren't really happy anyway and wish they could go back to their previous lives.

To conflict theorists, **ideology** is a powerful way of controlling large groups of people over an extended period of time. An ideology is a belief that, if internalized, benefits some people more than others. More than just a belief, an ideology has political and social consequences. As long as the elites get people to believe what they want them to believe, ordinary citizens will not fight the system that puts them at a disadvantage. To the contrary, many will even go to war and lay down their lives to protect that same system, being motivated by the ideological belief system they have internalized. Analyses of social life conducted from a conflict point of view try to highlight ideas in society benefiting one group (usually the ones that have more resources) more than others.

Symbolic Interactionist Theory

These perspectives have something in common: they make assumptions regarding the "true" nature of social life and interpret the social world from that perspective. A third sociological tradition, however, maintains that human life is not so predictable. To refer back to our island example, symbolic interactionists believe there is no essential nature to social life. If we replicate the experiment of putting a thousand people on several islands, symbolic interactionists believe we will see a variety of outcomes.

Human social life, then, is mostly unpredictable to symbolic interactionists. They do generally agree, though, that some common elements may appear in social groups over time. People on all of the islands in our experiment will eventually develop a common understanding or definition of what is actually happening on their island. They may dislike it or may embrace it, but over time most social groups develop a common definition of reality. This is accomplished as social groups begin to define collectively certain symbolic elements common to their experience. Trees, for example, might come to be defined in a certain way. On some islands they might be revered for their shade. On other islands they might be seen as a commodity to be exploited for firewood or housing materials. What is common to all, though, is development of shared understandings of the world humans inhabit. The same is true for nonmaterial symbols such as prestige, love, power, and religion. Through interaction (peaceful or not), all the people on the island begin to develop shared understandings of how things work. Thus, symbolic interactionists are fascinated with the actual process through which social groups develop shared meanings of symbols in their environment.

SUMMING UP

These three theoretical perspectives have been described here to give you examples of sociological thinking on the grandest and most abstract level. Considerable debate continues among sociologists as to the nature of social life. In some ways, this has frustrated the project of planning or building better societies because sociologists and others have yet to arrive at a common ground regarding the essential nature of social life—or, as symbolic interactionists stress, whether it even has one. On the other hand, some sociologists value the fact that there are multiple perspectives allowing them to view problems and interpret data diversely, enriching one's understanding of the complex nature of social relations.

More recently, most sociologists have been content to attempt to uncover patterns of social life that might be more short-lived or limited to only certain groups or societies rather than uncovering grand "essentials" of human group life. What behavioral relationship exists, for example, between sex and, say, drinking? Is there a connection between religiosity and a status quo orientation to society? If we ask questions such as these, there will always be, at the forefront of the investigation, development and refinement of sociological theory. Why would we expect these two variables to be related? In building theories of the "middle range" (Merton, 1968) in this manner, we are over time led to grander insights into the nature of social life. In this project you will attempt to apply your sociological imagination to understanding a relationship between two concepts.

DEVELOPING A THEORY FOR YOUR CLASS PROJECT

It's time to put all of this discussion together and apply it to your class project. Now that you know some of the differences between logic used in a casual manner and logic as part of the scientific method, you are in a better position to develop your own theory regarding the two topics or concepts accepted by your class earlier in the term.

As described earlier, you likely have some personal ideas on why you think the two concepts identified in your class discussion are related. For the purposes of illustration, let's assume your class chose to examine the relationship between gender (i.e., male and female) and attitude toward premarital sex. If you remember the earlier discussion about causal relationships, you should be able to identify the independent and dependent variables in this example. Attitude toward premarital sex would be the *dependent* variable because the implicit way in which the two variables (gender and attitude toward premarital sex) appear to be related is that one's attitude would depend on one's gender. Arguing the opposite— one's attitude toward premarital sex determines one's gender—is an example of illogical reasoning (gender precedes attitude toward premarital sex in time). Therefore, you are left to accept gender as the independent variable and attitude toward premarital sex as the dependent variable.

Now consider the two concepts your class decided you would use in your project for this semester. Your class may have already determined the independent and dependent variables. If not, take a moment to identify first which one should be the independent variable (that is, the cause that is going to bring about a change in the dependent variable). Write them here:

_____   _____

Independent variable   Dependent variable

Once you've done this, chances are you're already implicitly aware of the theory you have used to make sense of the supposed relationship between these two variables.

It's important to write out your explanation of *why and how* you think these two variables are related. Do that here so you can examine your ideas more closely.

The reason I feel these two variables are related is _____

_____

_____

_____

_____

It is equally important, however, to be sure to specify how you believe the two variables **covary**. That is, as the independent variable changes, what change in the dependent variable do you expect? In the example of gender and attitude toward premarital sex, one could hypothesize that men would have a more favorable attitude toward premarital sex than women. Of course, the opposite could also be hypothesized, that women would have a more favorable attitude toward premarital sex than men. The determining factor in specifying a hypothesis is ultimately the theory one uses to explain why the two variables should be related. It is necessary to make this thinking explicit. What explanation would you offer for the hypothesis that men have a more favorable attitude toward premarital sex than women?

SOCIAL FORCES

Remember that it is important in this process to exercise your sociological imagination. For example, it would be easy to suggest a "natural" or *biological* reason, for example that there is something inherent in males that makes them more favorably disposed to sex compared to women (and again, note that any responsible scientist would also make explicit what he thinks it is about male biology that would cause the scientist to propose such). Here, though, is a chance for you to think sociologically about "differences" between men and women. Consider those forces existing *outside* the individual—social forces. Is there anything different in how we raise boys and girls, for example, that might foster a greater attraction to the notion of premarital sex for men than women?

One might suggest boys are raised more often with fewer restrictions than girls are. In other words, there is a certain level of acceptability for boys to engage in activities that are seen by society to be somewhat deviant. The saying "boys will be boys" is an example of lower expectations for male morality than for female morality. On the other hand, girls are frequently raised with greater expectations and restrictions compared to their male counterparts. As a result, our sociological imagination would be able to account for this differently from how biologists are. Ultimately, more specific studies would need to be conducted to distinguish between biological and sociological models.

Being Specific

It is important to be as explicit as possible in developing a theory that explains a relationship between the two variables. Nothing taken for granted should be left unstated. This is because small differences in explanation can have potentially large implications. Consider the example of gender influencing attitude toward premarital sex. In stating a sociological explanation of why we think the two variables are related, we might be tempted to simply write, "I think the two variables are related because a double standard exists for men and women in our culture. Men generally learn that it's OK to be promiscuous; women don't. Thus, I would predict that more men will have favorable attitudes toward premarital sex than women."

What do you think of this theory? Does it make sense to you? Is it clear enough? Should more be added? At first glance, the explanation makes good sense. But think more carefully about what kinds of information are missing. First, from whom do men and women receive differing messages about promiscuity? their parents? friends? the media? These are all distinct influences. Someone could say the double standard is a part of our culture, but it's important to identify examples and make explicit the sources of this information.

Second, how do men and women learn or "internalize" these messages? Theories of learning vary considerably and the differences, again, are subtle but important. Are human beings basically open vessels, blank slates? Or do human beings learn primarily through role modeling—watching what other important people in their lives do and then seeking to copy the behavior? Perhaps human beings learn primarily through behavioral modification, a result of being rewarded or punished for certain actions. That is, when people act in a sexist manner and are rewarded for it, are they more likely to repeat the action than if they were scolded? The explanations are qualitatively different when it comes to the source of the variation between men and women.

Hypotheses are often modified according to these important theoretical distinctions. Making hypotheses explicit also presents opportunities for future research. That is, if a relationship were found between sex and attitude toward premarital sex, research in the future would first attempt to investigate the processes by which people come to learn double standards as suggested by the theory in the original study.

The lesson to take from all this is to be as explicit as possible when you offer an explanation or theory in your paper of why you think the two variables your class chose to research are related. Don't be afraid to make a commitment to what you think is going on. As human beings, some of us periodically suffer from ego involvement with our favorite theories. That is, we believe them so much we try to be vague enough to protect them from being discredited. But this is where science tries to rise above our human imperfections, by allowing our ideas to be tested and potentially falsified.

Take a look at the explanation you wrote down earlier in this chapter. What aspects of your theory need to be clarified? Make those changes. In addition to adding descriptions clarifying the processes through which you think one variable affects another, tying your explanation to one of the three grand theories described earlier in this chapter (structural functionalism, conflict theory, or symbolic interactionist theory) will further help to clarify your theory. This is because assumptions as to the nature of social relations are an integral part of each theory. Integrating your explanation to one of these major theories will help you understand what assumptions about social relations are implicit in your theory. This can help you improve it.

An Illustration

Here is an example for you to consider. Let's pretend a class wants to see if students with a variety of majors have differing patterns of alcohol consumption. They adopt the independent variable of *type of major* and the dependent variable of *number of days per week a student consumes alcohol.* The two types of majors they identify are business or the natural sciences on the one hand, and students majoring in the arts, humanities, or social sciences on the other.

What hypothesis would you develop with these two variables? What theory would you use to explain your hypothesis? Here is how one student described it:

> The hypothesis we are testing is the relationship between a student's type of major and the number of days per week a student drinks alcohol. The independent variable in this analysis will be the student's major. The dependent variable will be the number of days a student drinks each week. I believe that people in the science/business majors drink more frequently than people majoring in the arts/social sciences.
>
> The theory that leads me to believe this is structural functionalism. Emile Durkheim suggested that social practices exist in societies because they serve some type of social function. Durkheim believed that deviance is functional for society because it serves a social function. Durkheim said, "deviance promotes social unity" (Henslin, 2008:213). By this, he meant that we feel we are a part of a group by conforming to a specific group's principles. The people who want to be associated with a deviant group may be more inclined to be deviant in order to fit in.
>
> For the purposes of this study, I am identifying frequent drinking as deviant behavior. This theory of deviance does not fully explain, however, the greater proportion of frequent drinkers in the science/business field. In my belief, fields associated with science/business put more pressure on people than fields associated with arts/social sciences. As a way to cope with this greater pressure, students in science/business fields may develop a culture in which it is acceptable to drink more frequently than in the less stressful arts/social science fields. This leads me to believe that the more challenging a major is, the more people are inclined to drink because of the pressures associated.

Regardless of your opinion of this student's theory, notice that his explanation contains all of the necessary components specified earlier. First, he identifies the independent and dependent variables. Next, he articulates his hypothesis and specifies how he believes the two variables will covary. Third, he briefly describes a sociological theory and explains its relationship to his hypothesis. Finally, he makes explicit his ideas as to how and why the type of major and frequency of consuming alcohol may be related: it is due to high stress.

IMPROVING YOUR WORLD

In science, the strength and quality of any investigation ultimately depend on the quality of logic used to make sense of the information collected. At first it may feel like work to you, but understanding the importance of being specific can motivate you to do an excellent job. Poorly developed theories result in a poor or incorrect interpretation of collected data. Little is gained from projects in which the logic is flawed.

The cartoon in Figure 4.1 is a good illustration of a poorly articulated theory. Leaving processes vague is widely practiced in everyday interactions, but writing out exactly what we think is going on and subjecting it to scrutiny is one way science transcends everyday understandings of the world. Ultimately, the goal is that we will create an even better one.

Figure 4.1. Eliminating Mystification in Science.

Source: ScienceCartoonsPlus.com. Used with permission.

SUMMARY

Thinking sociologically means first considering those influences or factors existing outside the individual but within our social world. Rules, laws, norms, cultural conventions, and beliefs are all aspects of our social world that play a role in influencing both individual and group behavior. Our critical thinking skills are enhanced when we consider sociological explanations others may be less inclined to identify.

Science attempts to prevent common errors in thinking by use of logic made explicit so that others can check our own thought progression. Negativistic logic is used in science to err on the side of caution and not adopt theories and beliefs that are not supported by evidence. Specifying exactly how and why we believe one variable will affect another is a way to avoid mystification and add clarity to the ideas we test through the scientific method.

With this in mind, you should now be able to articulate and refine your own sociological theory about why and how you suspect the two variables identified by your class are related. This chapter challenged you to write down your explanation for the variables identified by your class and to revise this explanation to make sure it is specific and to the point, with nothing left to guesswork. You were also encouraged to integrate your explanation with one of the three major sociological theories reviewed in this chapter. A good example was given so you understand what is expected of you for your class assignment. Did you ever imagine yourself to be a sociological theorist? You are now!

REVIEW QUESTIONS

1. What is involved in thinking sociologically? How do sociological theories of human behavior differ from those of other disciplines?
2. What are four common logical errors made in everyday communication? Give an example of each type of error.
3. What techniques do scientists use to try to transcend these common errors? In your opinion, is the logic of science superior to commonly used logic? Why or why not?
4. Explain how a functionalist theorist, a conflict theorist, and a symbolic interactionist theorist might explain the existence of social class.
5. What steps are necessary in properly articulating a sociological theory that explains why and how two variables might be related?

KEY TERMS

Constructs Individual perceptions and assumptions regarding how the world is ordered.

Covary Two variables that change together. When one variable changes at a rate consistent with another, they are said to covary.

Empiricism The practice of testing beliefs, ideas, and theories through sensory input or observations of the world, as opposed to intuition, faith, or logic alone.

Falsification Before a study is undertaken, the practice of identifying the kind of information collected that would be interpreted as negating or failing to support a hypothesis.

Ideology A vision of society or a set of beliefs that have the consequence, if believed, of benefiting one group in society at the expense of another.

Illogical reasoning Deducing something such that one thought or idea does not meaningfully follow from the other; it is nonsensical.

Mechanical solidarity Social solidarity created through a sense of face-to-face relationships and kinship ties that, according to Durkheim, is typically found in traditional societies.

Negativistic logic An assumption of the scientific method whereby every statement is assumed to be false until incontrovertible proof renders the negative position untenable.

Nonrational Aspects of life that have not been examined through the use of logic.

Organic solidarity Social solidarity created through the realization that various parts of society are interdependent for survival and success. According to Durkheim, organic solidarity is typical in modern societies.

Positivistic logic A process of inquiry involving first adopting certain beliefs or perspectives and then gathering supporting information.

Self-fulfilling prophecy A process in which the expectations of others so affect an individual that the person becomes what others expect.

Sociological imagination A way of thinking about the world that sees personal problems as the result of public issues.

Tautologies Statements that are true by definition and thus cannot be disproved.

5

Research Design 1

Concepts and Planning

LEARNING OBJECTIVES

- Identify the four main steps involved in designing research projects.
- Think through the issues involved in designing reliable and valid research in the first two steps.
- Understand how and why compromises are often made in research projects, and learn to assess how various compromises affect the trustworthiness of the results.

How would you go about gathering information to test your class hypothesis if you were the principal researcher responsible for carrying out the study? What method would you use? a survey? interviews? an experiment of some sort? Would you try to gather information from individuals, groups, households, organizations, or all of society? Would you gather data only once, or several times over a period of days, weeks, or longer?

The goal of any research project is to gather data in such a way that others trust the evidence you gather. You want to avoid having someone look at your study after it's completed and say, "This study isn't very good. The researcher didn't design it in such a way that the findings are trustworthy." How does one go about designing a project that is rigorous enough to gain the respect of other scientists?

Designing research involves four critical steps: (1) defining concepts, (2) planning the study, (3) data collection, and (4) sampling. This chapter introduces you to critical issues involved in the first two of these steps, while the next chapter covers steps three and four. The discussion of each step concludes with an application of the material to your class project.

Compromises are made in every research project because of practical constraints of time, money, or other limited resources. This doesn't mean that such studies are worthless. Rather, by knowing the critical issues involved in research design one can take into account certain shortcomings and comprehend under what conditions the results might be meaningful. Once familiar with the issues of research design covered in this chapter and the next, you'll have the ability to assess the relative merits of your class's research design.

Before turning to a discussion of the four steps of research design, we must introduce the issues of validity and reliability. In all stages, designing a research project that is both valid and reliable is the ultimate goal.

VALIDITY AND RELIABILITY

Much planning and strategy goes into designing research projects to build *valid* and *reliable* data collection methods. These two terms are important enough to merit focusing on them for a moment. If you think about it, scientists try to gather information about the world in a way that is more valid than simply commonsense ways of knowing. **Validity** refers to accuracy. Though there are many steps in the scientific process that are concerned with accuracy, a major issue in any study is **measurement validity**. That is, great care must be taken in measuring attitudes or behaviors so as to make measurement as accurate as possible.

An example from natural science illustrates the concept of measurement validity. Suppose we wanted to find out the real outside temperature, down to the degree. We could go outside and "feel" how warm or cold it is and estimate the real temperature in degrees. Alternatively, we could use a thermometer. Which way of knowing do you think would be more valid (or accurate)? The thermometer would be a more precise, and thus more valid, way of measuring because it shows exactly what the temperature is in degrees.

Similarly, in trying to measure the attitudes of a large group of people living in a city, would relying on your own informal impressions of the attitudes of others be more valid than the results of a survey of city residents, or less so? Because a survey would collect more information from the people to whom we are interested in generalizing, it would likely produce more accurate, or valid, results than merely relying on one's informal impressions. This depends, of course, on how well the questions in the survey are phrased. Formal impressions, though, are often less precise than information collected through a survey. People typically tend to spend time with others who are similar to them in important ways and assume most others they have not met are similar as well. This is not always the case.

Reliability refers to how much a measure can be trusted to produce the same results in repeated measures of the same thing. For example, if a weighing scale produced a different answer every time you stepped on it in succession, you would say the scale is unreliable. A reliable scale gives the same answer time after time (so long as your weight does not change). In social science, developing reliable measures of attitudes or behavior is critical to collecting quality information.

You might try this experiment sometime. The next time you're a passenger in a car on a road with no traffic, try to estimate the speed of the vehicle without looking at the speedometer. Most of us are not very good at estimating speed, so a speedometer is a more reliable way of measuring speed than people's informal impressions. More than one driver has been distracted, only to look at the speedometer and realize that she is traveling ten miles per hour or more faster than she thought.

In designing research projects, then, care must be taken to ensure collection of data that are both valid and reliable. This means making careful choices during the research design process. Again, time, money, and other resources often force researchers to make less-than-desirable compromises. A constant tension exists between doing credible research on the one hand and working with available resources on the other.

STEPS IN RESEARCH DESIGN

STEP ONE: DEFINE CONCEPTS

To illustrate how decisions are made in the process of research design, let's choose an example to work with. Suppose you want to conduct some research on the impact of corporal punishment (that is, spanking) on a person's development. A researcher might hypothesize that a child who is spanked will turn out to be better-adjusted than a child who is not spanked. Can you identify the independent and dependent variables in this example? The hypothesis suggests that a person's development is dependent on whether or not he is spanked. Therefore, spanking is the independent variable and a person's development the dependent variable.

Creating Nominal Definitions

Suppose you are the principal investigator for this study. How would you design a research project that would collect quality information to inform this hypothesis? Step one is to carefully define the concepts used in the study. Researchers refer to this step as creating a **nominal definition**. A nominal definition is simply a specific definition of a concept that the researcher will use for the purposes of the study. For example, what constitutes spanking and what doesn't? Would one swat with an open hand on the buttocks be considered spanking? What about a dozen swats? Would it make a difference if the spanking session went on for, say, five minutes or so? Is it a spanking if the child is hit anywhere other than on the buttocks? At what point does hitting a child become something other than spanking, even abuse? Would swats with a tool, such as a belt or board, constitute spanking or child abuse? Questions like these need to be answered so a specific nominal definition of spanking can be rendered.

Similarly, a nominal definition would be created for the dependent variable, or what we mean by a person's development. What would be accepted as a positive developmental outcome, and what would be considered unsuccessful? Are we concerned about a person's intellectual, emotional, or social development, or all three? A nominal definition describes a concept in such a way that it is ultimately measurable. Critics can take to task the nominal definition one chooses to use in a study, but they cannot criticize a researcher for being too vague if he or she makes explicit the nominal definitions in the process of the research.

Variables

Because nominal definitions are of necessity more specific than concepts, a variable (which is essentially a measurable concept) can then be developed from each nominal definition. Variables must be described in such a way that they are intuitively measurable and that they contain the potential for real variation. This means that, in a given study, one would expect a variety of responses to the same question. Recall from an earlier chapter the distinction between a variable and a constant. A constant is an aspect of a population that doesn't change. For example, a researcher might want to compare the attitudes of individuals currently imprisoned with those of people not in prison, but interview only prisoners for the research. In this example, imprisonment would be a constant rather than a variable because it is expected that all prisoners would indicate they are in prison. By contrast, variables must show variation in response.

The Process of Defining Concepts

For now, it may help to think of the process of defining concepts as one going from very general or abstract concepts to the very specific, measurable operationalization seen in Figure 5.1.

The final step in this process of defining concepts is the process of **operationalization** (the subject of Chapter Seven). Operationalization refers to the process of deciding exactly how a variable will be measured, right down to the specific wording of a question. The decision on how to precisely measure a variable is called an **operational definition**.

Let's return to the example of spanking to illustrate this process of moving from the general to the specific. Suppose we have a theory that various forms of punishment of children will affect overall development in adulthood. The ideas of punishment of children and overall development are our concepts. They are abstract and could be further defined in several ways. A commitment would have to be made by being specific about the meaning of these concepts. Let's say we make the decision to define punishment of children as the use of spanking specifically, while overall development is further defined as a person being a functioning, responsible member of society. These become the nominal definitions of our concepts.

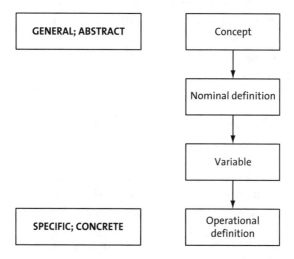

Figure 5.1. Concept Definition: From General to Specific.

Further clarification of the nominal definitions is warranted, so we define spanking to mean hitting a child on the buttocks between one and ten times with the intention of inflicting physical pain on the child. Anything else, by definition, would not be spanking. Built into this definition is the assumption that anything over ten strikes constitutes, say, abuse and not spanking. The second variable—being a functioning, responsible member of society—would be further clarified by identifying one or more items we take as evidence of this. Let's decide on three indicators: (1) meaningful employment, (2) living on one's own, and (3) lack of criminal record. Recognize that other indicators could be chosen, but these three will be used to illustrate the decision-making process.

A variable can now be developed from our nominal definition of the use of spanking by simply identifying the variation as either experiencing or not experiencing spanking while growing up. Let's call the variable *spanking*; its attributes (or categories) are having been spanked or not having been spanked as a child. A variable also needs to be created for the concept involving overall development. Let's call the variable *adjustment* and decide that it will comprise three indicators of adjustment: (1) meaningful employment, (2) independent living, and (3) no criminal record. Scores will be recorded on each of these indicators for every respondent and then added together into one score.

We'll leave the task of operationalizing these variables to Chapter Seven.

Distinguishing Concepts and Variables

Students are sometimes surprised at the difference between a concept identified in class and the variable eventually identified as an indicator of the concept. That is, people manage to think of other dimensions of a concept not included in a particular variable. If this is the case for you, you're noticing the tension in the difference between conceptualization and measurement, or between concepts and variables. The difference between the two is the level of abstraction. If you're unsure about the difference between a concept and a variable, recognize that it is sometimes subtle, pertaining to the amount of uncertainty, complexity, or ambiguity of what constitutes the concept and what you ultimately decide you will focus on to measure in your study.

Sex is a good example to illustrate this tension. As a variable, sex seems pretty straightforward; one takes a look at the person he or she is interviewing and discerns whether the person is male or female. Or one asks the person to self-report sex. It seems pretty straightforward.

As a concept, though, it is appropriate to ask what exactly we mean by sex. Is the presence of male or female *genitalia* the feature that makes someone male or female? If so, what does one do with hermaphrodites, people born with a combination of some male and female genitalia? Conceptually, you might decide instead that sex is only indirectly related to biological markers, because ultimately sex is a matter of *personal identity*. This would help explain why some people choose to engage in cross-dressing, because their sex identity is at odds with their biological makeup. Or perhaps you'd prefer a third option, believing that sex is ultimately determined by the combination of X and Y *chromosomes* within an individual. The point of this brief discussion is to demonstrate that even a seemingly self-evident concept such as sex is not as straightforward as it might seem at first glance at the conceptual level. Sociologists typically use the word *sex* to refer to any biological indicators and *gender* to connote the socially shared notions as to how men and women are expected to think or behave.

Does this illustrate for you how even "simple" concepts such as sex are actually fairly complex? To identify those issues is to discuss something at the conceptual level. Ultimately, a researcher must make the decision as to how she or he will nominally define sex so that it can be measured for the purposes of the study. Others may criticize the nominal decision adopted, but they cannot criticize consistent use of the chosen definition.

Specifying Your Class Hypothesis

Once concepts have been specified as variables, a formal hypothesis can be created. A **hypothesis** is a supposed relationship between two or more *variables.* The word *supposed* is used because hypotheses are developed before data are collected. It is a guess about the nature of the social world. Notice also that a hypothesis is a statement created once concepts have been made specific enough to be called variables. Concepts are linked together by a unifying theory. Variables are linked together by a hypothesis. The difference in language used is in the measure of specificity.

Earlier chapters have already challenged you to think of your concepts as variables and arrange them in the form of a hypothesis. Although your class has identified two variables, it is up to you to specify how *you* feel the two variables covary. If you have not already done so, write down your guess as to how you think your independent variable will affect the dependent variable. For the hypothesis that sex affects alcohol consumption for example, one would need to specify whether men or women (the categories of the independent variable) would be expected to consume more alcohol (alcohol consumption being more consumed or less consumed).

STEP TWO: PLAN THE STUDY

Once the concepts have been clearly defined, data collection techniques must be designed such that information collected will clearly shed light on the hypothesis being tested. The intent here is to plan a project in which the data are reliable and trustworthy. Good research designs build in enough controls to be respectable in the eyes of other scientists. That said, some research designs are clearly better (meaning, more valid and reliable) than others. Researchers sometimes use weaker designs when resources are limited or when exploring new potential relationships between concepts.

Longitudinal Studies

Consider again the example of conducting a study on the effects of spanking on adult development. In dealing with a topic involving the effects of something that happened in a child's life, it is best to design a research project where information would be collected at various points in a person's life during growth from infancy to adulthood. A design taking multiple observations over time is superior to one that merely asks adults questions about their childhood; the latter method would depend on the quality of the memory of those being interviewed. Interviewing parents as well as children would also gather additional valuable data by attempting to discern whether spanking has an impact on a person's development. You might anticipate that conducting a research project of this magnitude is both expensive and time-consuming. As time passes, people move away, or pass away, or decide that they no longer want to take part in research projects. A good research design in which data are collected over time (called a **longitudinal study**) would not only plan for multiple years of data collection but would also start with a large enough sample of people so that a good number will still be around years later.

If a study like this sounds complicated and involved, that's because it is. Ultimately, though, the information collected through a carefully designed study produces more reliable data than just informal impressions, or even studies that attempt to collect data at one point in time.

The One-Shot Case Study

There is a substantial body of literature built up around the issues involved in designing quality research studies (see, for example, Campbell and Stanley,1966). You will be exposed to some of these designs if you take a research methods course in your undergraduate career. I mention the issue here only to point out that doing research as we will do it for this class is not the only way in which research is carried out. The design we are using in your class project is the simplest research design, called the **one-shot case study**. It is so called because data are collected at a single point in time, using a method called the structured interview. You'll analyze the data you collect to see if the two variables in your class hypothesis covary.

There are some advantages to using a one-shot case study. It is quick, fairly easy, and relatively inexpensive to carry out such a study. Because data are gathered at one point in time, there are no concerns about things changing or people moving away. However, a serious limitation of the one-shot case study is that it is difficult to establish causality between two variables. Because both the independent and dependent variables are measured at the same time, we cannot determine with certainty that the independent variable occurred before the dependent variable. They may covary, but it will be difficult to demonstrate causality.

Correlation and Causation

A distinction needs to be made here between correlation and causation. **Correlation** refers to the covariation of two variables; as one (that is, the independent variable) changes, a change in the second variable (the dependent variable) is observed. If it is observed that more children who were spanked are well-adjusted as adults than those who were not spanked, the two variables are described as being correlated. Correlation is a necessary but insufficient condition for establishing causality between two variables. **Causation** occurs when the independent variable is responsible for a change in the dependent variable.

Two variables may be correlated that are not actually causally related. That is, the change in the independent variable does not *cause* the observed change in the dependent variable. Both variables may happen to change at the same time, but in fact a third variable causes the change in each of the variables. A correlation caused by the effect of a third variable is called a **spurious correlation.** We'll return to this topic in a moment.

Can you think of an example in which two variables might covary without one affecting the other? Let's say a relationship is found between family structure and juvenile delinquency. We observe in our data that children raised in single-parent homes are arrested more often for delinquent acts than kids raised in two-parent family homes. Does this mean that family structure *causes* juvenile delinquency? Is it possible that the reverse is true—that is, a juvenile's involvement in delinquent activities puts enough stress on a marriage that the parents end up divorcing? Which comes first: family structure or juvenile delinquency? If information on both variables is collected at the same time, it is virtually impossible to distinguish which is the cause and which is the effect.

A difficulty in establishing the time ordering of the independent and dependent variables is a major shortcoming of a one-shot case study. One could ask in the interviews if involvement in delinquent activities came before or after a divorce, but human memory is imperfect and subject to forgetting (Chan, 2009). And of course, parents simply may not know when their child started her delinquency career.

How to Establish Causality

Good research designs satisfy the three major criteria for establishing causality. First, a correlation between the independent and dependent variables must be established. Second, the time order of the variables must be obvious or observed; a change in the independent variable must occur before a change in the dependent variable. Third, all other possible explanations for the correlation must be examined and discounted. If all three of these criteria are met, it is assumed (at least for the present time) that the independent variable *causes* the change in the dependent variable.

It is worth noting, however, that one can never ultimately *prove* causality because there may always be a third variable causing the covariation that no one has thought to identify. This is why scientists do not speak of *proving* or *disproving* a certain theory. In the pure negativistic spirit of science, the best we can do is to fail to come up with any other explanation for why two variables would be related in any way other than a causal fashion, and to tentatively conclude that causality must exist between the two variables.

The Research Design for Your Class Project

As mentioned earlier, a one-shot case study research design will be employed in this class project. Data will be collected in a single effort (extending over several days). Recall that the one-shot case study design is the simplest type of research to execute. Because the primary purpose of this study is to give you some experience in "doing" social research, the one-shot case study is sufficient to give you an opportunity to collect data and sensitize you to some of the issues involved. Research designs more complex than the one-shot case study require additional time, expense, and work on your part, without necessarily imparting any additional insights into the process of social science. In addition, other designs typically require approval from an institutional review board. Application, review, and approval processes can sometimes take weeks. Thus the one-shot case study is the best design for your class project.

SUMMARY

The trust that others place in a study is directly related to the quality of its research design. Defining concepts clearly and specifically, first as nominal definitions and then as variables, is a key part of the process. Choosing a research design that collects the best-quality data to inform the research question is also important. However, decisions like these are always made in a context of limited resources. Compromises often have to be made, potentially affecting both the validity and the reliability of the project. Better studies are able to demonstrate causality by establishing a correlation, making sure that a change in the independent variable precedes that observed in the dependent variable, and eliminating other plausible explanations as to why the correlation might exist.

Compromises in research design are made in many studies, and your class project is no different. It will be up to you to decide whether the research design is credible enough for you to trust the results. Keep in mind that the ultimate goal of your class exercise is to give you experience in social science data collection. It's already a success if you're thinking more about what makes information more, rather than less, credible and trustworthy.

REVIEW QUESTIONS

1. What are the four steps of research design? What critical decisions need to be made in the first two steps?
2. Define *validity* and *reliability*. Why are they important in scientific research?
3. Describe the difference between correlation and causation. What three criteria need to be met in order to establish causality between two variables?

KEY TERMS

Causation   When a change in an independent variable *causes* a change in the dependent variable.

Correlation   An observed covariation between two variables; as one (the independent variable) changes, a change in the second variable (the dependent variable) is also observed.

Hypothesis   A supposed relationship between two or more variables.

Longitudinal study   A study that involves repeated measures over an extended period of time.

Measurement validity   Exists when an indicator measures what it is intended to measure.

Nominal definition   A specific definition of a concept that the researcher will use for the purposes of the study.

One-shot case study   A study that involves collecting data at one point in time only.

Operational definition   The actual manner in which a variable is measured. In survey research, this often takes the form of a specific question or set of questions.

Operationalization   The process of deciding exactly how a variable will be measured.

Reliability   The extent to which a measure produces the same results in repeated trials of measuring the same thing.

Spurious correlation   A correlation between two variables caused by the effect of a third variable.

Validity   The accuracy of a study or measure.

6

Research Design 2

Methods and Sampling

LEARNING OBJECTIVES

- Understand the importance of research methods and sampling in the overall research design.
- Increase your critical thinking skills by considering the advantages and disadvantages of various data gathering techniques.
- Improve your analytical skills by evaluating the usefulness of published research according to the type of sampling method used.

In the previous chapter, steps one and two of research design were described, and their relevance to your class research project was noted. This chapter describes the final two steps of designing research, which involve selection of data collection methods, identification of a population, and sampling techniques. This information will reveal the logic behind the steps chosen for your own class research project. You're moving ever closer to the point where you will have a chance to collect your own data.

STEP THREE: CHOOSE A DATA COLLECTION METHOD

Deciding on the data collection methods to use in a study is critical to the overall research design. There are many data collection options available to researchers. Ask yourself what data collection method you might use for your class project if we choose to conduct something other than interviews. Each method has its own strengths and weaknesses, and better research designs incorporate more than just one method into the overall design. Experiments, surveys, interviews, unobtrusive measures such as examination of diaries or newspapers, and participant observation are just some of the methods commonly used by sociologists. A data collection method should be carefully selected to supply the best information to answer one's research question. Some methods are better at answering certain types of questions than others.

Think again about the example in the last chapter. What data collection method would be best suited for finding out if there is a relationship between spanking and a person's long-term development? If a survey is used at one point in time to ask people about their experience with spanking as a child, then we are relying on people's memory for information. Chances are their recollection of frequency or intensity of spanking may be incorrect. Indeed, the odds are an adult will not remember at all if he or she was spanked in the first few years of life. Consequently there must be better ways to study this relationship than a survey done at one point in time. Surveys as well as interviews could be administered more than once. Which method would elicit the best data?

Experiments, by contrast, use direct observation rather than relying on people to report their experiences. This approach results in greater accuracy, but an experiment would take years to complete and the participants would presumably have to be raised in a laboratory if watched continuously until they grew into adulthood. Ultimately, the integrity of the research design must be balanced with practical concerns of limited time and resources.

Data collection is an integral part of the overall research design, though how social scientists collect data varies greatly from study to study. As mentioned before, better studies use more than one method of data collection, in part to see whether the responses received through one method are similar to those derived from another method. The information collected is considered to be more reliable if the results are similar even when collected with two or more methods. Researchers also use more than one method to get different kinds of information. For example, descriptions gathered through interviews are typically much richer and deeper than responses in surveys. It is important to carefully select research methodologies, within one's resources, that offer the best information to answer the research question.

Let's consider some of the advantages and disadvantages of five of the most popular methods used by sociologists.

SURVEYS

Surveys are the most commonly used research method among sociologists. Surveys are mailed out or handed out, although they are increasingly being made available on the Internet. All surveys require a participant to read and answer a series of questions or indicate opinions on certain statements. Surveys are used frequently because of their practical advantages. In fact, every ten years the U.S. government attempts to collect information from every person living in the United States. It's called the U.S. Census, in which people are (currently) required to respond to a mailed survey and either mail it in or submit responses online.

You can no doubt anticipate why surveys are so popular. They are easy and cost-effective to use and distribute. They allow quick access to information from potentially millions of respondents. The information collected can be easily analyzed in a fairly short period of time. In essence, surveys are popular largely for practical, rather than methodological, reasons.

Surveys have their shortcomings, of course. Only a small percent of people receiving surveys actually complete and return them. The accuracy of information in surveys depends almost entirely on the honesty of the people filling out the questionnaire and their willingness to answer every question. Because no researcher is present to make clarifications while the survey is completed, people may misunderstand questions when reading them and answer accordingly. Researchers have no idea when or on which questions this might occur, so considerable care must be taken in constructing questions to phrase them in a way that makes sense to the people who will receive them.

INTERVIEWS

A variation of the survey is the face-to-face or telephone interview. In this data collection format an actual person asks another for the information required by the study. There are at least three ways to conduct interviews: structured (or standardized), semistructured, and unstructured. In studies using fully *structured interviews,* all the questions to be asked are written out ahead of time. All possible responses are frequently also written down so the interviewee simply indicates the response that best resembles the person's opinion or behavior. The interviewer does not waver much from simply asking the written questions and recording the reply. This is to ensure that all interviewees receive the same questions in the same way.

At the other end of the spectrum, *unstructured interviews* are usually used in qualitative data collection, and often in conjunction with participant observation. In unstructured interviewing, the researcher has only a general idea of the topics he or she wants to ask of interviewees. The questions, the order in which they are asked, and the phrasing all vary from interview to interview. Here, the interviewer wants most of all to get the interviewee to talk. Emphasis is on discovering new ideas, thoughts, and social processes that the interviewer is not aware of, in an inductive fashion. There is a good deal of emphasis on **probing** new issues that the interviewee mentions as part of the interview. As a result, every interview can be quite different.

In between these two interviewing techniques is one called the *semistructured interview.* Here, the interviewer has a clear list of questions, but they may be both closed-ended and open-ended. There is a definite structure to the interview and an order to the questions asked, but the interviewer is allowed to clarify matters for the interviewee and may even ask additional questions to probe or get more information on topics of interest. Ultimately, the purposes of the study dictate the form of interviewing taken by the research.

Interviews are excellent for increasing the response rate because it's more difficult for people to refuse a request from another person than it is to throw away a paper survey. Depending on how formal the study, interviewers can also clarify things to those who appear to not understand various questions. Interviews also allow the researcher access to the nonverbal communication of interviewees, and the interviewer can attempt to make sense of responses to questions that people stumble over or pause for a long time before answering. None of this information is accessible in collecting data with a survey.

Interviews, too, have their disadvantages. Because a human being is asking the questions, the data collection process is potentially influenced by subjective interpersonal factors. Depending on the question, some interviewees may give a different response to an older male than to, say, a younger female. Good interviewer training helps to minimize problems like these, but they cannot be completely eliminated. Because interviews are administered orally, they take a great deal of time to complete compared to a survey, making it more expensive to conduct these studies.

From a pedagogical point of view, interviews allow a student to ask questions directly of other human beings and observe their thought processes and responses firsthand. This gives the combined experience of collecting data and doing so in a manner that involves face-to-face interaction. Interviews are an excellent learning tool to use in the course of this class study.

UNOBTRUSIVE MEASURES

A major weakness of both surveys and interviews is that they are potentially **reactive**. That is, the data, or information desired can be changed simply because of the attempt to collect the information. For example, interviews are reactive in that a real, live person asks the questions of another human being. Subjective factors such as stereotyping or sexism and general notions of privacy, may influence the interview process and bias the responses given. Similarly, surveys are reactive in that they may ask for opinions on issues when a respondent may not yet have formed one. Requiring the respondent to answer requires forming an opinion, therefore changing how the respondent previously thought.

The strength of unobtrusive measures is that the information collected doesn't change in attempting to measure it. This is because unobtrusive measures collect information from artifacts left behind by human beings, rather than from the people themselves. Diaries, journals, newspapers, and music lyrics are examples of items that can be studied, but information can be gathered from less obvious sources too. Webb, Campbell, Schwartz, and Sechrest (1966) measured the amount of dirt around the floor of various exhibits at the Chicago Metropolitan Museum, inferring that dirtier floors were an indication of greater walking traffic and thus greater interest in an exhibit than with nearby floors that were relatively pristine. Webb and his associates even measured the amount of mucus on glass cases, inferring that the greater the amount of mucus and slime, the greater the interest in the exhibit (as people put their fingers or noses to the glass to get a closer look).

All of these artifacts can be studied to catch a glimpse of human behavior. The fact that they are nonreactive (or unobtrusive) is a strong point and is often the only means social scientists have of trying to discern what was important to people after the fact. We can't go back in history to observe people, but they did leave artifacts and writings that can be analyzed. The biggest weakness to nonobtrusive measures, though, is that one must trust the inference being made. For example, are song lyrics the authentic voice and opinion of the singer, or are lyrics constructed to maximize album sales? Do people put their genuine feelings down in their diaries, or do they record things that they hope someone else will someday read? Do people record in a diary or journal what typically happens in their lives, or what is unusual and stands out? How do we know, in other words, that our inferences are correct?

This point can be illustrated in the story of a captain of a ship and his first mate during the days of European world exploration. The captain was incensed that the first mate was often drunk, and he recorded in the ship's log "The first mate was drunk today" every time it occurred. The first mate's turn came to keep the ship's log after a month at sea. Angered at what the captain had recorded, the first mate got his revenge simply by recording once, "The captain was sober today." Obviously, someone reading the ship's log would infer that the captain's sobriety was an unusual, rather than typical, occurrence. Similarly, inferences made while using unobtrusive measures must always be made with caution.

EXPERIMENTS

Laboratory experiments are generally the most respected research method. Much of the useful information that has influenced our physical lives in modern society (as with pharmaceuticals, medical advances, and technological innovations) has been tested through carefully controlled laboratory experimentation. Social scientists use this method as well when appropriate. Good experiments have a number of advantages over the other methods discussed so far. Experiments rely primarily on direct observation of behavior rather than people merely reporting what they think and feel. An experiment is a controlled situation, free of most other potential influences on behavior. Once the independent variable is introduced into the experiment, changes in behavior can be directly observed. This means that the problem of time ordering discussed earlier is satisfied because the experimenters control introduction of the independent variable. This builds the case for causality.

Most experiments contain both a control group and an experimental group. The latter is exposed to the independent variable while the control group is not. At the end of the experiment measures are taken of people in both groups. Any difference in results is attributed to the effect of the independent variable. If there are no differences between the groups, it is assumed that the independent variable had no effect.

Not all social science questions can be tested in a laboratory, of course, although more questions can likely be tested in this way than one might imagine (Zelditch, 1969). But experiments are potentially flawed by the aspect that is their biggest strength: they are controlled situations in an artificial environment. This may be fine for testing chemical reactions or even biological processes, but these phenomena lack a human consciousness. Human beings respond to their environment (real or artificial). Therefore, how do you know that the way people act in an artificial laboratory setting will be the way they act in the real world?

One way in which sociologists and others have attempted to solve this problem with experiments is to create interesting research designs called *quasi-experimental methods* (Campbell and Stanley, 1966). These methods follow the same logic as experiments and include a control and experimental group, but the study is carried out in a real-world setting. To methodological purists, these studies are seen to be inferior to the laboratory experiment because the same amount of control is not built in. For many sociologists, however, quasi-experimental methods incorporate a better real-world application than the artificiality of the laboratory.

PARTICIPANT OBSERVATION

Participant observation is a unique method of information gathering compared to the others described here. This is in part because participant observation is often used as an exploratory data-gathering tool, as distinct from a hypothesis-testing method. Participant observation may be used when a researcher has no real idea of what she or he will find in a particular social setting. As a result, an inductive, rather than deductive, logic is used with participant observation. Data gathering starts by developing a broad research question, visiting the area where the social activity of interest takes place, and taking as many field notes as possible. Data can be gathered on one particular *setting* or on a type of people involved in one type of *activity* but in multiple settings. As the researcher revisits the setting or people being studied, field notes accumulate over time. They become the data to be analyzed. They are also the basis from which a theory is eventually generated.

Participant observation has been used in quite a variety of social situations. Some of its most interesting applications have been in the area of deviance and crime. Sociologists have studied street gangs (Brotherton, 2000), mental institutions (Rosenhan, 1973), homosexual behavior in public restrooms (Humphreys, 1970), deviant musical subcultures such as heavy metal (Friesen, 1990), and more using this method. Its strength is the fact that the researcher both observes and experiences what is going on in the setting, getting a genuine firsthand appreciation of the emotional sense of the group being studied. Processes are observed over time so cause-and-effect relationships are often directly observed, just as in quasi-experimental designs.

Like other methods, participant observation has its drawbacks. Collecting information of this type is incredibly time-consuming. Researchers typically spend months, and sometimes years, with a group before feeling that they have a full understanding of what they are observing. Pages of field notes are generated, only a fraction of which are used to arrive at a particular conclusion. The level of subjectivity of an individual researcher is also a concern. Because we are human beings first and researchers second, we are selective in what we pay attention to. How can we be sure that another researcher in the same setting would come to the same conclusions as the first? Finally, participant observation is plagued with the same problem as most other methods: it is reactive. A researcher interacting with other human beings causes them to react to who the researcher is and what she or he does. In short, the researcher potentially changes what happens in the setting simply by being there.

Despite these shortcomings, participant observation continues to be one of the best tools to make discoveries not easily brought to light through other methods. Being exposed to the conversations and patterns of behavior of social groups over time produces some of the most detailed information we have about social life.

Social researchers make use of methods other than those described here. Selecting the most appropriate method to gather quality data that will inform a particular research question is the most important issue for investigators. If time and resources allow, investigating an issue using a combination of methods produces the richest information.

A RESEARCH METHOD FOR YOUR CLASS PROJECT

Would you use a method other than interviewing if you were leading your class through a project of this nature? What would be the advantages and disadvantages of your chosen method? Decisions made at this point are important because each method has inherent advantages and disadvantages. As mentioned before, practical considerations also influence the inevitable selection of one's methodology.

Structured interviews will be used for your class's one-shot case study, for several reasons. Compared to the other methods, interviews offer the best combination of experience and expediency for learning purposes. A survey or study using unobtrusive measures, for example, does not give you the opportunity to gather information directly from other human beings and observe them thinking about their responses. Experiments are involved and typically expensive, while participant observation studies require a good deal of time and sophistication in making interpretations of social events. Interviews therefore offer a good opportunity to learn about doing social science without the project becoming overwhelming. *Structured interviews* require interviewees only to ask questions in a prearranged format, without the additional stress of trying to pry more information out of people than what is asked for. Be aware, though, of the inherent weaknesses in interviewing so efforts can be made to overcome them.

STEP FOUR: IDENTIFY YOUR POPULATION AND SAMPLING METHOD

IDENTIFYING YOUR POPULATION

As a budding social scientist, give some thought to the group that you are ultimately interested in learning more about, and the best way to go about collecting that information. The group one is interested in studying is called a **population**. Your technique of finding people for your study would no doubt differ if your population were, say, pregnant women as opposed to all residents of a geographic area. How would information be collected to increase confidence that the results actually represent the characteristics of, say, the entire U.S. population? Ideally, wouldn't you want to collect information from every person in the United States? This means more than three hundred million people—quite an undertaking! No wonder the U.S. government attempts to do so only every ten years.

Imagine for a moment all of the practical problems involved in getting information from everyone in the United States. The population changes every day. People immigrate daily to the United States, and some migrate out. Babies are born and people pass away. How can you collect quality data on an ever-changing population? Speaking of babies, perhaps trying to get a one-month-old to fill out a survey or respond to an interview is a little unreasonable. You may want to establish an age minimum (say, fifteen years old) and not go below that.

You'll also want to define what you mean by the "United States of America." Do U.S. territories such as Puerto Rico and American Samoa count as part of your population? Then there are the people who are virtually inaccessible, such as those who are part of the U.S. population but living in military bases around the world, or traveling, or living in isolated parts of the country. Should we include or exclude them in the study? It may seem frustrating, but clearly identifying the group—the population you are interested in studying—is an essential step in social research. This is true whether you are attempting to assess the views of an entire country or a small street gang.

Aside from simply defining your population, practical problems exist in gathering information from everyone in a population. Some will refuse to participate, and there are laws that protect their right to do so. This is fine if it's only a few people, but what if the number of nonparticipants is very large? Would you still have confidence that your results represent all of the United States? What if you noticed that people who were a part of religious cults were mostly the ones refusing to take part in your study? *Not* hearing from certain types of groups would almost surely bias your results.

As you can see, there are many practical difficulties with attempting to get information from everyone in the United States. In fact, despite heroic efforts, the U.S. Census gathers information from only about 70 percent of the U.S. population in a given census year.

Sampling

With all of the difficulties in collecting information from an entire population, wouldn't it be nice if one could just gather information from a fraction of the people in a population and yet be relatively sure the views of those selected actually represent the views of all? This very question has intrigued social scientists for some time. The issue is called **sampling**. How could a sample of people from a population be drawn such that their views represent those of the entire population? For this class project, your population is all the students at your educational institution. Would it be possible to gather information from a small group of students and feel confident that their responses accurately reflect the responses of all students?

Owing to the difficulties in trying to gather information from a population of thousands or more, social scientists have refined the process of sampling to . . . well, a science. You'll learn more about the intricacies of scientific sampling if you take a course in research methods. Here, however, I'd like to give you just enough information about the principles of scientific sampling to understand how much or how little trust you can have in the sample of students on your campus from which you'll gather information. This will make you a better consumer of information presented to you in the news and on the Internet, as well as evaluating the relative worth of the information collected in this assignment. Knowing the nature of a sample of a particular study helps you decide just how trustworthy the results are.

Samples of populations are taken in order to reduce the considerable expense and difficulty of trying to collect information from every person in the entire population. A good sample represents the same proportions of people and opinions in the overall population.

For example, let's say that we took a poll of the U.S. population and found that about 90 percent of Americans are in favor of interracial marriage. How would we draw a sample of Americans so that we could be reasonably sure that close to 90 percent of people included in our sample held the same opinion?

Random Samples

The key to selecting a good sample is actually found in the principle of **randomization**. That is, if the people included in your sample are selected randomly from a list of everyone included in the population, that sample will almost always represent the proportions found in the total population. This is a difficult concept to grasp for some, because it means essentially trusting the principles of sampling rather than controlling or measuring the equivalency of the sample in some way. The principle of randomness or probability sampling, though, has been demonstrated to work.

Evidence of this can be seen in the accuracy of polls conducted to predict the outcome of presidential elections. Pollsters incorporate the principle of randomness into the way they sample. Pollsters are repeatedly able to predict the outcome of national elections within plus or minus three percentage points by interviewing between 1,000 and 1,500 of the roughly 150 million people who vote in the United States. That's an incredible testament to the power of accuracy in sampling methods.

The most important point of taking a good random sample is that *every person or unit of analysis in the population must have an equal chance of being included in the sample.* This is a critical point. Suppose you wanted to take a random sample of everyone attending your college. How would you do it? You could go to a major building like the student center and ask students questions as they come through the door. But would that be a random sample? Would everyone in the university have an equal chance of being included in your sample? Depending on the time of day or day of the week, some students may not set foot in the student center. Indeed, some students may never visit the student center at all. You could try to get to other places around campus and interview students, but part-time students, commuter students, online students, and others would still be less likely to be included in your study since it is likely they spend less time on campus than any students living in residence or close to campus.

To ensure equal opportunity of inclusion and thus a proper sample, a list of every person or unit in the population must be generated. Because the actual people or units making up the population change frequently, researchers handle this by creating a list of units in the population at a particular point in time. In larger populations such as cities, states, or countries, it is understood that these population lists are approximate or robust. This is less of a problem in populations of thousands or more. Selecting a sample from a list of everyone in the population satisfies the condition of equal opportunity because every name or unit on the list has an equal chance of being selected. How is this ensured? Every name on the list is first numbered, and a list of random numbers is then consulted or generated by computer. Each person identified by the randomly selected numbers then becomes a part of the sample.

Of course, the fact that a person's name shows up on a randomly selected sample does not guarantee that the person will agree to participate in the study. Here too is another challenge to proper sampling: it is imperative that information be collected from all or almost all of the people selected in the sampling process. The larger the number of people in the sample refusing to participate, the greater the doubt that the responses from those in the sample truly represent the larger population. This is because there could be a systematic reason as to certain people choosing not to participate, thus biasing the study by excluding certain *types* of individuals. Great care must thus be taken to encourage all people selected in the sample to participate in the study while at the same time balancing their right to choose to not participate for whatever reason.

There are several variations of random samples that are also effective methods of collecting representative data, though they are quite a bit more complex than simple random sampling. Two of them are stratified random samples and probability cluster samples (among others). From a scientific point of view, only samples using the principle of randomness can be trusted to represent the views of the broader population. Even then, close attention must be paid to the refusal rate in the random sample, making sure that it is small. No other sampling method, no matter how sophisticated, can ultimately be trusted to represent the views of the broader population. This is a critical criterion regarding the difference between studies with good generalizability and those with limited applicability.

EXPERIMENTS AND GENERALIZABILITY

A special qualification needs to be made regarding experiments. You might recall that experiments typically use a small number of people in carefully controlled conditions. Generalizing results to the broader population from a small group of people must be done with great care. Experiments have two qualities that increase the trust we might have in the generalizability of their results. First, they are carried out in carefully controlled conditions, including controlled introduction of the independent variable. Careful observations are then made of its effect. Because most other possible behavioral influences have been eliminated, experimental results are more respected than results from dissimilar studies.

Second, experimenters use randomization to assign subjects to experimental and control groups. That means that experimenters make a list of all the people to take part in the experiment and from that list randomly assign people to one group or the other. This generally has the effect of making the two groups roughly equivalent. Any differences noted between the experimental and control groups after the introduction of the independent variable can then be attributed to the impact of the independent variable on the experimental group. If experiments are replicated with a variety of participants, their results are often considered to be generalizable.

Note that testing on diverse participants is important for ensuring the generalizability of experimental findings. In fact, some have accused scientists of having an **androcentric**, or male-centered, bias. Indeed, most of the classic scientific experiments on child development were based entirely on the observation of boys alone. Carol Gilligan (1982) developed a distinctly different developmental theory from those of the famous child development specialists Lawrence Kohlberg and Erik Erikson. Kohlberg and Erikson developed their theories by observing only boys; Gilligan observed girls to offset this bias. Tavris (1992) gives many examples of the androcentric bias, including a study on the effects of diet on breast cancer which included no women. Still, journals are filled with published studies carried out on groups of people who are selected not because they are representative members of a population but because they are those most accessible to researchers. The number of psychology studies conducted on students enrolled in introductory psychology courses, for example, likely outnumbers studies conducted on any other group.

This last point illustrates how important it is to use your own growing knowledge of good scientific practice to evaluate studies that you come across or read about in the newspaper. Though researchers are aware of the standards that make for high-quality studies and trustworthy results, most studies fall short in some respects. This is most often due to constraints of time, lack of funding, limited access to certain populations, and other pragmatic concerns. Knowing the standards of good science helps make you a better consumer of information and helps you decide how trustworthy the information is by letting you see potential weaknesses in the research design or sampling method. This ultimately helps you make better decisions for your life.

UNITS OF ANALYSIS

Selecting a population to study is highly important because it is the entire group that is the focus of your study. Identifying a population also helps in clarifying in the researcher's mind which group is being studied. This then helps the researcher make wiser decisions if sampling is required. It is important to note here that not all populations worthy of study are made up only of individual human beings. Information is frequently sought about other **units of analysis** as well. A unit of analysis is the particular entity whose characteristics are ultimately of interest.

Sociologists regularly study the performance of *organizations*, for example, which are a different unit of analysis from individual people. Although individuals ultimately do the work necessary to make organizations "real," their concerted, organized, collective actions directed toward a particular organizational goal are a different type of social reality from merely the actions of individuals themselves. Therefore, businesses or organizations in a certain area or of a certain type could make up a population. Think of other possibilities: *groups* such as gangs in a particular city, or families living in an apartment complex. For each of these examples, the focus is on a social unit rather than simply individuals.

DEFINING YOUR POPULATION

For your class project, the population of interest is all students attending school at your educational institution. Unless your instructor gives you different information, let's further define a student at your educational institution as *anyone who is enrolled in at least one class on campus this semester.* This will include both part-time and full-time students but exclude students who are taking a break from their studies, are studying abroad, or are taking courses only on the Internet. Because our focus is on students, our unit of analysis is the individual.

Think about the generalizability of your research for a moment. Let's suppose we find a strong relationship between your class's independent and dependent variables, in the way that you have specified the hypothesis. Would we be able to say with scientific certainty that the results are true for, say, students at other educational institutions? for people in their late teens and twenties, regardless of whether or not they are enrolled in school? Would the results be true for the population of the entire country?

From a scientific point of view, the answer is an unequivocal no. The results of your class study cannot be assumed to be true of anyone else. This is because the population you collect information on is only students enrolled at your institution. Speaking scientifically, there might be some characteristics unique to students on your campus not shared by others who live in the same city or state, or even those who attend college at other institutions. People in those populations do not have an equal chance of being included in the study compared to students at your campus. Therefore we cannot say with any scientific confidence that these results are generalizable to any people other than those students on your campus.

THE SAMPLING TECHNIQUE

In fact, the results of your study would be generalizable to students on your campus *only* if we drew a random sample. Refer back to the discussion in the previous chapter of what is involved in selecting such a sample. Because taking a scientific random sample from all students at your college would be time-consuming, difficult, and expensive, we will use a nonrandom type of sampling method called a **sample of convenience**. That is, you will simply interview any person you can find who fits the criteria for our population. Drawing a sample of convenience is much simpler than drawing a random sample. However, a shortcoming of a sample of convenience is that the results cannot be trusted to represent the entire population (all students at your educational institution). If the study is completed carefully, *you will know nevertheless that the results are likely true for those from whom information was collected.* There is no scientific basis, though, to trust that the results are true for any others, on your campus or any other. This is an important point.

It is true that people included in our study might be included by chance (that is, you just happen to see someone whom you walk up to and ask to interview). This does *not* mean, however, that our sample is "random." Remember, in a truly random sample everyone has the same chance of being included in the study. Obviously, those people in close geographic proximity to you when you are looking for someone to interview have a better chance of being interviewed than those who are not close to you. Students in my first-year classes, for example, typically interview more first-year students than others.

Although the results of this study are limited to those from whom information has been collected, remember that the primary purpose of the project is your own education. That is, you'll be learning about social science as you complete it. Remember, too, that the results should be true at least for the people from whom we collected information. This, in and of itself, is interesting. In fact, I encourage you to test the impressions you form after completing your own interviews with the overall class results. They are not always the same; forming impressions by talking with a few people is not always as accurate as gathering information from many people.

SUMMARY

Selecting a research method, identifying a population, and using a sampling procedure are part of the decisions involved in research design, in addition to clarifying concepts and planning your study described in the previous chapter. Every research method has advantages and disadvantages. The latter can sometimes be compensated for by using more than one data collection method or by using the method with care so as to minimize potential disadvantages.

Because the intent of your class project is to give you a taste of social science data collection, most of these steps have already been completed for you. It is critical to understand the issues involved in each step, however, as well as their relation to each other. This will help you do well on the written portion of your project and hone your critical thinking skills as a soon-to-be college graduate.

Your class project will take the form of a one-shot case study, using standardized interviewing as the data collection method. Your population is all students enrolled at your educational institution, and the sampling method to be used is a sample of convenience. The next step is to understand the process of operationalization, covered in Chapter Seven.

REVIEW QUESTIONS

1. What research method would be most appropriate for testing the effect of a new drug that potentially keeps people calm during stressful situations? Explain.
2. What type of sampling method is best suited for generalizing to a broader population? Why?
3. How are the issues of validity and reliability relevant to research methods and sampling? Explain.

KEY TERMS

Androcentric Male-centered.

Population A group that is the focus of an investigation.

Probing A practice in interviews where the interviewer prompts the interviewee to share additional information.

Randomization In sampling, randomization refers to the principle of every unit of the population having an equal chance of being included in the sample.

Reactive A situation in social research where the information being gathered may be changed simply because of the data collection method.

Sample of convenience A sample generated simply by gathering information from units most easily accessed by the researcher.

Sampling Learning about a population by studying a subset of its units.

Unit of analysis A social entity whose behavior is the ultimate focus of the research.

7

The Interview Schedule

Operationalization

LEARNING OBJECTIVES

- Learn how important details are in developing questions and statements for use in surveys and interviews.
- Gain knowledge by familiarizing yourself with the issues involved in measuring variables.
- Consider the importance of question ordering in creating survey and interview instruments.

After familiarizing yourself with the previous two chapters, you should by now have formed the impression that there is much involved in research design. At times, ideas appearing to be sound at the conceptual level sometimes fall apart logically as one simply thinks through the process of measurement and potential falsification. For those ideas surviving the conceptualization process, moving from general to specific, a great deal of time and effort is put into measuring the idea responsibly and carefully. In addition, you must examine the construction of the survey or interview itself, including the ordering of the questions, which requires a good deal of time and effort. This, of course, is how it should be if science is going to transcend everyday, casual ways of thinking about things, right?

Operationalization is tied closely to the research method you choose for collecting your information. How one chooses to measure, say, peer pressure, depends on whether we use an experimental method, a survey, or an interview. Decisions on how to operationalize variables are always made in the context of how the research is designed and the methods employed. You already know that the method used for this study will be a structured interview, and that a list of questions will be developed in an effort to gain information about our variables that we need if we are to have meaningful data to analyze and compare. A good deal of thought needs to go into developing useful questions for interviews and surveys.

Your instructor will likely create the questions that ultimately measure the variables included in your class hypothesis. That is, she or he will take the two concepts you identified in class, turn them into variables, and develop one or more questions for your interviews that attempt to measure what you want to find out. However, your instructor may ask for some input from you regarding the question or questions to ask that measure your variables. This chapter gives you some examples of how variables are operationalized (measured) and demonstrates some of the issues that need to be addressed in this process.

Knowing what is involved in operationalizing variables makes you a better thinker. It helps you think through claims about studies that you hear or read about, because you'll know that claims made in some reports are difficult to support, given the challenging task of operationalizing variables. This in turn leaves you less likely to be misled by confusing claims and more likely to want to ask questions before accepting the claims of others outright. In short, knowing how variables are operationalized makes you a better consumer of information.

OPERATIONALIZING VARIABLES

There is real skill involved in doing a good job of operationalizing variables. Do you think you might be good at it? Chapter Five introduced the process of moving from a concept to a nominal definition to a variable. In operationalizing, the challenge is to take a variable and, in the context of an interview questionnaire (also known as an **interview schedule**), develop the exact wording on a question or set of questions that will measure the variable in question.

AN EXAMPLE: AGE

Suppose we wanted to operationalize the variable *age*. What question would you ask in an interview to have the interviewee reveal her correct age? This would be straightforward:

> How old are you?

If this question were posed to a sample of people living in the United States, would every respondent be as specific as you hope? Would some be more likely to round off their age, saying "oh, fifty" when in fact they might be forty-eight years of age, or even fifty-two? If so, we might want to ask the question to elicit more precise responses.

> What is your age in years?

This is a better question in that it specifies how the answer should be expressed. However, this operationalization creates another potential problem. By adding the phrase "in years," it emphasizes one's real age. The United States is generally a culture that values youth more than age. We know from other studies that some groups (older women in particular) are more likely to be influenced by this cultural bias and report their age as less than their actual age. This is not so big a problem with traditional college students, most of whom are younger anyway, but it can cause problems if validity is important to the researcher. Interestingly, researchers have found an operationalization of age that elicits fewer errors or nontruths:

> In what year were you born?

Apparently, people are more likely to report the true year in which they were born than to reveal their true age.

Look at the operationalization of age once more. If you were interviewing someone and read this question to her, would you discover any problem with it? In particular, where would you record the response of the interviewee? If more than one interviewer is taking part in the study, some may write the answer below the question, others to the right of the question, and still others perhaps in the margin. Therefore, operationalizing variables also includes the mundane task of inserting a space in which the answer can be recorded:

In what year were you born? _____

To be specific, one might also want to indicate to the interviewer that the year should be fully expressed in four digits, rather than two.

In what year were you born? _____ _____ _____ _____

Of course, depending on your purpose in asking this question, it may be sufficient instead to create closed-ended response categories where the interviewee simply indicates the response that represents age. It could look like this:

Which category best represents your age in years?
_____ 0–20
_____ 21–40
_____ 41–60
_____ 61–80
_____ 81 or more

Operationalizing age in a way that essentially groups the data has the advantage of ensuring greater uniformity of response and decreasing the amount of misrepresentation because people do not have to reveal their exact age. However, because the responses are grouped, one can never ultimately determine the exact age of respondents from these data. Unless one is sure that more specific information won't be needed, it's wise to collect more specific information rather than less.

All these issues are part of the process of operationalization. Asking poor questions leads to collecting invalid or unreliable data at least some of the time. As a result, giving careful thought to the wording of questions and possible responses is part of the process of operationalization. My favorite example is a survey for which I was hired to analyze the results after they had been collected. One of the questions on the survey asked people for their marital status, in an open-ended fashion:

Marital status: _____

The person who created the survey obviously anticipated that people would write in a status like single, married, divorced, separated, or widowed. However, about 20 percent of the people wrote in simply "yes"! I was faced with the problem of interpreting those responses reliably. I presumed that people who wrote in "yes" were married, but ultimately I could not tell for sure. Asking good questions ensures uniform and accurate responses, increasing the validity and reliability of the study.

A SECOND EXAMPLE: RACE

Are you ready to try another one? Before reading any further, try your hand at writing a question to measure a person's race. What question would you ask? What possible answers would you include as a response to this question?

Race is a particularly difficult variable to measure. This is because residents of the United States tend to use appearance or skin tone to determine a person's race. This can be problematic, because there are many persons of African ancestry who are lighter-skinned than dark-skinned Caucasians. On the Italian peninsula, for example, the farther south one travels the darker the skin of the inhabitants. Yet all Italians are categorized as white or Caucasian by ancestry.

Categorizing Hispanics by skin tone is similarly confusing. The skin tone of Hispanics is generally darker than that of many Caucasians living in the United States (mostly because non-Hispanic white Americans trace their ancestry to the lighter-skinned northern Europeans). Most Hispanics, of course, have European ancestry, stemming from Spanish conquistadors who produced offspring with indigenous populations in the New World. Some African ancestry is also interwoven into the composition of Hispanics as union with former African slaves likewise took place. How should Hispanics be categorized?

The U.S. Bureau of the Census identifies Hispanics as Caucasians, by virtue of their Spanish heritage. Census publications routinely distinguish Hispanic whites from non-Hispanic whites. So if it is not race that distinguishes Hispanics, what does? It's certainly not a shared culture. Hispanics in the United States come from a variety of countries with hugely divergent histories, cultures, and celebrations. Puerto Ricans have little in common with Cubans, who in turn have little in common with Mexicans. Just watch the look of consternation on the face of someone of Cuban ancestry when you say with pride that you took part in Cinco de Mayo celebrations—a Mexican holiday!

Hispanics in the United States are primarily a *linguistic* group. That is, they come from countries where Spanish is usually the dominant language and where there was a history of Spanish or Portuguese colonization. Most Hispanics in the United States speak Spanish as their first language, though this is changing as Hispanics assimilate over generations, become fluent in English, and even lose the ability to speak Spanish. This linguistic categorization holds for most, but not all, Hispanics, which is why the qualification of Spanish or Portuguese colonization is included. People from the very populous country of Brazil, for example, speak Portuguese instead of Spanish, but for various reasons they are included under the Hispanic label in the United States.

Getting back to our challenge, then, how would you word a question in an interview or survey that would accurately measure this ambiguous concept of race? Because of all of the inherent difficulties with this question, the U.S. Bureau of the Census all but gave up trying to consistently categorize individuals by race or ethnicity and instead created a question that lists several racial and ethnic groups and simply instructs people filling out the form to "check all that apply." Respondents now categorize themselves using their own subjective evaluation of their heritage and identity. Multiple answers were also allowed so people of varied backgrounds could check off more than one category and acknowledge all of the important parts of themselves with which they identify rather than forcing them into only one category that may not feel entirely correct.

Although this type of measure makes some sense to the person filling out the question, it is obviously not a question that categorizes people consistently. A person might be more in touch with her African ancestry in one decade when she fills out the survey and checks off "black," but she may be more in touch with, say, her Asian roots in the next decade and check off "Asian." From a scientific point of view, categorizing the human population into various racial categories is ultimately a futile exercise; there is no meaningful scientific system of racial categorization (Bamshad and Olson, 2003, Rothenberg, 2008). Despite this, race remains a significant social construction and a genuine influence in how some people treat others. This makes the notion of race particularly difficult to operationalize.

I have used two examples here, age and race, that at face value might appear to be easy to measure in a survey or interview schedule. On closer examination, though, they are fraught with ambiguity. This should illustrate the many challenging decisions that must be made in operationalizing different variables. A researcher must ultimately make these decisions in the course of research and then explain exactly in the write-up how the variables are measured so others can intelligibly interpret the results.

THE PROCESS OF OPERATIONALIZATION

Now that you've seen some of the inherent challenges in measuring even what appears to be the simplest of variables, let's go through the process of conceptualizing something that you might measure in your class project, turning your concept into a variable, and finally operationalizing your variable by deciding exactly the wording of the question you might ask on a survey or interview.

CONCEPTUALIZATION

Alcohol consumption is a popular concept to investigate among students. A second concept such as religiosity or sex would need to be paired with the concept of alcohol consumption, but consider it on its own for a moment. At the conceptual level, it is understood that many people in the United States consume alcohol from time to time. The reasons for alcohol consumption vary, of course. Some drink only on special occasions, others more frequently to be sociable. Some drink as an entertainment activity in and of itself, and still others drink with the goal of eventual drunkenness. Some drink to escape or cope with problems in their lives; others drink to gain status among friends or peers. Of course, some people don't drink at all.

DEVELOPING A NOMINAL DEFINITION

These differences may be important, depending on the focus of your study. Suppose you were simply interested in measuring the range of drinking behavior by quantity and would like to know how little or how much students drink on your campus. Once a focus on quantity is set, we have defined our concept in a way that is potentially measurable. This is referred to as a nominal definition of our concept, making specific how a researcher defines a concept for the purpose of a particular study.

Recognize that we could adopt other nominal definitions of drinking for the purposes of a study. Drinking could be nominally defined as the amount consumed at a typical drinking occasion, or how many people have ever encountered problems in their life as a result of their drinking behavior. You can likely think of other ways in which a researcher could focus on aspects of drinking behavior.

Aside from behavior, one could nominally define drinking as an *attitude*. A nominal definition could focus on whether or not respondents think having, say, more than three drinks in a typical drinking occasion is excessive or not, or even if they believe drinking alcoholic beverages is a healthy or moral thing to do. A researcher could nominally define drinking attitudes as largely dealing with how often, as opposed to how much, a person feels one should imbibe.

IDENTIFYING A VARIABLE

Variables are developed from a nominal definition of a concept and are selected in terms of their relevance to the concept to be measured and the overall purpose of the study. For the purpose of illustration, suppose you are most interested in examining the frequency of drinking occasions rather than how much is consumed on those occasions. Once this decision is made, it becomes apparent that drinking frequency should be measured in terms of a span of time. It is reasonable to assume that the frequency of alcohol consumption would vary weekly among individuals. This variable might be called *weekly frequency of alcohol consumption*.

OPERATIONAL DEFINITIONS

The next step is to develop specific questions that actually measure the nominal definition or variable. This is, as you have heard, called the process of operationalization and entails deciding how you will measure what you want to measure. What question or questions could be developed to measure how frequently people consume alcoholic beverages? There are a number of ways to operationalize our variable. Which of these do you think would most accurately measure what we are trying to measure?

1. How many times a day do you typically consume alcohol?
2. Please indicate on how many days out of seven you consume alcohol in a typical week.
3. Most college students concentrate their drinking activities on weekends. On how many of the past four weekends did you spend time consuming alcoholic beverages?

CONSIDERING YOUR AUDIENCE

If you've looked at these three questions, you've likely formed an opinion that one option produces better information than the other two. You might even come up with a fourth option of your own that you feel does a better job than those listed. The point here is to illustrate that choices need to be made in the process of operationalization, and that these choices are important. Better questions produce better-quality data.

You might be tempted to ask all the questions and see what results are produced. This is an option, but a researcher must also balance the desire for good-quality data with more pragmatic concerns. Asking too many questions makes the interview longer and increases the number of people who refuse to participate or who end the interview early. It is wise to ask fewer good questions than many questions whose quality is dubious.

Selecting a particular operationalization is contingent on a number of factors. For example, one must consider the level of sophistication of the people who will be asked the interview questions. Would you word the questions the same way, using the same language, if you were asking about drinking frequency among, say, the homeless? among hip hop artists? among high schoolers? Some audiences have a larger vocabulary than others, and many social groups develop their own distinct phrases or terms that have special meaning to that group alone. Being sensitive to and using language to accurately convey what is being asked is a goal of the researcher. Therefore, the wording and phrasing of questions depends in part on the characteristics of the audience to whom they will be posed.

CLOSED-ENDED VS. OPEN-ENDED ITEMS

Researchers can also choose to operationalize variables using closed-ended or open-ended question types. **Closed-ended questions** are those that provide a list of possible responses. The interviewee simply selects the one that is most appropriate to the situation.

For example, here is a closed-ended question that could be asked in an attempt to measure religious affiliation:

What is your religious affiliation?
1. Christian (Catholic, Protestant, or Orthodox)
2. Jewish
3. Muslim
4. None
5. Other (please specify) _____

Note that all the possible responses have already been identified, including an "Other" category. Any respondent not fitting into the categories already listed could give the interviewer an answer and the interviewer would write it in the space under "Other."

Open-ended questions are those in which the responses are not specified ahead of time by the researcher. This is often done in exploratory research or to investigate a concept about which the researcher does not know much. In these cases, it is important to report exactly the information offered by the respondent being interviewed instead of attempting to force the person to choose responses that may not accurately measure an attitude or behavior. Open-ended questions can ask for a simple single response, as in "What year were you born?" Alternatively, more detailed and lengthy responses can be required. Imagine the responses one might get with this open-ended question: "Describe your childhood experience. Be sure to discuss whether it was happy or unhappy and why. Refer to your relationship with your parents, your experiences in school and with friends, and any other aspects you feel were important."

Closed-ended questions are used more often than open-ended questions, for several reasons. They yield quick and convenient responses that are neatly categorized ahead of time by the researcher into categories that are both mutually exclusive and exhaustive. Once responses are received, they can be quickly entered into the computer and analyzed. All the responses to open-ended questions must be listed, assigned a number, and then entered into the computer. It is often difficult to categorize responses to open-ended questions because some people answer fairly vaguely, others give too much detail, and still others appear to contradict themselves in their own answers. Still, open-ended questions are the best route to let respondents speak for themselves by allowing them to answer the question in their own words.

For your class interview, it is likely that your instructor will choose to use only closed-ended questions. This will make things easier to understand and process. Because your class will likely develop a hypothesis using variables that are fairly common in social research, there will not be a great need to develop open-ended questions to probe new areas. If you like the idea of using open-ended questions, however, you might think about doing your own study at some point for honors or as a senior thesis in your major.

SINGLE AND MULTIPLE INDICATORS

Choosing the best operationalization of a variable also depends on how many questions you might want to ask to measure a single variable. As was mentioned above, it's true that the shorter the list of questions the greater the likelihood you will have people answering all of them. But sometimes a particular concept or variable might be complex and thus need more than one question to adequately tap into it. A single question is called an **indicator** for a particular variable. Asking more than one question, or posing more than one statement with which interviewees can agree or disagree, is using multiple indicators to measure a single variable. Complex variables, such as a person's overall happiness, are more accurately measured using multiple indicators instead of only one; each indicator allows us to make an assessment that may permeate different aspects of a person's life.

Do you think it might be necessary to use multiple indicators to measure one or both of the variables your class has chosen to research for this project? The most common use of multiple indicators in social science is a technique that has come to be known as the Likert-type format. This consists of a list of statements, often opinions, that all deal with the same subject or variable. For each statement, the respondent indicates to what extent he agrees or disagrees. The number of possible answers varies, but the continuum is usually spread between *strongly agree* at one end and *strongly disagree* at the other. If there are five possible responses (for example, strongly disagree, disagree, neutral or undecided, agree, strongly agree), numbers from one to five can be assigned to the answers. Once the respondent has answered all the questions, the numbers that correspond to answers for the five statements can be added together.

Here is an example of five such statements:

For each of the next five statements, please say if you strongly disagree, disagree, are neutral or undecided, agree, or strongly agree.

	SD	D	N/U	A	SA
A. There is something wrong or unnatural about homosexuality.	1	2	3	4	5
B. I would feel uncomfortable sitting next to a homosexual.	1	2	3	4	5
C. Homosexuals should not be allowed to hold public office.	1	2	3	4	5
D. Children are more at risk having a homosexual as a teacher.	1	2	3	4	5
E. I would be disappointed if one of my children was a homosexual.	1	2	3	4	5

What variable are these statements attempting to measure? You'd be correct if you guessed homophobia. Notice that, for each statement, the higher the score the greater the homophobia, and the lower the score the lower the feelings of homophobia. By scoring the five items in this manner, it becomes possible to add the score on the items together. Notice that the lowest score on all five items combined is 5, which would occur if someone answered strongly disagree to all five items. Alternatively, the highest score someone could receive would be 25 by answering strongly agree to all five items.

Adding the five items together, then, we've created a scale of homophobia, which ranges from 5 to 25. This is a more complex measure of homophobia than simply asking a single question. Notice that, in the five items given here, we tapped into attitudes toward physical proximity to homosexuals, homosexuals as teachers, holding public office, and having a homosexual child, in addition to asking a question about homosexuality in general. This should give us a fuller understanding of the depth of feeling people have regarding homosexuality, certainly more than if we had asked only one of these items in our interview. Scale creation also produces a larger amount of variation among respondents because a range of 20 responses (25 minus 5) is larger than a range of 5 (the maximum for any single indicator in the scale). This can be helpful in trying to make subtle distinctions among respondents, such as identifying the strongly homophobic from those only moderately so.

If you choose to major in sociology or some other social science, you'll gain additional knowledge on sophisticated techniques for further testing and refining indexes and scales. By pretesting these questions first with a small but diverse group of people, the usefulness of each individual item in the scale can be examined. Items that don't produce a good deal of variation, or those items that vary quite differently from the others, are usually eliminated so that a scale or index measuring only one concept is produced. The overall reliability of the scale can even be calculated and further improved through statistical analysis.

THE INTERVIEW SCHEDULE

Surveys and interviews are commonplace in our society. Chances are you have already completed many of them in your lifetime. There is also a good chance that, at some time in the future, you will be asked to or desire to collect information from other people. This discussion introduces you to some of the more important things to consider in developing a list of questions that will ultimately be used to gather information from human subjects.

Once all the variables to be measured have been operationalized, additional thought must be given to the ordering of the questions on the questionnaire. Indeed, the order of the questions is as important as the questions themselves. The list of questions asked of a respondent is, as we saw earlier, called the interview schedule. Typically, the interview schedule begins with the least sensitive questions and ends with those that are the most sensitive. This is done so the interviewer has time to build **rapport**, or a sense of trust, with the person she or he is interviewing. By beginning the interview with simple demographic questions, the interviewee is given a chance to feel comfortable with the question-and-answer format, thereby reducing any stress the person may be experiencing. This feeling is enhanced if the interviewer responds affirmatively and appreciatively to the interviewee's responses. By the time more sensitive questions are asked later in the interview, there should be enough trust that the interviewee feels comfortable answering all the questions, and truthfully.

OVERALL LAYOUT

Thought must be given to the overall layout of the interview schedule. You may think it important only that the questions be handed to someone to complete in survey fashion, but it is equally important to pay attention to presentation and format in a situation where an interviewer uses the schedule to pose questions to an interviewee. Interviewers themselves can become confused or disoriented by a poorly organized schedule, even though they may be quite familiar with the overall goals of the project. Creating an easy-to-follow list of questions that are well laid out is a way to ensure that questions are asked in order and responses are properly recorded.

Introductions, instructions, and points of clarification that are to be communicated to the interviewee during the interview should all be clearly written into the interview schedule. This is done so the interviewee does not need to rely on memory to communicate important information to all the respondents, and so each respondent receives the same information. This ensures uniformity of instruction and thereby of responses. Writing out instructions is even more important in studies where multiple interviewers are employed. The interview schedule should be a complete document containing all of the information necessary to carry out the interview professionally. Do this even if only one person is going to act as the interviewer, because he or she might fall ill or encounter circumstances making it impossible to complete the study. Someone else can then quickly fill in, stepping into the shoes of the principal interviewer and completing a credible study.

The next section covers instructions used in the interview schedule for this assignment. As should be evident, instructions in square parentheses are included for the student who serves as the interviewer, as well as the exact words she should say to the person she is interviewing. Because the directions are clear and explicit, all the students who perform interviews know exactly what to do. A good rule of thumb in creating instructions is to state the obvious. Instructions such as these are also covered in interviewer training, the subject of Chapter Eight.

INTRODUCTION TO SOCIOLOGY INTERVIEW

[TO THE INTERVIEWER: Find a person who is currently a student at our university who has not already been interviewed by another class member. Say to the person: *"I'm doing an informal survey for a sociology class. May I ask you a few questions? The information is confidential and your name will not be associated with this project."* (If the response is positive, move if necessary to a place where no one else is close by. Then say: *"My name is _____. Just remember, although I would like to get all of the information I need, you can choose to not answer any question."*]

Instructions to be read to interviewees should also be inserted into the body of the interview schedule. This helps to introduce new questions, so that the interviewee can focus or get oriented on a particular subject, and to have a sense of progress. The questions listed in the previous section on homophobia, for example, could be prefaced with this brief comment:

> I'm now going to give you five statements dealing with the subject of homosexuality. For each statement, please say if you strongly disagree, disagree, are neutral or undecided, agree, or strongly agree.

This statement is enough to let the interviewee know the next few questions have a particular focus, and there are five appropriate choices with which to respond.

CONTINGENCY QUESTIONS

Contingency questions are another important dynamic to consider in questionnaire and interview schedule construction. Contingency questions are those that redirect the interviewee to additional questions, depending on the response to the contingency question. For example, a researcher might be interested in finding out people's attitude toward living in a residence on campus. The researcher will first want to sort the students who do live on campus from those who do not, because asking questions about residence life does not apply to those living off campus. The question is asked:

> Q. 20: Do you live on campus or off campus? (check one)
> _____ on campus
> _____ off campus

At this point, the researcher wants to pose, say, five more questions to those who live on campus but not to those who live off campus. Instructions in brackets are added after each response to direct the interviewer to the next question appropriate for the particular person being interviewed:

> Q. 20: Do you live on campus or off campus? (check one)
> _____ on campus [go on to question 21]
> _____ off campus [skip to question 26]

It should be obvious that the five questions following number 20 deal with issues related to on-campus housing, while question 26 would be the first that once again applies to all interviewees regardless of where they reside.

It is unlikely that your instructor will permit contingency questions to be used in your class interview project because the total number of people that your class will interview is likely to be relatively small. The disadvantage of contingency questions is that they further decrease the total number of people who will answer the questions that apply only to some study participants and not others. In this example, only those living on campus would respond to questions 21 through 25—a smaller number than all who participated in the study. This is not so big a problem in larger studies where a thousand or more people respond to various questions, contingency or not. Just the same, I'm describing questions of this type because some in your class will no doubt want to ask questions that are contingency-based. Now that you know what they are, you can identify them if someone in your class suggests such a question, and you can explain why it might be best to avoid using such questions if your class sample size is relatively small.

PROCESSING RESPONSES FROM INTERVIEWS

Most researchers today eventually face the need to enter a large amount of information they have collected into a computer. Computers offer powerful, sophisticated, and accurate processing and condensing of data in a fraction of the time it would take human beings to do the same amount of work. Researchers are thus challenged with finding a quick and easy way to get the information from the completed interview schedules into a database.

Today there are a variety of options for data entry for surveys and interviews. Telephone interviewers increasingly enter the responses of interviewees directly. Software programs enable these interviewers to read questions directly from their screen and enter the response. The machine automatically codes the response for the researcher and represents it in the database so as to facilitate data analysis. For the most part, however, researchers find themselves having to enter data as a separate step in their research process.

Virtually all responses received from interviewees, whether from closed-ended or open-ended questions, are eventually turned into numbers. This greatly facilitates data analysis and organization. For example, consider this question:

> 3. What is your religious affiliation? (check one)
> _____ Christian
> _____ Jewish
> _____ Muslim
> _____ None
> _____ Other (please specify) _____

To enter responses to this question, a researcher would number the responses, usually in ascending order. A response of "Christian" is entered as a 1, "Jewish" as a 2, and so on. Any answers written into the "Other" response are assigned a separate number of their own after all interviews are completed. Say, for example, someone identified her religious affiliation as Buddhist. The interviewer would place a check mark in the blank of "Other" and then write in Buddhist. During data entry, the response is entered as a 5 and, in a record of coding (called a **codebook**), it is recorded that a 5 means Buddhist. If someone else identifies himself as a Hindu, the interviewer again checks off "Other" but this time writes "Hindu" in the space provided. The person doing data entry codes Hindu as a 6 (not a 5) and records this new datum in the codebook. The same is done for any other religions written in the "Other" category. In this way, every response can be separately identified once data analysis is under way.

PRECODING DATA

Imagine you are the person responsible for entering data. Each time you look at this question on religious affiliation, you need to refer to the codebook to find out the number assigned to the particular response checked off, and then enter it. You might think this could be figured out fairly quickly, but someone doing data entry for answers to dozens of questions can easily forget what the codes are between interviews. Considerable time is saved if the responses are already numbered. This is called **precoding**. Our example looks like this if it is precoded:

> 3. What is your religious affiliation? (circle one number)
> 1 Christian
> 2 Jewish
> 3 Muslim
> 4 None
> Other (please specify) _____

Do you see the difference? Each response is assigned a number, and the interviewer is instructed to circle one of the numbers. Now, during data entry the code for each response is immediately apparent (save for the written Other responses) and can quickly be entered without searching through the codebook for the number that represents a particular response.

Precoding is more common on instruments such as interview schedules than it is on surveys. This is because interview schedules are seen only by trained interviewers who are taught to understand precoding and can circle the appropriate response. Without this training, precoded answers sometimes confuse people, who may circle more than one number or believe that the number stands for something other than the answer. Indeed, some survey respondents may think that the number indicates how many people in their family identify themselves with a particular religion. So they circle a number and then circle a particular religion. This might sound a bit ridiculous, but remember, it is the job of the person designing the research to anticipate the problems any question may pose and then structure the question in a way that is going to be clear to all respondents.

Because your class will use an interview schedule that only you will see and fill out, your instructor will likely precode the questions on the interview schedule for you. This will make your data entry much easier once you have completed all of the interviews. Details on how to enter the data are shared in Chapter Nine.

SUMMARY

Operationalization involves making the tough decision of how to measure precisely what you want to measure. Although your instructor has likely done this for you, thinking through choices in operationalization helps you be a better consumer of research and truth claims made by others in society. As in other stages of research, validity and reliability are ongoing goals in operationalization. The sophistication of those being interviewed and their familiarity with the study subject needs to be considered in creating interview questions.

Care must also be taken to order questions so as to build rapport. Make sure the layout is professional and clear. Develop instructions for both interviewer and interviewee alike. Consider whether questions should be closed-ended or open-ended, and precoded. Paying attention to detail before the interview takes place greatly increases the chance of collecting information that is both valid and reliable.

REVIEW QUESTIONS

1. What advice would you give to someone who is creating questions to ask in an interview?
2. Why is the layout of a survey or interview important?
3. What kinds of instructions should a researcher include in an interview? for whom? why?
4. What is precoding? Why would a researcher precode a survey or interview?

KEY TERMS

Closed-ended questions Questions in an interview or survey with a predetermined and limited number of possible responses.

Codebook A document separate from an interview, listing all variables measured in the study, the question or questions asked to measure the variable, and a number assigned to every possible response to every question.

Contingency questions Questions determining whether or not other questions in a survey or interview will be asked of the interviewee.

Indicator The actual question or item used to measure a variable.

Interview schedule The complete list of questions and instructions constituting the content of an interview.

Open-ended questions Questions asked of an interviewee with no predetermined responses or categories created.

Precoding The process of identifying numerical values or codes directly on the interview schedule so as to facilitate data entry.

Rapport The feeling of trust and comfort the interviewee has toward the interviewer.

8

Conducting Ethical Interviews

LEARNING OBJECTIVES

- Learn what people are capable of doing to one another if they view human beings as anything less than equals.
- Understand the development of ethical research standards in light of important historical examples that shouldn't be repeated.
- Internalize the principles of ethical research so as to conduct your class research project with respect and dignity.

The preceding chapters have focused on critical issues for conducting credible scientific research. Research done with human subjects, however, requires that extra caution be taken so as not to cause physical or emotional harm to the people with whom the researcher comes into contact. Researchers are first and foremost human beings, susceptible to their own human strengths and failings. As you will see in this chapter, researchers need to be reminded that treating their subjects with respect is *more* important than gathering good-quality data. It's a difficult position to take for some, because studies could be conducted producing invaluable information for all of humankind by inflicting harm on a smaller number of human beings. Should compromises be made in those instances? How does one know when one has crossed an ethical line? Where are the lines drawn?

YOUR OWN ETHICAL CHALLENGE

This issue has direct application to the interview project you are conducting for this class. As a researcher, you will be placed in a position of having influence over another human being. Like it or not, responsibility comes with being a researcher. As you conduct your interviews, you will come to realize the substantial power you have in influencing how people might respond to the questions you ask. Just by how you phrase questions, or the manner in which you react to the answers you receive from others, you can potentially influence (and thus bias) the data collection process.

For example, if you ask people about their political affiliation and scowl when they mention a political party you do not support, you let the interviewees know that you disapprove of their choice. They might then change their answers to upcoming questions in a way that they think will agree with your views. Or they may react negatively to your disapproval of an answer and give future responses more extreme than they might otherwise be. This is an ethical issue as much as a methodological one. By reacting negatively to people's opinions or manipulating them to answer in a certain way, we are using social pressure to coerce people to answer as we wish. Is using coercion ethical?

Aside from your having the potential to influence answers, an additional problem is that the people you interview will also be sharing personal attitudes and information. Depending on the questions asked in your interviews, some of it might be embarrassing if it were to become public knowledge. Telling your friends or roommate about the responses of a person you interviewed, especially if your listener knows who the respondent is, would be a violation of the trust or confidentiality placed in you by the person you interviewed.

So how do you conduct ethical research? What does ethical research look like? As you'll see, this is an important question researchers must answer before entering the data collection stage of their work. This way, mistakes that compromise the rights of the individuals can be prevented. I present a few notorious examples of ethical violations in the name of science. If you are offended by the research design in any of the examples given here, ask yourself what it is about the research that you find offensive. You'll likely find your notion articulated in the ethical principles identified in the section that follows.

ETHICAL ABUSES IN RESEARCH

THE TUSKEGEE EXPERIMENT

In 1932, the U. S. Public Health Service conducted the Tuskegee Syphilis Study in Alabama to study how syphilis develops over time if left untreated. Researchers selected 399 poor and virtually illiterate African American men, mostly sharecroppers, for the study because they had syphilis and were poor and black. For the next forty years researchers studied the men, giving them free medical exams and aspirin and free lunches as an incentive to come back for examinations. None of the men was accurately informed of his condition. Instead, researchers told them they were suffering from "bad blood"—and didn't even tell them that they were part of a larger study.

No cure was available for syphilis when the study began, but researchers offered the men no treatments that would alleviate the development of the disease even after a cure was found. It wasn't until 1972 that someone working on the project leaked information to the media about what was happening. It took until 1997 before President Bill Clinton formally apologized to the eight remaining survivors (Reverby, 2000). The fact that these men were left to suffer for years when treatment was available to alleviate their pain and increase their longevity is one way in which this study is seen as unethical.

NAZI EXPERIMENTS

World War II was a major catalyst for a worldwide movement to articulate a set of common standards to which people of the world would hold their governments and each other accountable. When the gates of concentration camps were swung open by the Allied forces and journalists were allowed to take and publish photos, the world reacted with revulsion at what was found inside. Photos of piles of naked, emaciated human bodies caused mass horror all around the world. The attempted mass genocide of Jews, Gypsies, and homosexuals motivated leaders of various bodies around the world to push their respective political leaders to work cooperatively with leaders from other nations to agree to an ethical code that would apply around the world, regardless of nation, religion, or values.

Morsink (1999) notes that letters from individuals and groups around the world encouraged world leaders to develop a universal standard of human rights. Jews, Catholics, and Protestants joined together to call for peace and respect for human rights, as did labor organizations and many others. The result was creation, and later ratification, of the 1948 United Nations Declaration of Human Rights.

Nazi physicians reporting on their research activities at trial in Nuremberg, Germany, only added fuel to the fire. Physicians had forced people to drink seawater to see how long they would survive, immersed others in icy water to see how long a pilot might survive hypothermia after being shot down, and placed others in vacuum chambers to find how the human body responds to high altitude. Castration and sterilization experiments were numerous, as were unnecessary limb and bone transplants. Still others were injected with a variety of pathogens and diseases to experiment with cures. The toll on the human subjects was significant. Hundreds died, and many others lived with painful illnesses or deep psychological or physical scars for years to come (Annas and Grodin, 1992).

These inhumane experiments illustrate the capacity for human beings—even those dedicated to healing and the preservation of quality of life—to be distracted from honoring and respecting all human life in the name of powerful ideology, such as ethnocentrism, nationalism, or racism. Many Nazi doctors, excited with the possibility of developing knowledge that would help soldiers and leaders from their own country succeed in their military goals, eagerly pursued experiments that ended up causing significant pain and loss of life to thousands. The end goal of nationalistic pride and success overrode their professional goals of enhancing human life.

THE MILGRAM EXPERIMENTS

Nationalism isn't the only kind of ideology that can override one's empathic sensibilities. The otherwise pure quest for knowledge can sometimes cause researchers to overlook the possible impact of research design on participants. Stanley Milgram (1963) at Yale University conducted one such study. Like many people at the time, Milgram was surprised to learn about the level of cruelty guards displayed toward Nazi concentration camp inmates. Many non-Germans adopted a racist explanation for the behavior: there was something innate in the German mind that made them capable of doing cruel and despicable things to others, something that wasn't found in other people of the world. At the Nuremberg trials, however, German guards frequently asserted that they were merely following orders in torturing or otherwise harming inmates. Could it be that people easily defer to authority and inflict pain on others instead of following their own personal sensibilities that they might be harming another human being?

Milgram set up an experiment to test this. People recruited off the street were assigned to one of two roles: teacher or learner. In every case, the "learner" was actually someone (a confederate) working for the experimenter. People recruited for the experiment didn't know this and thought they had been randomly assigned the role of teacher. The learner was an older, gray-haired, grandfatherly person, strapped into a chair in another room with his hand on a shock plate. The "teacher" watched as this older man was strapped into the chair and told that the teacher would be administering an electric shock every time the learner gave an incorrect answer. Before experimentation began, the elderly man would mention he had a heart condition.

Milgram set the teacher up at a control panel in the adjacent room, along with a list of questions printed on paper. The teacher was instructed to read one question at a time through a microphone to the learner in the other room. If the learner answered correctly, the teacher would let him know and go on to the next question. If the learner answered incorrectly, the teacher was to say "incorrect" and apply an electric shock. In reality the learner was not being shocked at all, but the teacher had every reason to believe that he was administering a shock. The control panel consisted of a series of thirty buttons in a row, labeled "slight shock" and "15 volts" on the left end to "danger: severe shock," "XXX," and "450 volts" on the other. The teacher was instructed to administer increasing levels of shock to the learner.

The experiment proceeded well at first, with the learner answering most questions correctly. Soon, however, the learner was answering incorrectly with increasing frequency. Each time, the teacher was expected to administer a harsher electric shock as "punishment." As the shocks grew more severe, the learner began to yell loudly and complain about the pain. He would yell that he didn't want to continue the experiment anymore and needed to stop. Eventually, the learner stopped responding entirely, presumably falling into a state of unconsciousness brought on by a possible heart attack.

Results

What would you do if you were in the role of the teacher? How far would you go in shocking the learner before your conscience would cause you to stop? At various stages of the experiment, participants in the role of teacher protested about what was happening to the older gentleman. Each time, Milgram would respond, "The experiment must continue" or "You have no choice; you must go on." Ultimately, 65 percent of the participants in one version of the study ended up administering the full series of shocks! The results of Milgram's studies confirmed the claim of the German guards: more often than not, people ignore their own personal principles of ethical behavior and follow the directions of an authority figure—whether an experimenter or a military officer.

The results of the Milgram studies are fascinating in and of themselves. The ethical issue of the research, however, involved the aftermath of the testing. People given the role of teacher in the experiment had been placed in a situation where they experienced a great deal of psychological stress and discomfort. Some found it difficult to challenge the authority of an experimenter from a prestigious university and continued harming another human being. Despite debriefing sessions after the experiment, where the subjects were introduced to the learner and the purpose of the experiment was explained, many participants were bothered for months afterward with bad dreams and other stressed-induced symptoms.

Some went on to struggle with guilt after realizing what they were potentially capable of doing to another human being. To be sure, the public reacted negatively to putting someone under that kind of stress for the sake of research. Today's university human subject review boards would rarely approve a research design of this nature because of the potential risk the research design poses to participants of inducing unreasonable and inhumane stress.

THE DEVELOPMENT OF STANDARDS

Experiences such as these alarmed the common sensibilities of regular citizens, but it took the horrifying attempts of institutionalized genocide in World War II to create worldwide momentum for articulating a set of minimum standards for treatment of human beings under any circumstances, including war or research. This international concern for human rights overshadowed the Nuremberg trials, where leading Nazis were held accountable in an international court for their role in orchestrating the genocide. As mentioned earlier, the testimony of Nazi scientists during the trial also revealed that previously trusted professionals could be swept away by ideological or patriotic fervor, to the point where they would cause irrevocable harm or death in service to the cause.

PROFESSIONAL ETHICAL STANDARDS

Over time, international and domestic government initiatives pushed members of professional organizations and research-driven institutions to articulate a set of standards for treating clients and research subjects that would not be compromised even for the sake of information. These standards today promote protection from physical or psychological harm, maintenance of privacy and confidentiality, freedom from coercion, and informed consent. Most professional associations add other basic human rights to their own code of ethics, but these four are common to virtually all. The American Sociological Association's Statement of Ethics includes directives regarding proper treatment and dissemination of data, acting in a professional manner, and more. It can be accessed at http://www.asanet .org/cs/root/leftnav/ethics/code_of_ethics_table_of_contents.

You'll want to pay attention to these principles in preparing to collect information from other human beings, even fellow students on your campus. How would you go about doing this in an ethical manner? Conversely, what might you do during the course of this study that would constitute an ethical violation? It is critically important that you understand these principles and respect them. Although this is a class exercise, you will be dealing with human subjects who are fully entitled to be treated respectfully and ethically.

Protection from Harm

Above all, researchers must take every precaution to protect people participating in research from any kind of harm resulting from participation in the study. They should be no worse off than otherwise for having participated in the study. Today, subjecting research participants to potential physical harm is rare because of heightened sensitivity to issues regarding human rights. The greater potential is to cause psychological harm, either directly or indirectly, from research activities that can cause stress, abuse, or even a loss of self-esteem. The Milgram study is an example of research that created a great deal of stress, even if unintentionally.

Is it appropriate to cause embarrassment in subjects, or anxiety, or stress? or create a situation where they are forced to choose between unethical actions? Most of us would agree that forcing such a choice is unethical because such disposition causes discomfort. If severe, embarrassment or stress can have lasting effects. From the research point of view, however, things are different. How else might researchers studying the effects of embarrassment, stress, or anxiety in certain situations otherwise produce meaningful and helpful studies if they are not allowed to create these conditions in their research? Is humankind not ultimately the benefactor of knowledge produced from such studies? Today, most ethics boards carefully examine proposed research designs and may approve experimentation if the psychological "harm" is short-lived, is mild, and can be eliminated through proper debriefing. Your instructor will help guide your class to select a topic that can be researched in a way that does not cause stress in the students you gather information from, and will phrase questions in a way that will be respectful.

Maintenance of Privacy

There is less privacy in our society today than there has been for many years (Staples 1997). Much of our personal information is stored in databases that we are unaware of. Data mining companies often collect the information we furnish on surveys or contest entry forms, aggregate it with other statistics about us, and then sell the data to marketing companies. Today people paste private information and photos on public Internet sites such as MySpace and Facebook, seldom realizing how quickly a posted photo can be copied by an acquaintance and distributed to others who may eventually post the photo on other public sites. We are frequently on camera in most stores, and we often willingly comply by sharing personal information such as a zip code requested by a store cashier. Staples (1997) refers to these occurrences as **meticulous rituals of surveillance**.

In a world of public access to private information, it might be difficult for some to grasp the importance of respecting privacy for its own sake. Some argue that they have nothing to hide and therefore nothing to fear. But this is not the point. Many regard **privacy**—the ability to control information about oneself—as a human right. People who will answer questions for your class interview project are releasing information about themselves because they will be informed that it is to be used only for educational purposes. It is therefore unethical for the interviewers to release the information in any other form or capacity. The aggregate data should not even be shared without every interviewed person first being informed of how the information is to be used and then giving consent to participate in the study.

More important, respecting participants' privacy also means keeping information you collect during the interview process to yourself. We'll deal with this issue again in the next section, but it bears repeating that the information must be treated confidentially. Whether you know the person you are interviewing or not, her response to your questions should not be shared with friends, relatives, roommates, classmates, or anyone else for that matter. This is true not only for the semester in which you collect the data, but forever. The identity of the person and her responses should remain private, regardless of how sensitive or impersonal *you* may feel the information is. Be prepared to handle information maturely.

Freedom from Coercion

A fundamental human right, recognized in the United Nations Declaration of Human Rights of 1948, is the right to self-determination. This means human beings have the right to make choices about their lives and not be restricted or forced into certain activities simply because someone else wants something from them. As long as people do not infringe on this same human right attributed to others, they should be free to make choices for themselves. This human right is violated, obviously, if someone is forced or coerced to do something he does not want to do.

Physical force is only one mechanism by which people are forced to do things they do not want to do. Slavery is an obvious example. Subtler expressions of power are often used to coerce people into taking part in studies without their consent. University professors periodically require students enrolled in their courses to reveal confidential information about themselves in surveys; their grades may be lowered if they choose not to participate. Is this ethical? A guiding principle of data collection in organizations is that a person should not be coerced if the exercise has no direct personal benefit (such as an opportunity to learn) to himself or herself.

Sometimes *withholding* information can be considered coercive. If an authority figure such as a police officer or a professor asks you for information, you might feel compelled to comply because we have generally been taught to trust authority figures.

But what if they ask for information that we do not want to give and are not required to give by law? We have a right to refuse to answer. Sometimes we need to be informed that we have a choice.

Subjects participating in research studies today are almost always informed that they can choose not to participate, that they may end their participation in the study at any point, and that they can choose to not answer any question at any time. Protecting these rights can be quite inconvenient from a data collection standpoint; information taken from someone who refuses to answer a critical question or drops out of a study early is basically worthless. Protecting the human right to self-determination, however, is *more* important than gathering quality data for a particular study.

People should not be coerced, and they should not have to reveal information if the sharing is not germane to what they are seeking. This means if a student's participation in a study is not an essential part of the learning goals of a particular course, she should not be required to participate. This applies to your class research project; you will ask for voluntary participation from other students at your school but will not make it mandatory. You will also inform them that they are free to choose not to answer any question.

Informed Consent

The Tuskegee experiment illustrated an ethical breach of informed consent. That is, no one should be inducted into an experiment without first being fully informed of the nature and purpose of the study, his role in the study, and how the information will be used. Consent to participate should be sought only after full disclosure. Of course, protection of this human right creates a fundamental research issue: if someone is informed about the topic of study, he may become more self-aware about that topic as far as his behavior is concerned and may then act differently than he would otherwise. This in turn draws the validity of the research results into question.

This issue is particularly important in doing experimental research with human subjects. Because of this, most **institutional review boards** today allow some deception to occur in experimental research, but only if the deception is essential for producing important results, no major stress or anxiety is produced in subjects as a result of the deception, and subjects are debriefed after the experiment so they learn the true nature of the experiment. This form of mild deception is common today, so much so that, if you agree to participate in an experiment you can be fairly sure that whatever the researchers suggest the focus of the research to be is *not* what it really is! A compromise is made as a result between protecting human rights and gaining valid information from experimental research.

In survey and interview research, informed consent is most frequently secured at the beginning of data collection. Subjects are told about the purpose of the research, how the data will be used, how long the survey or interview will take to complete, and that they can choose not to participate at any time. In fact, you'll be informing the people you interview of their rights in this regard before you ask them the first question.

INSTITUTIONAL REVIEW BOARDS

Aside from the code of ethics statements that most professionals are bound to follow by dint of their membership in professional organizations, virtually all universities and research organizations have created their own institutional review boards (or IRBs) as an additional precaution to protecting human subjects involved in research projects. Researchers typically submit a proposal to the IRB before any other actions are taken. Experts in research methods on the IRB review the proposal, looking for any potential danger of doing harm or otherwise violating the rights of individuals who might be involved in the research. This additional precautionary step is meant to protect human subjects from any researcher who might be so interested in getting good-quality results that she or he does not anticipate all of the potential risks involved in the proposed research.

Many IRBs insist on providing interviewees with a written letter that informs them of their rights during the interview process. IRBs prefer to have potential interviewees then sign the form to show that they have been familiarized with their rights. Exhibit 8.1 is an example of the letter that my university uses to obtain informed consent. This is fine in principle, but you can likely imagine some situations where insisting that a person sign an official-looking letter might actually reduce the number of people who consent to taking part in a study.

An example was the research I engaged in for my master's thesis. I conducted a year's worth of research on the heavy metal music subculture in a large city. Most of my research took place in heavy metal bars and concert venues. I applied for research funds to assist with data collection and received some modest funds, but the university insisted that I give a written consent form to every heavy metal listener I interviewed. Can you imagine trying to get someone in a darkened bar, with music blaring from a live band, to read and sign an interview consent form? It was an unreasonable expectation. As a result, I modified my research slightly so that I gained more information from "casual conversations" with people in the setting rather than from formally defined interviews. This tension between getting good-quality information from people on the one hand and making sure that their rights are respected on the other is an ongoing challenge in data collection. Both are important, but human rights more so.

Most universities make exceptions to applying for formal IRB review if a research project is relatively small, does not involve people off campus, is for pedagogical purposes only, and does not deal with overly sensitive topics. Your instructor will find this out for you and will fill out the necessary IRB application if your university requires it.

EXHIBIT 8.1 EXAMPLE OF AN INFORMED CONSENT LETTER

INFORMED CONSENT
THE UNIVERSITY OF TAMPA

Project Title
Principal Investigator
Address and Phone
Purpose of Project
Procedures
Risks and Benefits
Confidentiality

CONDITIONS OF PARTICIPATION

Participating in this project is voluntary, and refusal to participate or withdrawing from participation at any time during the project will involve no penalty or loss of benefits to which the subject is otherwise entitled. The principal investigator may terminate participation of a subject or the project entirely without regard to the subject's consent. In the event of questions or difficulties of any kind during or following participation, the subject may contact the principal investigator as indicated above.

CONSENT

I have read the above information and my questions and concerns, if any, have been responded to satisfactorily by project staff. I believe I understand the purpose, benefits, and risks, if any, of the study, and give my informed and free consent to be a participant.

_____

Signature   Date

This research project has been approved by the Institutional Review Board for the Protection of Human Subjects of the University of Tampa.

SUMMARY

There have been tragic historical examples of harm being inflicted on other human beings, even in the name of science. Ultimately, collective values protect us from harm. Inspired by the human rights movement, professional associations, universities, and research organizations have developed their own codes of ethics and have institutionalized ways to enforce and protect them. Germane to all are protection from physical or psychological harm, maintenance of privacy and confidentiality, freedom from coercion, and informed consent.

Protecting these rights is a responsibility for you as you proceed with completing your class's research project. Treat others as you want to be treated, by honoring these basic human rights.

REVIEW QUESTIONS

1. In your opinion, what ethical principles were violated in the Tuskegee experiment? the Milgram study? the Nazi experiments?
2. What historical experience was the catalyst for articulation of a Universal Declaration of Human Rights? Has the human rights movement had any impact in establishing professional codes of ethics for conducting research? Explain.
3. What four ethical standards are common to all codes of ethics today? What other rights would you want protected if you were taking part in a research study?
4. What is an IRB? What role does it play in protecting human rights in research?

KEY TERMS

Institutional Review Board A board at a research institution, consisting of experienced social researchers, that protects human rights by reviewing research proposals before they are carried out.

Meticulous rituals of surveillance Daily activities in which we are asked by store personnel, online sites, and the like to reveal personal information about ourselves.

Privacy Freedom from intrusion into one's own life or activities.

9

How to Be a Good Interviewer

LEARNING OBJECTIVES

- Understand the importance of your role as an interviewer to ensure the validity and reliability of the data you collect.
- Examine behaviors that will produce poor data.
- Discern how to perform interviews professionally, thereby collecting quality data.
- Form your own opinions on the usefulness of interviewing as a data-gathering tool.

This chapter gives you the tools you need to complete the interviews for your class project. Consider it a crash course in interviewer training. Good interviewers are professional, are consistent when interviewing different people, and quickly build rapport with those they interview. This is essential to collecting valid and reliable data, which is your goal for this part of the project. Because multiple people will be conducting interviews in this project, it is also important that everyone in your class approach this task as uniformly as possible. Otherwise, variation in responses might be produced by the uniqueness of the several interviewers, which produces **measurement error**.

FIRST PREP: AN ATTITUDE OF INQUIRY

Before beginning your interviews, take a few minutes to review the questions on the interview schedule. For each question, *estimate how you think the overall results will turn out.* Record your estimate on a separate piece of paper and save it to examine after the data have been collected and compiled. If your interview contains a question on sex, for example, estimate the percentages of men and women you think will end up being interviewed. By making these estimations, you'll be giving yourself an opportunity to be impressed with the data collected. The responses you get from other students may surprise you—or perhaps they'll be in line with what you expect.

For some, writing down expectations before collecting data can be personally threatening. This is because they don't like putting themselves in a position where they might find out their impressions are wrong. Know that even academics and other researchers who design studies are often surprised by research results. This process of making explicit one's assumptions about the nature of the social universe and then comparing those impressions to collected information is the essence of the scientific method. It allows us to rise above our favored ideas and beliefs to confront a broader reality that we might not have been aware of.

In fact, finding results that run counter to one's own beliefs actually becomes an *enjoyable* part of the process of discovery. Contrary findings often stimulate more questions and can help spur on new and important discoveries or relationships. Researchers too often relish presenting the results of their own studies at a scientific conference that surprise or amaze their peers. Finding relationships between two or more variables that few have suspected or noticed before is a big part of the joy of discovery of science. More than one scientist has grown in notoriety by being the first person to demonstrate a meaningful connection between two or more important variables.

Rising above **ego involvement** with our favorite theories or ideas is consequently essential to doing science, as is rising above commonly accepted notions of who human beings are or how they behave. All this means adopting a spirit of honesty and humility, a willingness to contrast new information and evidence with our personal preferences and biases. The rewards in terms of personal growth, knowledge, and wisdom can be amazing. Do you have what it takes to be a social scientist?

A NOTE ABOUT INTERVIEWS

There are inherent strengths and weaknesses in any type of data collection method. Interviews are no different. We're using interviews for your class project, as opposed to surveys, experiments, content analyses, or other options, for several reasons. Remember that the ultimate goal of this project is to give you a taste of what it is like to share in the joy of discovery in doing social scientific research. You've formulated a hypothesis about how the social world works in terms of cause and effect. The next step is to move to the process of data collection to test your hypothesis.

We're also using interviews because they are a method that gives you some experience in both qualitative and quantitative aspects of data collection. Asking someone questions face-to-face exposes you to the challenges and benefits of gathering information from others, without biasing how they answer. This qualitative component of data collection is dynamic and must be approached carefully. We'll review good ways of interviewing. Coding people's responses into numerical values so they can be entered and analyzed by computer is the quantitative aspect to interviews. Your instructor will likely put numbers beside each possible response on your interviews and then enter the data to produce the tables you will analyze. Interviewing exposes you to a wider variety of issues involved with data collection than most other methods, meaning you'll learn more from the experience.

CRITICAL ISSUES: VALIDITY AND RELIABILITY REVISITED

You're about to interview one or more people on your campus. What are your goals as you ask the questions? How do you know if you've achieved your goals? Is there any way you could "mess up" the interview? What is involved in doing a good interview? Here's an opportunity to think through these issues before you start asking questions.

VALIDITY

Recall that measurement validity was defined earlier as *actually measuring what you want to measure.* This is a critical issue in any study, regardless of method. In interviewing, validity most often has to do with the wording of the questions on the interview schedule. You won't have much control over this because your instructor has likely prepared the questions for you. You should, however, read them over and ask yourself whether the questions are worded so as to truly measure the variable of interest. It should not be considered a problem if you decide a question could be reworded because the class project is ultimately a learning exercise.

To take an obvious example, which of these questions would elicit answers that more accurately measure the variable *country of birth*?

      A. In what country were you born? _____

      B. What is your favorite color? _____

I do hope you selected A as the better question to discern someone's country of birth. Question B appears to have nothing to do with one's country of birth, and even if it did A would still elicit a more specific and accurate answer than B ever would. In other words, A is a more *valid measure* of country of birth than is B.

I trust this obvious example demonstrates that some questions produce more valid responses than others. But it is often difficult to choose how questions are worded because the differences are subtler than in the obvious example. Sometimes the validity of a question can be established *only after* the data collection is completed and the results are compared to other established measures of the variable in question.

Your challenge as an interviewer is to produce validity by getting a *true* or honest answer for every question from every person you interview. Take this as a personal challenge. In the interview, it is only you, the other person, and the questions to which you want real answers. What do you, the interviewer, need to do to motivate the other person to tell you the truth? Part of the answer lies in establishing rapport, which is discussed later. The rest of the answer is best described by considering the issue of reliability.

RELIABILITY

Reliability means *getting the same results with the same instrument over repeated measures of the same thing.* When interviewing, questions asked during the research process are posed in such a way that an interviewee would always answer in the same manner. To clarify this, imagine how questions might be asked that would produce *unreliable* answers. Let's say that one question asks if a person's family is upper-class, middle-class, or lower-class. Could you ask the question such that it might elicit an incorrect response? If you curl your nose and scowl when you recited the choice "lower-class," the interviewee could get the idea that you think being from the lower class is disgusting. Some people from a lower socioeconomic class thus might give an incorrect answer so as not to experience your disapproval.

Now, imagine you scowl only when asking some people the question but don't scowl when asking others. This obviously influences the amount of trust one can have in your interviewing techniques because some of the responses you record are inaccurate while others are accurate. In other words, asking questions in a different way, with varying tone of voice or nonverbal gestures, makes the data collection unreliable. To keep it reliable, the question should be posed to all the people you interview in as similar a fashion as possible. This means carefully reading the question word for word and not deviating or adding your own interpretation.

This is even more critical when an interviewing project involves more than one interviewer, as is the case with your class project because everyone in your class will be interviewing other students. How can we try to ensure that all students will ask the questions in the same manner? Going through interviewer training as a class and reviewing each question can increase the standardization and thereby the reliability of the study.

HOW TO COLLECT UNRELIABLE DATA

You can no doubt anticipate other behaviors in which you or a classmate engage during an interview that would produce *unreliable* data. Varying how you conduct interviews is enough to draw the quality of the data into question. Because this class project involves more than one interviewer, it is imperative that all interviewers conduct interviews similarly. This means doing the interviews as you are instructed in class and as described in the next section.

This is illustrated by first pointing out the errors that some make when they *don't* follow the instructions on how to conduct good-quality interviews. These errors are usually committed by interviewers who don't pay attention to details, aren't interested in improving their skills through a project, or don't understand the importance of uniform data collection.

If you purposely want to gather information through interviews that is *invalid* and *unreliable*, here are some things you can do:

- Don't familiarize yourself with the interview questions before you go out to interview. (This way you're sure to make mistakes in some interviews as you read through the questions for the first time.)
- Act as if you don't care about the project or the person you are interviewing. (This indicates to the interviewees that the project is not important, so they in turn won't think much about the answers they give. Rushing through the interview is a great way to communicate your lack of concern over the quality of their answers.)

- Go through the interview too slowly. (This indicates that you don't care about being respectful of the interviewee's time. Interviewees will become bored and end the interview early or give quick answers with no thought behind them so they can get through the interview.)
- Interview only people you know. (People you know are aware of your opinions and may answer dishonestly on some items because they don't want to upset you or have you think poorly of them if their opinion differs from your own.)
- Change how you ask the questions from interview to interview. (This ensures that people respond differently to the same question.)
- Don't interview people at all, but instead hand them the list of interview questions to read and fill out on their own. (This turns the experience into a survey instead of an interview, thus drawing into question whether the people you gather information from really understand the questions in the same way.)

Can you think of other things to do to render the collected data unreliable or invalid? Remember, the more this is the case, the less trustworthy the data are.

HOW TO CONDUCT A GREAT INTERVIEW

It should be obvious from the previous section that collecting good-quality data requires some effort and planning. Would you like to find out whether there is support for your hypothesis for this project? This can be discerned only if quality data are collected. The success of this aspect of the research is completely in your hands and those of your class-mates. Attention to detail is needed at every step of the interview process: preparation, administration, and termination.

PREPARING FOR THE INTERVIEW

Good information can be obtained through interviewing if you take some time to think through things that might distract someone from otherwise being honest with you, and take steps to avoid committing those errors. Most people who agree to an interview don't mind sharing their thoughts with another person. They love the opportunity to talk about themselves! So good interviewing often involves *not getting in the way* of someone other-wise talking honestly about himself.

As interviewers, we want to present ourselves in as neutral a way as possible so the person can focus more on his answers than on us. The practices described here are simply good communication. Make use of these interviewing techniques whenever you meet new people or get together with friends and family, and you'll find that the quality of your relationships and dialogue will increase. Go ahead and try it!

Empathy is the ability to put yourself in someone else's shoes to the point where you understand the choices she has made or is facing. You may not agree with her choices, but to be empathic is to understand, as a human being, why someone would make the choices she has made. Being empathic can increase the quality of responses you get from someone else, because the person senses you are being nonjudgmental. This creates security whereby a person is more apt to reveal true feelings in an interview. Empathy is a powerful data collection tool. It enables us to understand and accept even those with experiences quite different from our own.

Using your empathic skills for a moment, imagine being interviewed on campus by another student. What might the person interviewing you do, say, or wear to *distract* you from answering every question fully and honestly? Take a moment to jot down anything that comes to mind.

Dress

Is there something you could wear that might draw more attention to yourself than to the interview questions? Messages on T-shirts or clothing—even name brands and logos—can be distracting. Some types of clothing hints at your social status, or your political or even religious views. You'll want to avoid a display of such cues because people may make assumptions about who you are as a person, and then choose to answer some questions more along the lines of how they think you would answer rather than how they really feel.

Generally, the more neutral the clothing you wear, the better. Clothing that is revealing, too tight, or too big can be a distraction. Some may even take offense. Shirts or blouses with solid colors or subtle patterns should be preferred over those with messages or images of celebrities or political leaders. Name-brand clothing is attractive only to some people. Name brands can evoke jealousy or even anger in those who cannot afford them or who do not agree with the heavy emphasis on consumption in American society. Interviewers wearing clothes that are neutral in color are less likely to get in the way of data collection than those who wear clothes designed to attract attention. Give some thought to the selection of your clothing before you begin interviewing.

Similarly, think about other visual clues you might normally include in your presentation of self that you would not want to wear while interviewing. How you style your hair, the number of visible piercings or tattoos you sport, and even the amount of make-up you wear should be carefully considered. Many students dress in a manner that expresses their unique sense of individuality (and, sometimes, lack of sleep). The question to ask in getting dressed for interviews: "How can I present myself in a way that will not distract the person I am interviewing from the questions I pose?" Dress casually, but neatly and neutrally.

Be Prepared

Read through the questions several times before interviewing someone for your class project. You'll want to pay particular attention to any instructions to give to the interviewee and how responses should be recorded for each question. Read the question aloud at least once, imagining the possible responses of interviewees. If your instructor approves, consider conducting a practice interview with a classmate, roommate, or friend. You're ready to interview when you can smoothly move through the interview without a long pause or confusion on your part.

CONDUCTING THE INTERVIEW

With preparation out of the way, you're ready to think through the challenges you'll face while actually conducting the interviews. Pay attention to three important features: deportment, verbal communication, and pace.

Deportment

Deportment refers to actions and words, in short, how a person presents himself or herself to others. Some of these issues were addressed in the previous section about preparing for interviews. Here we consider other important aspects of verbal and nonverbal interpersonal communication.

Eye contact is one of the most important aspects of deportment. Looking another person in the eye while talking to him or as he responds to you communicates respect and interest. Conversely, looking down at your paper or at others passing by is a sure way to communicate that you are not interested in his response. Familiarizing yourself with the interview questions ensures that you'll need only to glance at the questions before asking them rather than focusing on the page more than on the person being interviewed. Let your continued eye contact communicate that you are interested in what he has to say.

Having your *shoulders squared* with the person is also good use of nonverbal communication. Sitting sideways while talking to a person communicates partial interest at best, while turning your body straight to the person communicates that she has your full attention. Similarly, *giving an affirming nod* or reaffirming "*Mmmm hmmm*" lets the other person know that you hear what she is saying. Above all, *smile, smile, smile.* It demonstrates that you like people, and that you like interacting with the person you are interviewing.

A popular expression these days, posed in the form of a question, is, "Do you *feel* me?" That is, have you listened such that you understand what I am *feeling* rather than saying? I call attention to *empathy* here once more to enforce its importance. During the interview it may be appropriate to ask yourself what the other person is feeling as he shares with you. It lets him know he is being understood.

Verbal Communication

Making a bit of small talk before the interview—asking how classes are going, or how the person likes attending your college or university—is a way to build rapport. **Rapport** (pronounced "rah-PORE") is basically the presence of trust and mutual respect between interviewer and interviewee. Sometimes it takes asking only one or two informal questions about the other person to establish a sense of rapport. This demonstrates your interest in the interviewee as a human being, apart from the information you hope to get from the person.

Several years ago I took a group of fifty high school students and chaperones to help build a school for the deaf in the highlands of Jamaica. Men (and sometimes women) in many parts of the world have rituals that establish a sense of rapport among strangers. New acquaintances usually shake hands in North America. In the parish of St. Elizabeth in Jamaica, men would actually greet other men by extending a fist. The other man would likewise form a fist and tap the top of the other man's fist, who would then do the same to the stranger. In a final gesture, the two men would touch the knuckles of their fists and actually say, "Respect, mon; respect." Rituals such as these vary from culture to culture but are common, especially among males. As a sociologist, I was impressed at the Jamaican protocol of verbalizing the need to establish respect—the intention of the ritual. It was a way to establish rapport between strangers.

Interviewees may be reluctant to answer all the questions posed to them, or answer questions fully and honestly, if rapport has not been established. Rapport is unlikely to develop if an interviewer fails to show interest in what the person being interviewed is saying, and more so if the interviewer exhibits any kind of judgment or moralizing in response to answers given. Judging, condemning, moralizing, or even showing surprise at responses are particularly effective at shutting down quality communication. A good rule of thumb in interviewing (or just talking with people) is that *they will reveal their deepest beliefs and ideas only if they feel safe and supported.* If you want people to keep secrets from you or be dishonest, then *judge* and devalue their opinions as they share them. Even silent judgment is sometimes communicated in our nonverbal gestures. People can be respected as human beings who are entitled to their own opinions, even if the opinions differ from our own.

Making a verbal comment in reaction to how a respondent answers a question can heavily bias the answers to other questions. It is important to treat the interviewee professionally and nonjudgmentally, conveying respect and interest. Remember that the interview really isn't about you; it's about the person you are interviewing. Avoid commenting on the responses in a way that reveals your own beliefs or attitudes (such as "Oh, I agree" or "good answer!"). Such responses indicate that you are indeed evaluating as they answer, which may intimidate the interviewee from answering questions honestly later in the interview if they feel you might disagree with their responses. The same is implied with responses that reveal your own surprise ("Really?" or "Are you sure?").

Of course, negative evaluations of their responses (such as "That's just wrong" or "No way!") will virtually ensure that the interviewee will answer dishonestly or end the interview early. It's best to either not respond, verbally or nonverbally, to a person's response or else give a simple affirming nod indicating that you have heard and recorded the response. Then quickly move onto the next question. Alternatively, simply saying "OK, thank you" to a response before moving on is a way to vary your responses but keep an interview moving.

Pace

Finally, demonstrate respect for the interviewee by keeping the interview moving. Read all instructions and questions carefully and clearly; that is, don't rush. Keep focused on moving through the interview. This is true even if the person being interviewed likes to talk. In the type of structured interview your class will do, it is good to politely start to ask the next question at an opportune time once the interviewee has provided the information you need. If a person is talking too much, wait until he or she takes a breath to cut in and say something like, "OK, thank you; we need to keep moving . . ." and then launch into the next question. Feel free to clarify a question or answer other questions that an interviewee might have, but always keep an eye on the time.

Ask questions in a neutral and unassuming manner. For example, first think about how you might ask this question in a way that biases the person's answer: "Do you feel it is OK for students to consume alcohol to the point where they are drunk?" Try saying the question aloud a few times, using a different tone of voice or inflection each time. Are various ways of asking likely to elicit different answers? If so, you'll want to choose the way of asking the question that is *least* likely to produce biased responses. As always, valid and reliable responses are preferred to those that are biased or inaccurate; we want more reasons to trust the data we collect and the conclusions eventually reached.

COMPLETING THE INTERVIEW

Be sure to take a moment to make eye contact and express a genuine thank-you to each person you interview. People volunteer to be interviewed largely to be kind. As a result of their volunteering, you will have data to process and will be able to learn more about the process of conducting sociological research. They've done you a favor, so let them know you are grateful and that their efforts and responses are valuable.

Expressing your thanks also leaves the volunteer with good feelings, about both you and the experience of being interviewed. This leaves them more likely to agree to being interviewed in the future. Marketers and others have tricked many people by using the interview process to push interviewees into buying something. Experiences like this decrease the likelihood that people will agree to participate in studies in the future. This is a problem for social researchers who select random samples and who need to collect information from virtually everyone selected for inclusion in the study.

Today marketers (and some social researchers) are resorting to offering incentives for people to participate in surveys and interviews. Gift certificates, candy, or entry into drawings for valuable prizes are now common means to entice people to agree to participate. This creates new problems of increasing the expenses of doing research and training the general population to not participate in studies unless they "get" something in return. It can also affect the reliability of the information collected; people who agree to participate in a study for the sake of some reward may differ from those who are not motivated to participate for any kind of tangible reward. In the end, it is most beneficial for society if people choose to volunteer for the sake of providing information that may end up helping us further improve the society in which we live.

REFLECTING ON INTERVIEWS

As you complete each interview, take a moment to record for yourself how the interview went. This helps you complete your final assignment, and it also helps you evaluate the validity and reliability of interviewing generally as a data collection tool. Include a brief description of the person you interviewed—age, sex, and any other variables that you think might be important to think about in regard to the interview process. Record also any unique experiences or questions the interviewee asked. Did she hesitate to answer any questions? Were there questions she found unclear, offensive, or perhaps too personal? Did she seem engaged or bored throughout the interview? These notes will be helpful when you are asked in the final assignment to reflect on interviews as a data collection method. Recall that much of the data and knowledge we have available today is the result of interviews. After gaining some experience in interviewing, what is your opinion about using this method as a way to collect information?

Give some thought also to other types of data collection methods you might use if we were not to choose interviews. You'll be asked to respond to a similar question in your final write-up of this assignment. You are now aware that there are different ways of collecting data in the social sciences, among them surveys, interviews, experiments, unobtrusive measures, participant observation, and more. Each methodology has strengths and weaknesses. If you were to do this study again, what method would you use, and why? Asking yourself this question can help reinforce in your own mind that there is no one best method of data collection. The optimal method often involves a compromise between the unique challenges of data collection in a particular project, combined with budgetary limitations, time constraints, and how accessible a population might be.

SUMMARY

This chapter contains specific training to help you conduct your interviews professionally and consistently. The tasks you need to perform are listed here. Once you have prepared yourself to perform the following, you're ready to conduct your interviews. Good luck!

- For each question on your interview schedule, anticipate the results by recording the percentage of students you expect will select each possible response.
- Dress in a casual, neat but neutral manner for the interviews.

- Be prepared by familiarizing yourself with the interview schedule, the instructions, and the order and wording of every question.
- When conducting interviews, practice good deportment by maintaining eye contact, using affirming verbal communication, and keeping up the pace without rushing.
- Be ready to thank the interviewee for his time and the information he has provided.
- After every interview, write down your observations and feelings regarding how it went.

REVIEW QUESTIONS

1. How is it possible to conduct interviews that are both valid and reliable?
2. What behaviors on the part of the interviewer would ensure collection of *un*reliable data for your class project?
3. How should one prepare for conducting interviews?
4. What should be kept in mind when performing professional interviews?

KEY TERMS

Deportment How a person presents himself or herself to others.

Ego involvement An error of human inquiry in which data are interpreted in a biased manner that affirms one's pet theories or ideas.

Empathy The ability to understand another's decisions and feelings.

Measurement error Variation in data caused by mistakes made in the data collection process.

Rapport (pronounced "rah-PORE") The presence of trust and mutual respect between interviewer and interviewee.

10

Entering Your Data into the Computer

By now you should have finished all of the assigned interviews. In this chapter, you learn how to take the information from your completed interview schedules, turn it into numbers, enter the numbers into the computer, correct any mistakes you made, and submit the data to the instructor. You'll do this for two important reasons. First, becoming familiar with the process of data entry and analysis makes you a better consumer of scientific information. You'll be aware of the decisions social scientists make that can potentially affect their conclusions. Second, knowing how to transform information gathered through interviewing to numbers suitable for computer analysis is a highly marketable skill. You'll gain more such skills if you major in sociology or most other social sciences.

As with doing the actual interviews, paying attention to detail when entering data is critical to handling the information responsibly. Trying to rush this part of the process will mean that mistakes happen, thereby reducing the confidence we will have in the validity of the data. At each step, pay close attention to what you are doing, and do it carefully.

USING SPSS

We'll be using a computer software application for this project known as **SPSS**. SPSS is one of the most popular statistical programs, and for good reason. It is a powerful program yet is relatively easy to use, and with it a user can perform incredibly complex analyses that would take months to do by hand with the same degree of accuracy. To avoid information overload, *you'll receive only enough information in this chapter to complete your assignment.* Be aware that you'll become familiar with only a fraction of the capabilities of SPSS. Once you have learned to enter data and perform simple analyses, the only thing stopping you from doing greater things in SPSS is the limit of your interest in learning more about the software. It is absolutely fascinating to take a set of data and find out new things about groups of people through statistical analysis. Indeed, I hope you experience the same joy of discovery through this class project. You'll shortly be analyzing information collected from a select group of people never before collected, and you'll have the opportunity to see whether your hypothesis about how you think the social world is ordered is actually supported by the data or not. Today, applications such as SPSS make this job faster and easier than ever.

Before entering the data, take a moment to write down your impressions of how you *think* the final results will turn out for each question. You were encouraged to do this before performing your interviews; take a moment again to record your guesses. Have your views changed? If so, in what way? What might have caused the change? Is it possible that gathering information from others is having an effect on the opinions you held earlier? Reflecting on how the data collection process informs our own opinions is a critical part of the process of doing social science. You'll have the opportunity to describe how your impressions changed in this process in the final paper you'll write on this project.

CODEBOOKS

When you conduct research by interviews or surveys, information collected from interviewees must be converted into *numerical data* in order to facilitate computer analysis. This process, called **quantification,** greatly assists in determining patterns in the responses of people who have been interviewed. Statistical analysis is best handled by software if the responses are coded into actual numbers. For example, you may want to know how many males and females were interviewed in your study. In a small study it might be feasible to look through all the interviews, one at a time, and make a mark on another piece of paper to record the sex of the respondent. But what if the study includes, say, more than fifteen thousand people? Or what if the study is part of the U.S. Census, where census officials attempt to collect information from every adult resident of the United States? You can see how this quickly becomes a time-consuming process.

Quantifying data allows us to enter data and perform both simple and complex analyses. Further, analysis is performed more quickly and accurately than any single human being could do, and for a fraction of the cost. If we entered a 1 for every male respondent and a 2 for every female respondent, the computer can quickly tally the total number of ones and twos in the study, thereby giving us the total number of men and women interviewed. It could also calculate other meaningful statistics, such as the *percentage* of all people interviewed who were males. On variables such as age, we can also calculate meaningful statistics such as the median, mean, range, standard deviation, and so on. You can see why it is helpful to quantify responses and enter that information as computer data.

The first step in quantifying data, then, is to create a codebook. A **codebook** is a document that lists every variable measured in the interview. It shows the exact question used to measure each variable and lists all of the responses that people made to that question. It assigns a numerical value, called a code, to each of those responses. It also assigns a code to questions that were not answered by the interviewee, or contingency questions that were not applicable to that person, and so on.

The codebook is a guide for data entry. Anyone entering data could, with the codebook, assign a numerical code to every response made by someone interviewed and enter it. Remember that, throughout the research process, collecting and analyzing data that are valid and reliable is extremely important. A codebook allows data to be entered reliably because any person coding a response in an interview schedule would assign it the same number.

Exhibit 10.1 contains some questions from a sample interview schedule. You see the difference between an interview schedule and its codebook by comparing Exhibit 10.1 to its corresponding codebook, depicted in Exhibit 10.2 below. Notice that most of the questions in Exhibit 10.1 are *closed-ended*. That is, for every question asked there

---

EXHIBIT 10.1 SAMPLE INTERVIEW SCHEDULE.

Interview number: _____

The first part of this survey asks for some general information about you.

1. How old are you? _____ (age in years)
2. What is your sex? (check one) _____ male _____ female
3. Were you born in this country? (check one) _____ yes _____ no
4. With which racial or ethnic group do you most closely identify? (check one)
   _____ White
   _____ Black
   _____ Hispanic
   _____ Asian
   _____ Other (please specify) _____
5. Are you considered a freshman, sophomore, junior, or senior? (check one)
   _____ freshman
   _____ sophomore
   _____ junior
   _____ senior
6. What is your religious affiliation? (check one)
   _____ Christian
   _____ Muslim
   _____ Jewish
   _____ Hindu
   _____ None
   _____ Other (specify) _____
7. How religious do you feel you are on a scale from 1 to 10, where 1 means not religious at all and 10 means very religious? (circle one number)
   1——2——3——4——5——6——7——8——9——10

EXHIBIT 10.2 CODEBOOK FOR SAMPLE INTERVIEW SCHEDULE.

Variable name: Question, Possible Responses, Codes

INTNUM   Interview number (001 to _____)

AGE   1. How old are you? _____ (age in years)
99 missing

SEX   2. What is your sex?
1 male
2 female
9 missing

COUNTRY 3. Were you born in this country?
1 yes
2 no
9 missing

RACE   4. With which racial or ethnic group do you most closely identify?
1 White
2 Black
3 Hispanic
4 Asian
5 Other (specify)
9 missing

YEAR   5. Are you considered a freshman, sophomore, junior, or senior?
1 freshman
2 sophomore
3 junior
4 senior
9 missing

RELIG   6. What is your religious affiliation?
1   Christian
2   Muslim
3   Jewish
4   Hindu
5   None
6   Other
99 missing

RELIG2   7. How religious do you feel you are on a scale from 1 to 10, where
1 means not religious at all and 10 means very religious?
____ (actual number between 1 and 10)
99 missing

are responses already listed. The interviewer reads all of the possible responses to the interviewee and simply checks off the one response the interviewee selects for himself or herself.

Notice also that the question for age is *open-ended*, in that not all of the age categories have been listed below the question. However, we know that the answers to the age question will be specific and that the interviewee will respond with a number. The interviewer would then simply record the answer.

You should be aware, of course, that some open-ended questions are more difficult to code or turn into numerical values than others. In fact, for most open-ended questions coding categories are created and included in the codebook *after* the data collection process has ended. This is because not all possible responses can be anticipated. For example, it would be virtually impossible to predict all possible answers to the question, "What are three major goals you hope to achieve in your lifetime?" Listing all of the responses after the data have been collected and then assigning a number to each response so it can be entered as a datum is the most accurate and reliable way of handling these types of open-ended questions.

PRECODING INTERVIEWS AND SURVEYS

It can take a long time to enter data from interviews, even with a codebook in hand. Speed and accuracy of data entry can be increased if an interview schedule is *precoded;* this topic was introduced in Chapter Nine. In precoding, a number replaces the blank line to the left of every possible response to a closed-ended question. Instead of placing a checkmark on the blank line, the interviewer simply circles the number beside the given response. Exhibit 10.3 depicts changes to the survey in Exhibit 10.1 after it has been precoded. Study this example closely, because your instructor will likely have you use a precoded interview schedule for this assignment.

In this type of survey, the interviewer simply circles the number of the appropriate response instead of placing a check mark in the corresponding blank. This may not seem like an important difference to you, but you'll discover how easy it is to enter data when you are using a precoded interview schedule. Instead of having to look up every checked-off response to see what number should be entered into the computer, the number is already circled on the original interview schedule. All that has to be done then is to carefully enter the actual number that is circled.

Precoding is more frequently done with interviews than surveys. This is because trained interviewers are the ones who actually fill out the interview schedule, whereas actual respondents complete surveys on their own. Assigning numbers to responses sometimes confuses individual respondents who complete a survey on their own. Even though you grouped data for some questions, you might find, for example, that people have circled

---

EXHIBIT 10.3 SAMPLE PRECODED INTERVIEW SCHEDULE.

Interview number _____
The first part of this survey asks for some general information about you.

1. How old are you? _____ (age in years)
2. What is your sex? (circle one) 1 male 2 female
3. Were you born in this country? (circle one) 1 yes 2 no
4. With which racial or ethnic group do you most closely identify? (circle one)
   1 White
   2 Black
   3 Hispanic
   4 Asian
   5 Other (please specify) _____
5. Are you considered a freshman, sophomore, junior, or senior at the university?
   (circle one)
   1 freshman
   2 sophomore
   3 junior
   4 senior
6. What is your religious affiliation? (circle one)
   1 Christian
   2 Muslim
   3 Jewish
   4 Hindu
   5 None
   6 Other (specify)_____
7. How religious do you feel you are on a scale from 1 to 10, where 1 means not
   religious at all and 10 means very religious? (circle one number)
   1——2——3——4——5——6——7——8——9——10

---

a number thinking it means something real rather than an arbitrarily assigned value in a
particular category. To illustrate, consider the question:

How many children do you have?

1 zero
2 one to three
3 four or more

Someone with one child, filling out the survey in haste, might accidentally circle the number 1 thinking it means "one child," when it actually means zero children. This greatly reduces the accuracy of responses. This is less of a problem in interviews, where interviewers like you are first trained in the interviewing techniques presented in the previous chapter and then familiarized with the questions in the interview schedule they will use. The lesson for you here should be obvious: familiarize yourself with the interview before attempting an actual interview to ensure accurate recording of responses.

PREPARING FOR DATA ENTRY

You will need these items to correctly enter your data:

1. *The class codebook.* For this class assignment your instructor will create the code-book needed to accurately enter your own data. Be sure to code the data consistently with the codebook. This will be an easy process if your interviews are precoded. Still, take care to accurately code every response in your survey.

2. *The SPSS data file with defined variables.* Your instructor will also make available to you an electronic SPSS data file in which all of the variables measured on your interview schedule are defined. Be sure you know how to access this file, and have it available when you open SPSS. Once in SPSS, you'll open the file from your instructor that includes all of your variables and begin entering your data, one interview at a time. After entering your data, you'll save the file and deliver it to your instructor as per instructions.

3. *Your completed interviews and assigned interview numbers.* Have your completed interviews on hand when you are ready to enter the data. If you have not already done so, *number each interview with the interview numbers assigned to you by your instructor.* Every student in your class will have a set of interview numbers so as to distinguish every case.

4. *A computer with a version of SPSS installed.* You may enter and save your data on your own computer if you have a version of SPSS installed. Otherwise, be sure to locate computers on your campus that have SPSS installed for your use.

5. *A USB flash drive or other storage device.* You will need a flash drive or other device on which to save your SPSS data file if working on a computer other than one on which you can save your work to the hard drive for future use.

ENTERING DATA: USING SPSS

Listen carefully to your instructor as she or he explains how to access the SPSS application on your campus. Many universities and colleges install SPSS on computers in labs accessible to students. You may be able to access SPSS only in a computer lab.

Alternatively, your instructor may have ordered a CD of the SPSS student version packaged with this book on CD. If not, copies of the student version of SPSS should be available for purchase through your campus bookstore. You can install the student version of SPSS on your own personal computer and do your data entry and analysis on your own machine.

STEP ONE: OPENING SPSS

Procedures for opening SPSS will differ slightly, depending on how the application is configured and the unique characteristics of various types of computers. Once at a computer on which SPSS is installed, double-click on the icon on the desktop to start the program, or click on the name of the program on the Start Menu in Windows or on the desktop on the Macintosh. SPSS is also accessible through the Applications folder in Windows Explorer or on your Macintosh.

Let's spend a few minutes becoming familiar with the SPSS environment. After doing this, we'll learn how to open the variable file prepared by your instructor so you can enter data from your interviews.

The Opening Screen

A dialogue box, such as the one pictured in Figure 10.1, may appear when you first open SPSS. If this is the case, simply click on Cancel at the bottom right of the box. This will

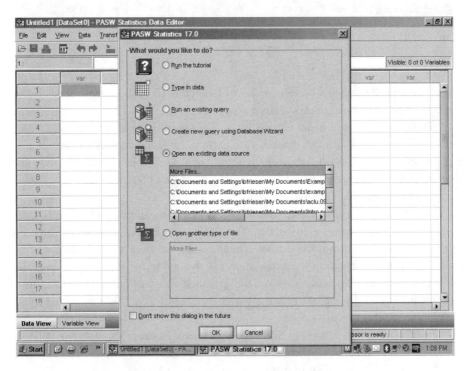

Figure 10.1. "What would you like to do?" Dialogue Box.

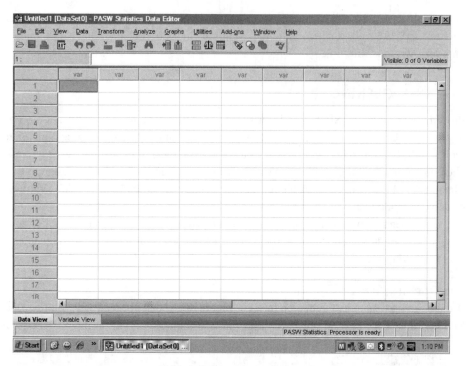

Figure 10.2. Data View.

present the main Data View screen as shown in Figure 10.2, the same screen that will appear if no dialogue box appears when you open SPSS.

Take note of the main menu options across the top of the screen, beginning with the word *File*. These menus furnish the means to perform functions in SPSS. Click on any of these menus and a drop-down menu will appear. In this class project we'll learn only about the menu options that are pertinent to your assignment (but you may want to explore the options that are available at another time).

You'll notice some similarities to the SPSS Data View screen and any spreadsheet application you may have used before. You can see in Figure 10.2 that information is organized in both columns and rows. Data are entered by row, with each row containing all of the information from one interview. Notice too that each column is titled "var" (shorthand for "variable"). In the file in which you will enter your data, the var in each column will be replaced by the variable name of a variable measured in your interview schedule.

Variables should be defined in SPSS before data are entered. Variables are defined in the Variable View screen. Click on the tab in the bottom left of the screen entitled *Variable View*. This opens a page similar to that shown in Figure 10.3.

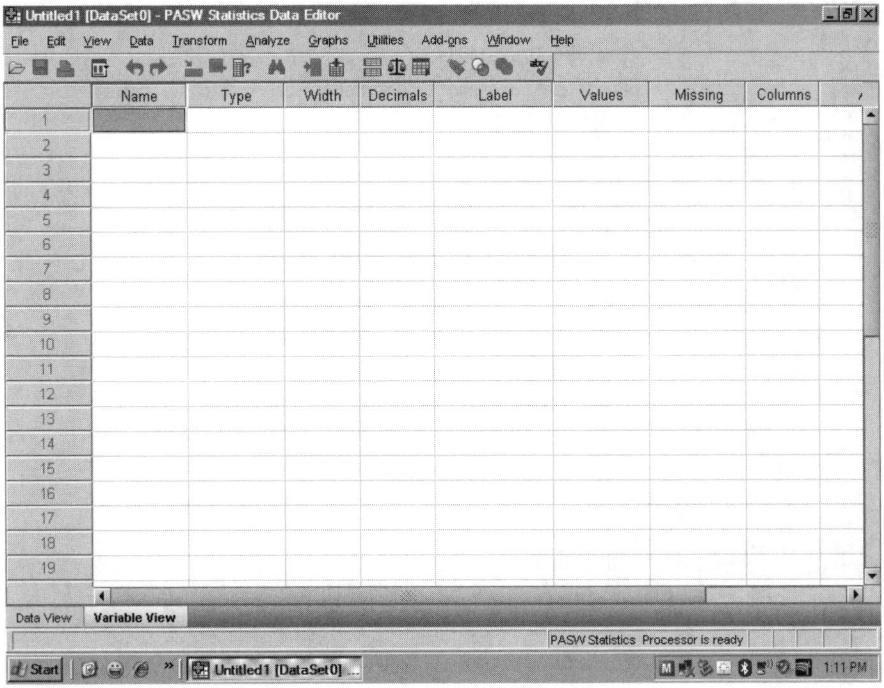

Figure 10.3. Variable View.

From this Variable View screen, you can create and edit all of the variables in your data file. Each column contains a piece of information about one particular variable. Information about each variable is entered by row, in the same manner as on the Data View screen. Each row contains all of the defining information for one variable in your dataset. Once a variable has been named and defined in the Variable View, its name will automatically appear in a column in the Data View screen. Go ahead and click on the Data View tab on the bottom left of your screen to return to the Data View page.

STEP TWO: ACCESSING AND OPENING THE VARIABLE FILE

Now that you're familiar with the two main screens in SPSS and how to toggle between them, let's open the variable file you'll use to enter your data. Your instructor has given you instructions on how to access this file. It may have been made available to you on a website or course software system such as Blackboard, or your instructor might have sent it to everyone in your class via email attachment.

To open your variable file, click on *File* in the upper-left corner of your screen. Click on *Open*, and then *Data*, as shown in Figure 10.4. This opens a dialogue box from which

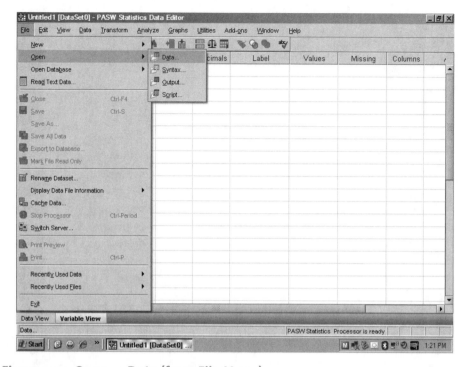

Figure 10.4. Open → Data (from File Menu).

you can access any files saved on any disk connected to your computer. Locate and high-light the file from your instructor that you have saved on your computer, and click *Open* in the dialogue box.

Once opened, the *Data View* screen of your variable file will look similar to Figure 10.5, though the variable names in your class data file will be different, matching the variables measured in your interview schedule.

Click on the *Variable View* tab at the bottom of your screen. Instead of seeing a blank screen as we did before, this time you should see each of the variables in your study, named and defined (Figure 10.6). Your instructor has prepared this SPSS file for you (be sure to say thank you!). If you want to know more about defining variables in SPSS, ask your instructor or consult a text on SPSS data analysis.

Save Your Data File

Save this file to your storage device once you have it opened, by clicking on *File* and then *Save As*. Choose to save the file to your storage device by first locating it at the top of the dialog box in the drop-down menu titled *Look in*. Important: follow any instructions

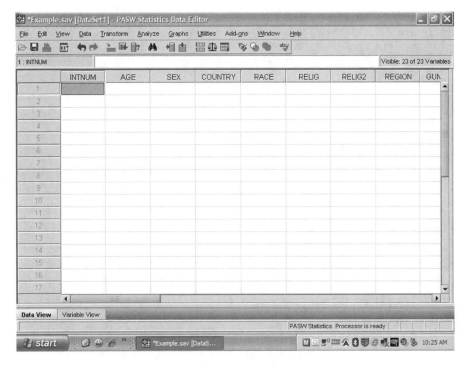

Figure 10.5. Sample Data File with Variable Names.

your instructor has given you regarding naming your data file. If no instructions have been forthcoming, save your data file in this format:

Your First Interview Number–Your Last Interview Number *Your last name*

Your instructor has given you an assigned set of interview numbers for you and you alone to use in numbering your interviews. Use the first and last assigned interview numbers to name your data file, separated by a dash, and followed by your last name. For example, a student named Lopez is assigned interview numbers 5 through 15; she would name the data file as:

005–015Lopez

Be sure to use all the digits supplied by your instructor for each case number. In this example, I used 005 instead of only 5.

Saving your file in this manner assists your instructor in merging the data files submitted by all the students in the class.

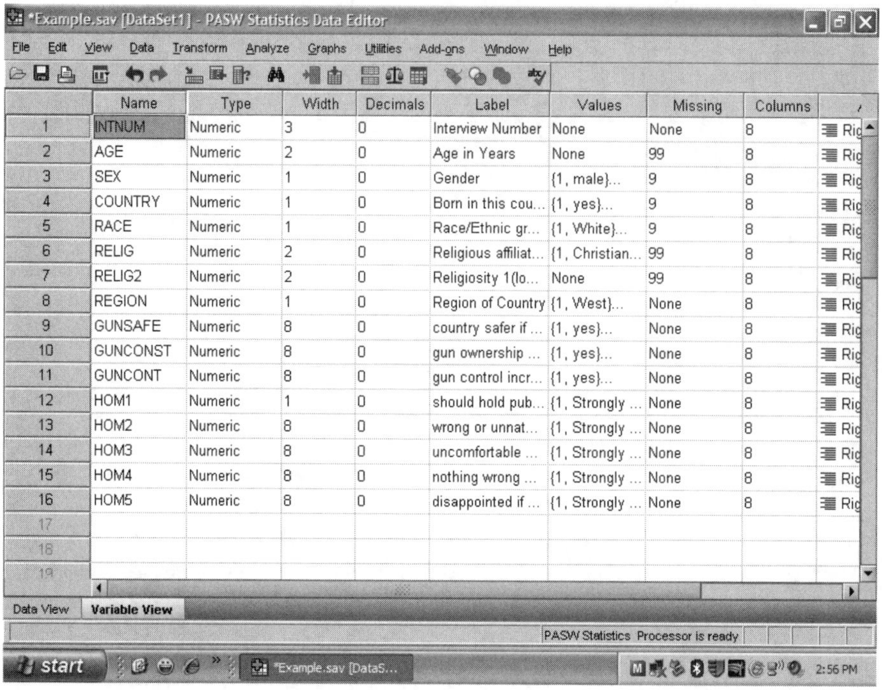

	Name	Type	Width	Decimals	Label	Values	Missing	Columns	
1	INTNUM	Numeric	3	0	Interview Number	None	None	8	Rig
2	AGE	Numeric	2	0	Age in Years	None	99	8	Rig
3	SEX	Numeric	1	0	Gender	{1, male}...	9	8	Rig
4	COUNTRY	Numeric	1	0	Born in this cou...	{1, yes}...	9	8	Rig
5	RACE	Numeric	1	0	Race/Ethnic gr...	{1, White}...	9	8	Rig
6	RELIG	Numeric	2	0	Religious affiliat...	{1, Christian...	99	8	Rig
7	RELIG2	Numeric	2	0	Religiosity 1(lo...	None	99	8	Rig
8	REGION	Numeric	1	0	Region of Country	{1, West}...	None	8	Rig
9	GUNSAFE	Numeric	8	0	country safer if ...	{1, yes}...	None	8	Rig
10	GUNCONST	Numeric	8	0	gun ownership ...	{1, yes}...	None	8	Rig
11	GUNCONT	Numeric	8	0	gun control incr...	{1, yes}...	None	8	Rig
12	HOM1	Numeric	1	0	should hold pub...	{1, Strongly ...	None	8	Rig
13	HOM2	Numeric	8	0	wrong or unnat...	{1, Strongly ...	None	8	Rig
14	HOM3	Numeric	8	0	uncomfortable ...	{1, Strongly ...	None	8	Rig
15	HOM4	Numeric	8	0	nothing wrong ...	{1, Strongly ...	None	8	Rig
16	HOM5	Numeric	8	0	disappointed if ...	{1, Strongly ...	None	8	Rig
17									
18									
19									

Figure 10.6. Data in Variable View.

STEP THREE: ENTERING YOUR DATA

Return to the Data View screen by clicking on the Data View tab at the bottom of your screen. Start entering data in the first row for one of your completed interviews by typing the value of the first variable. The first variable in your data file is the interview number or "case number" your instructor assigned. If your first interview is numbered, say, 21, type that number (21) into the first box in the first row.

Hit the Tab key to take you to the next box in the row. Enter the value for the second variable. If your second variable is Sex, for example, with values of 1 for male and 2 for female, enter the number as indicated in your first completed interview. If the person interviewed was male, you would have circled "1" in the precoded interview schedule. Simply enter the number 1 in the second box of the first row. Hit Tab to move your cursor to the next box on the right, and continue entering the values for all of the variables for one of your interviews.

If you are unsure of any value you are entering, check the codebook to clarify.

After you have finished entering all the information for one interview, begin entering your *second* interview on the second row in SPSS. Continue this process until all data have been entered from your interviews. It is particularly important to consult your codebook and follow the directions from your instructor in entering values for *missing information*. This is a critical issue about which you should know a little more.

Missing Data

In most studies involving surveys or interviews, a special problem in data entry is created when information is missing for one or more of the questions asked. This happens when a person refuses or fails to answer one or more questions, or when someone decides to end the interview early. Sometimes student interviewers who do not familiarize themselves with the interview schedule simply skip over a question. Regardless of the reason, **missing data**, for even one question, can be troublesome. If the information is missing for an important variable (such as the independent or dependent variable), it means the entire interview is essentially worthless. Without complete information on critical variables, the intended analysis simply cannot be performed on that interview.

Missing information can compromise the integrity of a research project. Missing data on a few interviews isn't usually problematic, unless the entire sample consists of only a few hundred cases or less. The smaller the sample, the greater the issue of missing cases becomes.

Besides reducing the overall number of valid interviews included in the analysis, the problem of missing data may have *systematic* causes. As examples, most of the people who do not answer one or more questions might, say, be male, or of the lower class, or minorities, or for some other systematic reason there is a shadow of doubt on the validity of the study.

The best way to deal with missing information is simply not to have any! However, you will recall from our chapter on ethics that no one should be forced to answer a question she does not want to answer. Further, if someone chooses to end the interview early and walk away without answering all of the questions, she must be allowed to do so. Indeed, if someone walks away without having answered most of the questions in the interview schedule, it is better to simply discard the interview entirely and start again with someone else. Given the primacy of honoring the rights of people who volunteer to participate in a study, how should missing cases be handled?

The study your class is conducting will likely be small enough to raise concern about missing values. In such a situation, researchers sometimes enter values for missing data. That is, they essentially "make up" answers for the questions people did not answer. Can this be done responsibly?

There are several ways in which researchers create responses for missing data (Babbie, 2007). One is to calculate a *mean* on the other responses received for a particular question and enter that for any missing cases. A second way is to simply have the computer enter a *random* valid number. If the possible responses for a question range between 1 and 5, for example, a randomly enter value between 1 and 5 for the missing data on that particular variable is acceptable. A third possibility is to attempt to *infer* a person's answer on the basis of how he answered similar questions. For example, someone who identified himself as being politically liberal would most likely be expected to vote Democrat in the United States. A fourth way, especially suitable in interviews, is to allow the *interviewer* to enter a value for any questions not answered by the interviewee. Because the interviewer has the most knowledge about the person and how he answered other questions, the interviewer's estimate of a person's response is often the best.

Your instructor will tell you which option to use for any missing information in your interviews. Depending on the circumstances, any of the four methods described is as good as any other. I have my students use the fourth method because each student had a chance to briefly interact with the interviewee. The interviewer heard the participant's responses to the other questions and also observed nonverbal cues during the interview. Thus the student interviewer has the most information for guessing how that individual would have answered any particular question.

It may not be perfect, but using this method likely creates less inaccurate data than other methods do. There may be other good reasons your instructor would choose another method for dealing with missing data. Remember that, for a study such as this one, the main purpose here is pedagogical. When you conduct a study of your own, you will be able make your own decision regarding how to handle missing information.

STEP FOUR: CLEANING THE DATA

Entering numbers, even in a situation like this one where they stand for something meaningful, can be a tedious process. Human beings, such as we are, are easily bored. Boredom leads to lack of attention, or an effort to hurry through the process. Errors are thus a common problem in data entry. This implies inaccurate information. The greater the amount of error in data entry, the less the results can be trusted. It is therefore important to engage in **data cleaning**—identifying and correcting errors made during the data entry process.

An error in data entry means an incorrect number was entered for a particular response given by an interviewee. Let's say males were coded as 1 and females as 2. You interviewed a female, but in entering your data into the computer you erroneously entered a 1 instead of a 2. This means in every part of the analysis where the responses of males and females are compared, any response from that particular female is interpreted as having been given by a male. As you can surmise, researchers want to do all they can to eliminate errors in data entry.

Make sure your dataset is free of errors, to save yourself some embarrassment. Your data will become part of a larger dataset where other students may know the interview numbers you and others have been assigned. Imagine the embarrassment of having the class analyze data that contain errors in *your* interview numbers. Take the time to make sure your data are clean before submitting them to your instructor.

Are you able to enter the data from your interviews without making a single error? Researchers have generated some operations to detect errors, but *nothing replaces careful and accurate data entry in the first place.* Looking for and correcting data entry errors—cleaning the data—is an essential part of any research project. We're all human, and part of the human condition is making errors. Be careful when you enter your data, but expect that your data will contain some errors that you will need to correct. There are two main types of data entry errors: those that are obvious and those that are not.

Correcting Obvious Data Entry Errors

The easiest data entry errors to detect are those where no value has been entered. Also easy to identify are meaningless codes or numbers in any column. To use the sex example again, if males have been coded as 1 and females as 2 you should see only ones and twos in the column of your sex variable in your dataset. Any number larger than a 2 is obviously an error.

These errors can be corrected by looking at the interview number in the first column of the dataset, then accessing the actual paper interview on which you recorded the interviewee's responses, and looking up the real code for the question about sex. You can then delete the incorrect number in the dataset and enter the correct one.

Finding a data entry error can lead you to identify other errors. Recall that when you entered data you hit Tab to move to the next column. Sometimes people in a hurry may miss the Tab key and enter not one but two numbers in a column for a variable where there should be only one. This essentially makes the rest of the data in that row incorrect because all numbers are off by one column. If you find a data entry error, recheck all of the values you entered in the dataset for that particular interview.

Looking down (or *eyeballing*) each variable column in the data set for meaningless numbers is one way to look for errors, and it is often sufficient for small datasets such as the one you created with the interviews you conducted. You may be interested to know that, in larger datasets, a more effective way to check for errors is to request from SPSS a printout of all of the values entered for every variable you have in your data set. A printout of all values for one variable is called a *frequency table.*

Table 10.1 is a sample frequency table for the variable *religious affiliation* in our example dataset. The values entered are listed in the first column. Notice that a number 17 appears, which does not correspond to any code assigned to the attributes of this variable. It is obvious that 17 was entered in error. A researcher would then track down the error in the dataset, reexamine the original interview schedule to determine what the correct code should be, and replace the 17 with the correct value.

Frequency tables are used in this manner to clean data in large datasets because errors are more easily identified in a small frequency table than they are in a column of data. Your instructor may use this method to look for data entry errors in the master dataset before making it available to the class.

Table 10.1. Frequency Distribution for Religious Affiliation.

	Frequency	Percent	Valid Percent	Cumulative Percent
1 Christianity	189	72.1	72.1	72.1
2 Islam	4	1.5	1.5	73.7
3 Judaism	12	4.6	4.6	78.2
4 Hinduism	2	.8	.8	79.0
5 none	46	17.6	17.6	96.6
6 other	1	.4	.4	96.9
7 Agnostic	5	1.9	1.9	98.9
8 Buddhist	1	.4	.4	99.2
9 Shintoism	1	.4	.4	99.6
17	1	.4	.4	100.0
Total	262	100.0	100.0	

Correcting Nonobvious Data Entry Errors

The most difficult data entry errors to detect are those described in the earlier example, where a meaningful but inaccurate code is erroneously entered in place of one that is accurate. This would happen if a 1 were entered for a female instead of a 2. For our purposes, the only way to detect errors of this kind is to compare the entered numbers with the actual completed interview. Do this before submitting your data file to your instructor.

In more involved projects, research project directors sometimes have two people separately enter the same interview data. A computer can then compare the two datasets and highlight any discrepancies. Because the number of interviews you have entered is relatively small, eyeballing the data and double-checking the numbers with the completed interviews are the two methods you'll use to make sure the data you have entered are clean.

STEP FIVE: SUBMITTING THE DATA TO YOUR INSTRUCTOR

Once you have entered all of your interviews into SPSS and corrected any errors you find, be sure to save your data to your storage device. *Do not* save your data to the hard drive of a computer in a public lab, because those drives are regularly cleaned. If you are using your own computer to enter your data, of course, you'll be able to save the data file directly to your hard drive. Remember to save it with a filename containing the first and last interview numbers and your last name.

Your instructor will also tell you what to do with your completed paper interviews. Remember to keep them in a secure place until you are instructed to dispose of them.

The information in both your SPSS file and paper interviews is confidential, so treat the documents as such by storing them in a place difficult for others to access.

Finally, you are now ready to submit the data to your instructor. He or she will give you directions on how to do this and may want you to send the file via email attachment, or submit it on a website such as Blackboard. SPSS files can be attached to email messages in the same way as any other electronic file. These procedures vary by email client. Contact your educational institution's IT helpdesk if you are unsure how to do this.

Be sure to send your instructor your actual data file and *not* any output file produced by SPSS. You can save output files for your own future reference if you wish, but remember that it is easy to reproduce output files again with SPSS.

SUMMARY

Completing the steps in this chapter means you now have some knowledge about how information is collected from individuals and converted into numbers for easy statistical analysis. These steps have also been an essential part of building a larger dataset for your class, the one that will actually be used to test your hypothesis. Your instructor will combine all of the data received from students enrolled in your class and make available to you a master dataset to use in testing your class hypothesis. You're almost ready to find out whether your guess about the nature of the social world is supported by the data you and your classmates collected. Are you interested in seeing whether there is evidence for your guess?

Indeed, this project was designed to bring you to this particular moment: the time when we let our collected data shed light on our assumptions about the nature of the social world. I hope the anticipation generates at least a little excitement for you. How will you react if the data contradict the hypothesis you created for this project? Sometimes our guesses are supported by the data, and sometimes not. It's easy to criticize the methods used to collect the data (indeed, criticism of this type can be valid), but the other possibility, of course, is that the hypothesis we formed is actually incorrect. In either case, we're faced with the challenge of synthesizing the information we've collected with our ideas about the social world. If the data are trustworthy, this means adjusting our attitudes, beliefs, or theories.

At this point, your instructor may do the rest of the statistical analysis for your class and produce the data tables needed to test your hypothesis. If this is the case, you can skip the next chapter, unless you'd like to know the steps she or he took to produce your finished cross-tabulation tables. If your instructor wants you to do the analysis, you'll want to carefully follow the steps outlined in the next chapter. Let's take a look and see whether there's support for your hypothesis.

REVIEW QUESTIONS

1. Why are computers used in data analysis? Why aren't informal impressions or hand counting sufficient for reporting results?
2. What is needed for preparing to enter data for the class assignment?
3. How are codebooks different from the surveys or interview schedules they represent?
4. Why are missing data a problem in data analysis? How can missing data be handled?
5. What is data cleaning? Why is it done?
6. What steps must be completed to enter the data for this assignment?

KEY TERMS

Codebook A guide for data entry in which the numerical values to be entered are indicated for every possible question response.

Data cleaning Identifying and correcting errors made during the data entry process.

Missing data Information that was not collected on one or more interview schedule items during the interview process, because of refusal or failure to answer or interviewer error.

Quantification The process of assigning numbers to collected information so as to facilitate computer data entry and analysis.

SPSS A proprietary statistical software package.

11

Data Analysis 1

Producing Frequencies and Collapsing Variables

LEARNING OBJECTIVES

- Learn how to produce and interpret frequency tables from your master dataset.
- Learn how to collapse discrete and continuous variables into fewer categories.
- Learn how to double-check your work to eliminate errors and produce reliable data transformations.

The disciplines of history and sociology are important in gleaning knowledge about the human condition. The methods of investigation used by historians and sociologists, however, can differ markedly. A good friend and former colleague of mine, a historian, was very skeptical of attempts to quantify human activities in the manner described in the last chapter. "You can get statistics to say whatever you want them to," she once exclaimed. Instead, she prefers her method of carefully reading multiple sources of information about a particular historical event or period and allowing the themes to inductively reveal themselves.

I suggested to her that more important than the method is the rigor with which one approaches the task. It would be just as easy for a historian to superimpose subjective ideas or beliefs on the sources being consulted, trusting one source more than another simply because it reaffirms a theory about what was happening at the time.

So it is with statistical analysis. An irresponsible or sloppy researcher can allow subjectivity to influence whatever he or she is doing, be it historical or quantitative analysis. Used responsibly, a variety of research methodologies can produce revealing and meaningful insights into a compendium of human activities. My historian friend graciously accepted my response, though she still prefers to make use of methods with which she is familiar. Of course, peers in the review process scrutinize any individual researcher's efforts, regardless of the method.

Perhaps this brief anecdote will help you reflect on your reservations about doing quantitative analysis. There are individuals attempting to discredit quantitative analysis, not necessarily because of any inherent flaws but because they may personally be struggling to gain competence with the method. Statistical analysis involves numbers, and numbers are used in mathematics. Those with a certain amount of math anxiety may approach statistical analysis with some fear and trepidation. Some find it easier simply to adopt the attitude that statistics do not "prove anything," or that quantitative analysis is inherently flawed.

Although there are some important criticisms of quantitative analysis (as with any method, for that matter), isn't it better to first understand and have some familiarity with statistical analysis before dismissing it outright? Indeed, letting you look inside the black box of quantitative analysis is one of the goals of this class project. You're getting some idea of how social research of this type is carried out. In this chapter, you learn how to produce reports known as frequency tables depicting the distribution of responses for every variable in our dataset. You also learn how to simplify variables by collapsing categories. This is an important preparatory step for the analysis to be conducted in the next chapter.

DATA ANALYSIS BEGINS WITH ASKING QUESTIONS

At the end of the last chapter, you sent your cleaned data file to your instructor, who created a master dataset by combining all submitted data files. Your instructor will show you how to access the master dataset so you can complete the steps in this chapter. Be sure that all steps completed in this chapter are carried out using the master dataset received from your instructor, *not* the smaller dataset that contains data only from the interviews you completed.

Data analysis is often driven by the research questions we seek to answer. What is the first thing you'd like to know, now that the data have been collected, entered, and cleaned? Would you like to get an idea as to the kinds of responses for each question in the interview? It might be interesting, for example, to see how many males and females were interviewed, or how many people categorized themselves as very religious or not religious at all. SPSS easily generates statistics detailing the responses for the questions asked of interviewees.

Producing *frequency distributions* is the most effective way to see variations in responses. Frequency distributions were briefly mentioned in the last chapter as a way to assist in cleaning large datasets. Running frequency distributions on cleaned data reveals the variety of responses collected for all the interview questions.

PART ONE: PRODUCING FREQUENCY TABLES

Make sure you are sitting at the computer with your class's master dataset opened in SPSS on the screen before you. Click on the word Analyze in the toolbar at the top of the screen. Next, click on Descriptive Statistics, and then Frequencies from the drop-down menu that appears (Figure 11.1).

A dialog box appears as shown in Figure 11.2. On the left of the dialog box is a list of the names of all the variables from the interview schedule.

You can request a frequency distribution on any variable by moving it from the list on the left to the box on the right side in the dialog window. To do this, highlight a variable name by clicking on it once, and then click on the arrow in between the two boxes. (Choose Display Variable Names by a right-click anywhere in the column if a Windows user, or Control-click if using a Mac.) Because we'd like to request frequency distributions

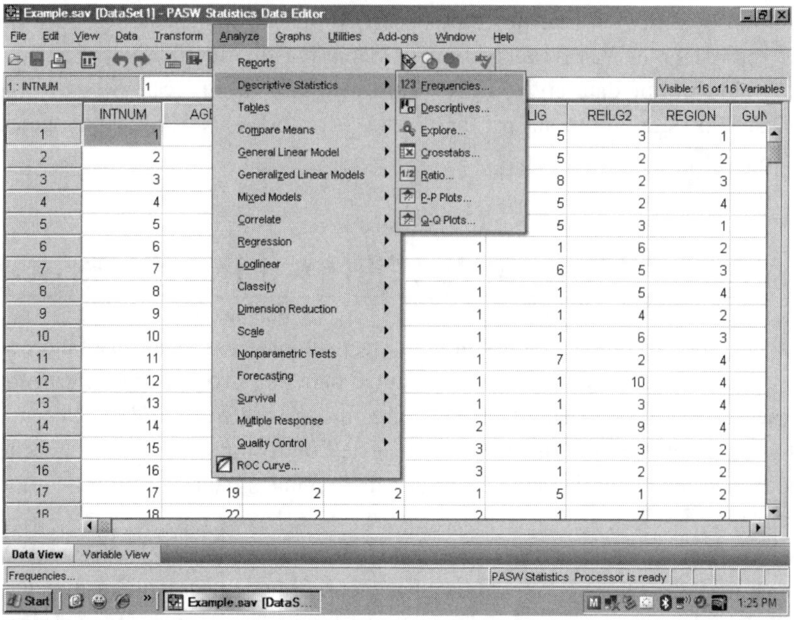

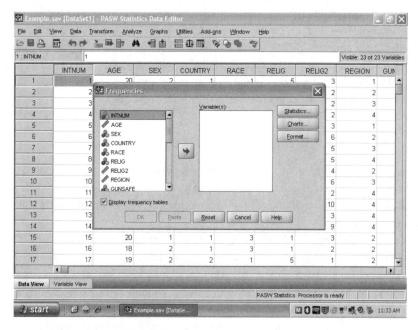

Figure 11.1. Analyze → Descriptive Statistics → Frequencies . . . Menu.

Figure 11.2. Frequencies Dialog Box.

for every variable in your data file, highlight all of the variable names in the left-hand box. You can do this by clicking once on the first variable name and, while holding down the Shift key, clicking on the Down arrow key to highlight all the variables in the list. Click on the arrow to the right and you'll see all of the variable names transferred to the column on the right. Once this is done, simply click OK at the bottom of the dialog box to execute the request.

SPSS does all of the calculations for you almost instantly and creates a new file called "output," which opens automatically on your computer. Scroll through the output file, and you'll see one frequency table produced for every variable. If your first variable is something like "interview number" or "case number," the first table will be fairly lengthy. Keep scrolling down until you see the other frequency tables.

Interpreting a Frequency Table

Table 11.1 shows an example of a frequency table for the variable Religious Affiliation for a fictional set of data. Let's examine the information in a frequency table to see how it is organized. The first column lists the actual values of the variable. If the first column of the frequency tables you have produced contains numbers only, you'll need to look at the codebook to discern what numbers were assigned to the various responses.

The second column in the table, called Frequency, reports the number of respondents in the sample that selected each response. In Table 11.1, 190 people indicated affiliation with a Christian religion. The third column, labeled Percent, calculates how many out of 100 each frequency represents. The 190 Christians, for example, represent 72.5 percent of all 262 of the respondents interviewed. There are no missing cases in this table.

Table 11.1. Frequency for Religious Affiliation.

	Frequency	Percent	Valid Percent	Cumulative Percent
Christian	190	72.5	72.5	72.5
Muslim	4	1.5	1.5	74.0
Jewish	12	4.6	4.6	78.6
Hinduism	2	.8	.8	79.4
None	46	17.6	17.6	96.9
Other	1	.4	.4	97.3
Agnostic	5	1.9	1.9	99.2
Buddhist	1	.4	.4	99.6
Shintoism	1	.4	.4	100.0
Total	262	100.0	100.0	

If there were, the Valid Percent column would calculate percentages by first excluding all missing cases. Finally, the Cumulative Percent column simply keeps a running total of the Valid Percent column by adding each successive number in the column. You can see that 74 percent of the sample indicated they were *either* Christian or Muslim. This is an important column that will be very useful a little later when we begin collapsing variables.

Now that you know how to interpret a frequency table, take some time to look at the distributions in the frequency tables you produced in SPSS. Are the distributions similar to or different from what you thought before we began this project? How about after you performed your own interviews? If any of the results surprise you, think about what might have caused the difference between your original impressions and the actual data. Surprises like this are common in social science.

If the results of the overall study are different from the impressions you formed after your interviews were completed, this may be due to sample size. The **law of large numbers** states that the larger the sample, the more accurate the results, or the less error there will be in representing the views or actions of the entire population. Generally speaking, interviewing the few people you did is less accurate than the results from the larger sample of students, assuming that no additional errors were made in collection of data.

Although a review of frequency distributions is interesting, it offers us little information needed to test the hypothesis we are exploring. To do this, we calculate and interpret cross-tabulation tables. Before doing so, we need to learn how to transform variables such that cross-tab data will be easily understood.

COLLAPSING VARIABLES

The analysis component of this exercise has been simplified to be as intuitive as possible. This is so you have the best chance of seeing the rudimentary characteristics of the comparative process in social science. As I mentioned, keep in mind that simplifying data analysis by using statistics or collapsing variables ultimately *loses* much of the rich information contained in the data. More sophisticated analytical techniques (covered in statistics courses) do a much better job of taking into account the diversity in the data while identifying data trends comprehensibly.

The collapsing process differs slightly for discrete and continuous variables. **Discrete variables** are those that have definite categories that cannot be easily divided. Sex, race, and religious affiliation are examples of discrete variables. Their categories, such as male and female for sex, cannot be easily divided into additional categories. They involve differences in *kind*. **Continuous variables**, on the other hand, are infinitely divisible. Age is an example of a continuous variable. A person's age can be expressed in years, or half years, or quarter years, and so on to infinity. Continuous variables involve differences of *degree*. For your class project you will need to determine whether your independent and dependent variables are discrete or continuous. You also need to do this for any other variables identified by your instructor.

COLLAPSING DISCRETE VARIABLES

Some of your variables first need to be transformed by collapsing them into just two categories or attributes. For example, several responses are possible for the variable Religious Affiliation, among them Christian, Jewish, Muslim, and so on. Collapsing involves reducing the number of attributes to only *two*. Because the majority of Americans identify themselves as Christian, creating two attributes entitled *Christian* and *non-Christian* would ensure that some cases fall into each category. Anyone indicating religious affiliation to be something other than Christian (including the nonreligious) would be counted in the non-Christian attribute.

A second issue is equally important: variation. That is, all of the concepts we are dealing with have been operationalized into *variables*. This means there must be *variation*, or some people in our study who fit into one of the attributes and others who fit into the second. If a study were conducted where everyone indicated her religious affiliation was Christian, it wouldn't be a variable at all, but a *constant*. There has to be at least one other attribute against which to make comparisons. This is important in doing a cross-tabulation analysis such as we will do for this assignment. In fact, social scientists aim for something called **maximum variability** when collapsing variables. Maximum variability occurs when an equal proportion of cases falls into each attribute of the variable. Maximum variability would occur for the variable Sex if 50 percent of the people sampled were males and 50 percent were females. If there were three attributes of a variable (say, upper, middle, and lower for a variable capturing social class), the maximum variability would be 33 percent of cases in each class.

This type of variability allows us to make the maximum number of comparisons between attributes of the variable. The more unbalanced the number of cases, the closer the variable comes to being a constant. This is less of a problem in large datasets where information has been collected from thousands of people, in which case a variable with even 10 percent or fewer of the cases in one attribute still means that thousands of comparisons can be made. But in small datasets such as the one collected for your class, maximum variability is an important issue. Too few cases in one of two attributes means that few comparisons can be made, and as a result any conclusions are tenuous. If a table is further split by a control variable (called *table elaboration*, explained in Chapter Thirteen), too few cases in one attribute of the independent or dependent variable means there will very likely be cells in a table that contain no cases at all. This is a bad situation because no analysis can then be performed.

Achieving something close to maximum variability is thus important for our class project. You may now be asking yourself if there are generally accepted cut-offs when collapsing variables into two categories. Is it acceptable to have 70 percent of the cases in one attribute and 30 percent in the other? How about an 80/20 split? Or 90/10? The answer is that it ultimately depends on the number of cases in your sample and your type of statistical analysis. In all cases, the larger the sample, the less likely it is that maximum variability will be an issue. When doing cross-tabulation analyses with small datasets such as we are doing, maximum variability is highly desirable. A rule of thumb to follow is that every cell in every table produced in the analysis must have more than five cases represented therein.

This would be a critical issue if we were doing a study that was eventually going to be published. Because this exercise is basically one designed to teach you about the excitement of collecting information and making discoveries, the rules of maximum variability can be slightly relaxed. For our purposes, in collapsing your variables for this project do your best to have no fewer than 30 percent of your cases in one attribute of any variable. This should ensure a reasonable number of cases in every cell for the analysis you will do.

A final important issue in collapsing variables is to make sure that the two new groups you create are theoretically meaningful for comparison. If one wanted to compare the responses of Americans who live closer to the West Coast versus the East Coast, it wouldn't make much sense to collapse a variable called Region of Country to include residents of, say, the Southeast and Midwest in one attribute and residents of the Northeast and West in the other. Instead, combining respondents who live in the West and Midwest into one attribute, and those who live in the Northeast and Southeast in the second attribute, would make good theoretical sense.

Using SPSS to Collapse a Discrete Variable

To demonstrate how to collapse a discrete variable using SPSS, let's walk through the same example. Consider the frequency distribution for the variable Region of Country as illustrated in Table 11.2. We are interested in collapsing this variable into two categories: East and West. To do this, we combine the categories of West and Midwest (values one and three) into one new group called West, while the categories of Southeast and Northeast (values two and four) will be collapsed into the new East category. Eyeballing the data, we see that we can get close to maximum variability with these two new categories.

With your dataset opened in SPSS, click on the Transform menu at the top of the screen. Click on Recode into Different Variables from the drop-down menu. A pop-up window opens, like the one displayed in Figure 11.3.

Table 11.2. Frequency Distribution for Region of Country.

	Frequency	Percent	Valid Percent	Cumulative Percent
1 West	57	21.8	21.8	21.8
2 Southeast	72	27.5	27.5	49.2
3 Midwest	65	24.8	24.8	74.0
4 Northeast	68	26.0	26.0	100.0
Total	262	100.0	100.0	

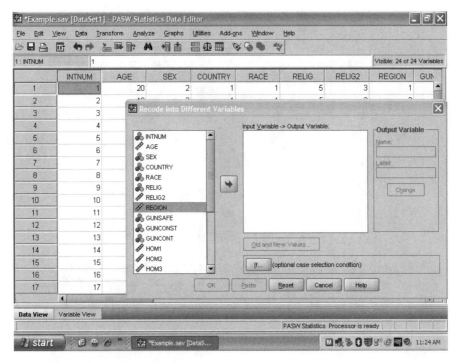

Figure 11.3. Recode into Different Variables Dialog Box.

Highlight the variable of interest (Region, in this case) by clicking on it. Click on the arrow to move it to the box on the right.

In the box on the upper-right-hand part titled "Name," enter the name you wish to call the new variable. Add a "c" to the old variable name to do this. For the variable Region used in the example in Figure 11.4, "Regionc" would be entered as the name of the new variable. The "c" in a variable name connotes that the variable has been *collapsed*.

In the box marked Label, a longer description can be supplied for the variable. This label will be printed out following the name of the variable on any output you produce in SPSS. "Region collapsed" would be all you have to enter in this example. Once this is done, click on Change. You will see the new variable name appear to the right of the old variable name in the white box in the center of the screen.

Next, click on the button entitled Old and New Values. The dialogue box depicted in Figure 11.5 appears. Notice that the box is split into two columns, labeled Old Value and New Value. The Old Value column has several options to indicate which of the codes in the uncollapsed variable should be included in one of the attributes of the new collapsed variable being created. The top of the New Value column has a box labeled Value, in which the new code should be entered.

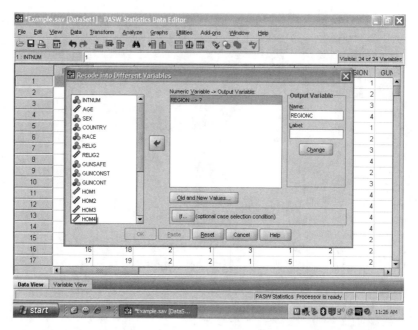

Figure 11.4. Recode into Different Variables Dialog Box, with Region Moved to Box on Right.

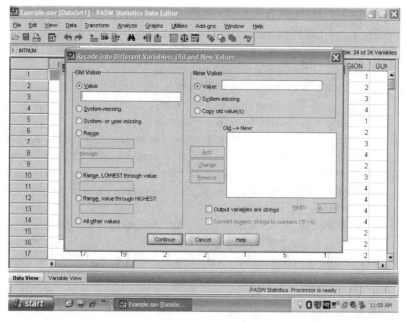

Figure 11.5. Old Value and New Value Dialog Box.

In the first option of the Old Value column, enter 1 for West. In the New Value column, enter 1 as well, to indicate the value of the new Regionc variable being created (see Figure 11.6). Clicking on the Add button will create a recode statement in the box at the lower right of the screen (it is important to create a recode statement for every old and new value, even when the values are the same. If you prefer, you can click on the Copy Old Value(s) option in the New Value column when the value of a code remains the same in the new variable).

Repeat this process for the second value of the old variable by entering 2 in the first option of the Old Value and 2 in the first option of the New Value column. Clicking on Add generates a second recode statement in the box. This is depicted in Figure 11.7.

Complete the process for the last two values of the variable Region. The old 3 will be recoded as 1 and the old 4 as 2. This produces a total of four recode statements, as shown in Figure 11.8.

Every old value of Region is now accounted for in the small box. Once this is done, click on Continue to return to the previous dialogue box. Once there, click on OK to have SPSS perform the operation. SPSS quickly makes all of the changes you specified, creates a new variable called Regionc, and opens the output file.

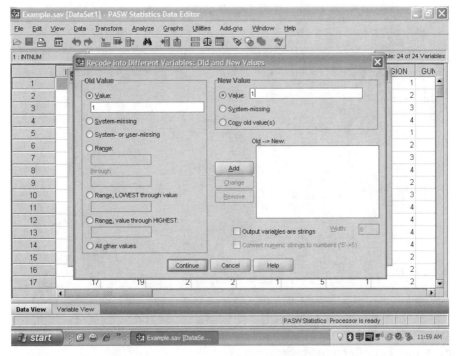

Figure 11.6. Old Value and New Value Dialog Box, with "1" Added in Both Columns.

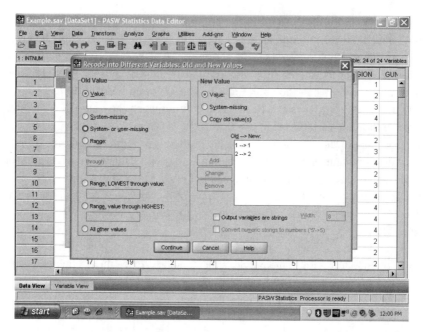

Figure 11.7. Two Recode Statements.

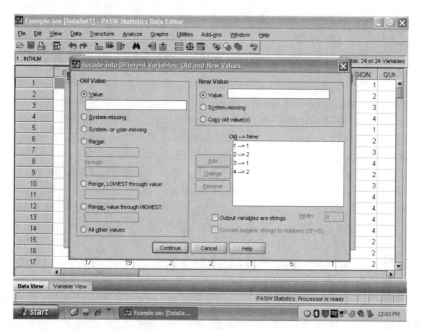

Figure 11.8. Four Recode Statements.

Now let's shrink the output file and then check to see if the variable was correctly transformed. To do this, make sure you are on the Data View screen in SPSS (if necessary, click on the tab labeled as such on the lower left of your screen). Scroll to the right to see the last column listed in the dataset, as depicted in Figure 11.9. You'll see that SPSS has added a new variable, named Regionc, to the end of your data file. You have created a new variable!

Defining Your New Variable

It is important to define every newly created variable *immediately* after it is created. To do this, click on the Variable View tab at the lower left of the screen. You'll see the new variable, Regionc, listed as the last variable at the bottom of the page, in row 17 (Figure 11.10).

Defining a new variable simply means making changes to the information in this row so that it correctly describes the characteristics of the new variable. For the purposes of this project, we'll need to change the information in only a few of these columns. Click on the Decimals column and either enter "0" or click on the Down arrow to reduce the number to zero. You'll want to do this for any variable you create where decimal places are not needed.

Next, click on the Values box in the row of your new variable (see Figure 11.10). Click on the small light gray box that appears. This opens a Value Labels dialog box, depicted in Figure 11.11. In this box you can describe the meaning of each new code or attribute of your

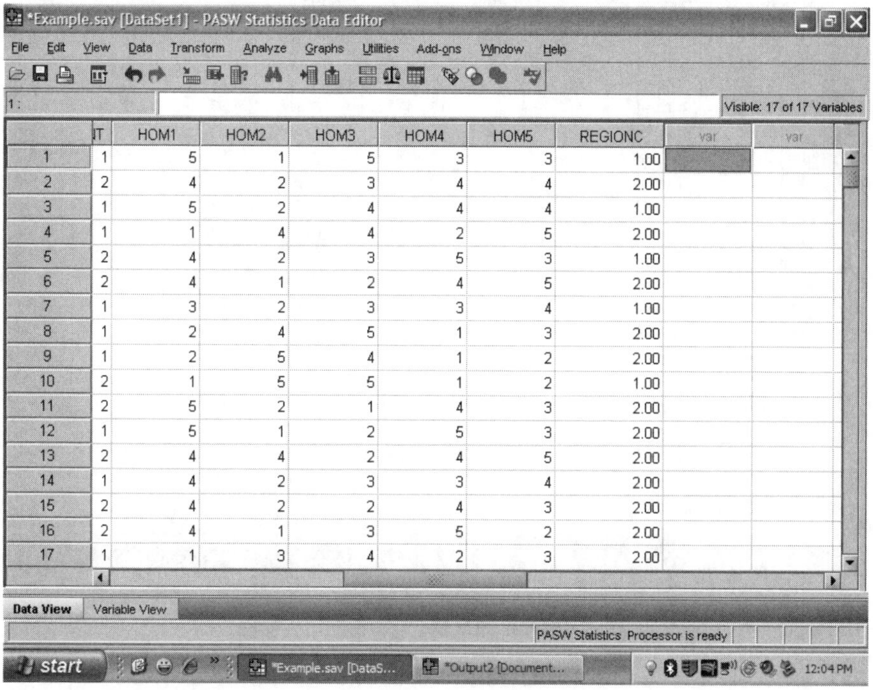

	IT	HOM1	HOM2	HOM3	HOM4	HOM5	REGIONC	var	var
1	1	5	1	5	3	3	1.00		
2	2	4	2	3	4	4	2.00		
3	1	5	2	4	4	4	1.00		
4	1	1	4	4	2	5	2.00		
5	2	4	2	3	5	3	1.00		
6	2	4	1	2	4	5	2.00		
7	1	3	2	3	3	4	1.00		
8	1	2	4	5	1	3	2.00		
9	1	2	5	4	1	2	2.00		
10	2	1	5	5	1	2	1.00		
11	2	5	2	1	4	3	2.00		
12	1	5	1	2	5	3	2.00		
13	2	4	4	2	4	5	2.00		
14	1	4	2	3	3	4	2.00		
15	2	4	2	2	4	3	2.00		
16	2	4	1	3	5	2	2.00		
17	1	1	3	4	2	3	2.00		

Figure 11.9. Data View Showing New Variable Regionc.

new variable. Recall that we recoded Regionc into only two categories, coded 1 and 2. Do you remember which value represented students from the West? This is why it is important to redefine variables as soon as they are created; it's easy to forget. Recall that 1 means West and 2 means East. Recording this in the Value Labels box carries the added advantage of having these labels show up on all output produced in SPSS, making interpretation of the tables easy.

Enter 1 in the Value box. In the Label box, enter West. Click on Add to see it appear in the large white area of the dialog box. You'll repeat the same process for each code or attribute of any new variable you create. Click on the Value box again. If necessary, delete the 1 and enter 2. Enter East in the Label box (deleting West if necessary). Once again, click on Add. Two statements, each defining a label for one value of the variable, should now appear in the large white area in the dialog box, as in Figure 11.11.

There are no other codes to label, so click OK to close the dialog box and return to the Variable View screen.

Pay close attention to any directions your instructor gives you on how to code missing cases. You will not need to enter a value in the Missing column if your instructor

	Name	Type	Width	Decimals	Label	Values	Missing	Columns	
1	INTNUM	Numeric	3	0	Interview Number	None	None	8	Rig
2	AGE	Numeric	2	0	Age in Years	None	99	8	Rig
3	SEX	Numeric	1	0	Gender	{1, male}...	9	8	Rig
4	COUNTRY	Numeric	1	0	Born in this cou...	{1, yes}...	9	8	Rig
5	RACE	Numeric	1	0	Race/Ethnic gr...	{1, White}...	9	8	Rig
6	RELIG	Numeric	2	0	Religious affiliat...	{1, Christian...	99	8	Rig
7	RELIG2	Numeric	2	0	Religiosity 1(lo...	None	99	8	Rig
8	REGION	Numeric	1	0	Region of Country	{1, West}...	None	8	Rig
9	GUNSAFE	Numeric	8	0	country safer if ...	{1, yes}...	None	8	Rig
10	GUNCONST	Numeric	8	0	gun ownership ...	{1, yes}...	None	8	Rig
11	GUNCONT	Numeric	8	0	gun control incr...	{1, yes}...	None	8	Rig
12	HOM1	Numeric	1	0	should hold pub...	{1, Strongly ...	None	8	Rig
13	HOM2	Numeric	8	0	wrong or unnat...	{1, Strongly ...	None	8	Rig
14	HOM3	Numeric	8	0	uncomfortable ...	{1, Strongly ...	None	8	Rig
15	HOM4	Numeric	8	0	nothing wrong ...	{1, Strongly ...	None	8	Rig
16	HOM5	Numeric	8	0	disappointed if ...	{1, Strongly ...	None	8	Rig
17	REGIONC	Numeric	8	2	Region Collapsed	None	None	10	Rig
18									
19									

Figure 11.10. Variable View with Regionc Created But Undefined.

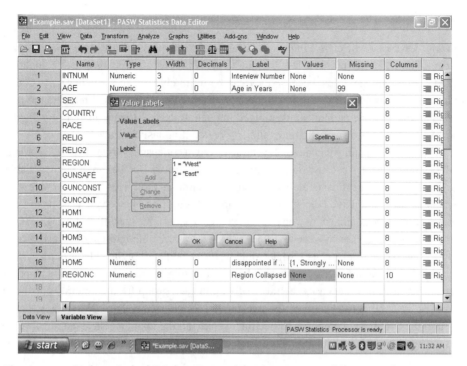

Figure 11.11. Values Label Dialog Box with New East and West Values.

informed you to fill in an answer for any questions not answered by an interviewee. On the other hand, your instructor may want you to fill in a special code or value for missing information. If so, enter this value in the Missing column. Clicking on the gray box in the Missing box will cause a dialog box to open. Enter the value or values as identified by your instructor and click OK.

The final column in the Variable View screen that needs attention is the Measures column. It is important to identify the level of measurement for every newly created variable. Click on the Measurement box and then on the Down arrow to see the list of options for this column. Discrete variables are differences in kind; they are always **nominal variables**. **Ordinal variables** are those whose attributes imply some kind of hierarchy—more or less of something, or stronger and weaker responses. **Interval variables** are continuous data that use an equal unit of measurement (such as years of age) for the intervals. SPSS substitutes the word Scale for interval level variables. Because our newly created Regionc variable reveals simple differences in kind (students from the West or East), nominal would be the correct designation in the Measures column.

COLLAPSING CONTINUOUS VARIABLES

If variables do not differ in kind, they differ by degree. That is, on some type of scale or continuum there is more or less of something. Variables such as these are sometimes called *continuous* variables, because they can be infinitely split into smaller parts. Think of temperature as an example of a continuous variable. You can measure temperature on a Celsius scale, but one degree can be divided into a half degree, then a quarter of a degree, and so on. The division can continue infinitely or "continuously," hence the name.

Maximum variability can more often be achieved in collapsing variables of this type than with discrete variables because the cut-offs for one category or another are more negotiable. For example, examine the cumulative percentage column in Table 11.3 for the variable Age. Recall that the Cumulative Percent column simply adds together the percentages in the Valid Percent column, beginning at the top of the table. Age is a variable that differs by degree (ages can increase or decrease by years). If you collapsed this variable into only two age groups (younger and older, for instance), what would be the cut-off age for the older group?

Recall that maximum variability and theoretical integrity are our goals. That is, approximately 50 percent of the cases should ideally be in each group for maximum comparison purposes, and the construction of the two groups should make sense. What ages should fall into the "younger" category? Notice that we are talking about a college campus where you expect the overall population to be younger than that of, say, the entire United States.

Table 11.3. Frequency Table for Age in Years.

	Frequency	Percent	Valid Percent	Cumulative Percent
17	1	.4	.4	.4
18	37	14.1	14.1	14.5
19	42	16.0	16.0	30.5
20	60	22.9	22.9	53.4
21	48	18.3	18.3	71.8
22	32	12.2	12.2	84.0
23	15	5.7	5.7	89.7
24	10	3.8	3.8	93.5
25	9	3.4	3.4	96.9
26	2	.8	.8	97.7
27	1	.4	.4	98.1
30	1	.4	.4	98.5
31	1	.4	.4	98.9
34	1	.4	.4	99.2
40	1	.4	.4	99.6
42	1	.4	.4	100.0
Total	262	100.0	100.0	

Thus the term *younger* should be relative to the group you are studying. Note that the Cumulative Percent column indicates that 53.4 percent of the sample is age twenty or younger. This cumulative percentage is as close to 50 percent (or maximum variability) as can be achieved with this variable. Subtracting 53.4 percent from 100 percent (the entire sample), you can deduce that 46.6 percent of the sample is twenty-one or older. Because the ideas of younger and older are relative to the college campus, you may decide it is acceptable to compare those who are twenty or younger to those who are older than twenty.

Collapsing Continuous Variables Using SPSS

Recoding continuous variables is relatively simple. Consider the data for the variable Religiosity, depicted in the frequency table in Table 11.4.

Respondents were asked to indicate how religious they are on a scale from 1 to 10, where 1 means not religious at all and 10 means very religious. One can see by studying the distribution that there is considerable variation in religiosity among the 262 people who answered the question; this is a good sign. Examining the Cumulative Percent column, we find that 58.4 percent of the sample indicated a religiosity between 1 and 5. Subtracting this number from a total of 100 percent indicates 41.6 percent of the sample having a religiosity between 6 and 10. This is a reasonable split when collapsing variables into two categories, which also has intuitive appeal because the ten-point scale is evenly divided.

Notice, however, that we could get closer to maximum variability by splitting the variable a little differently. A roughly 45–55 split could be achieved if categories 1 to 4 and 6 to 10 were collapsed. Which is the correct way to recode the variable? This is a judgment call on the part of the researcher. In a "real" study in which a cross-tabulation analysis is performed, a responsible researcher would create two new variables of religiosity by collapsing the variable both ways and then running cross-tabulations to see if the results vary

Table 11.4. Frequency Table for Religiosity.

	Frequency	Percent	Valid Percent	Cumulative Percent
1	36	13.7	13.7	13.7
2	23	8.8	8.8	22.5
3	29	11.1	11.1	33.6
4	31	11.8	11.8	45.4
5	34	13.0	13.0	58.4
6	31	11.8	11.8	70.2
7	30	11.5	11.5	81.7
8	25	9.5	9.5	91.2
9	13	5.0	5.0	96.2
10	10	3.8	3.8	100.0
Total	262	100.0	100.0	

substantially. For our purposes, we'll use the 1–5 and 6–10 groupings. In collapsing the variables, your instructor will likely give you specific information regarding the point at which to split the variable. If not, you'll make the decision on your own.

The process of collapsing a continuous variable in SPSS is similar to that described for collapsing a variable differing in kind, and it is simpler in some ways. This is because a range of values in the old variable can be identified at once and recoded as the new value.

Returning to the Data View in SPSS, click on the Transform menu at the top of the screen, and choose Recode into Different Variables. Highlight the variable you want to recode and move it into the Input Variable box. Enter a name for the new variable in the Name box on the right (adding a "c" to the end of the old variable name to show the new variable is a collapsed version of the old one). In the box marked Label, enter a fuller description of the variable, such as "Religiosity Collapsed." Click on the Change button to see the new variable name appear to the right of the old variable name in the large white box on the left. Your dialog box should resemble that in Figure 11.12.

Once this is complete, click on the Old and New Values button. As described earlier, notice that the dialog box that appears is split into two columns labeled Old Value and New Value (refer back to Figure 11.5). The Old Value column has several options for you to indicate which of the old values you want to recode. Two options on this list that will make your job easier in this instance are the "Range, LOWEST through value" and "Range, value through HIGHEST" options, each followed by a blank line in which to enter a value. In this example, I wish to collapse the variable Religiosity into just two categories. Values 1 through 5 in the old variable make up one category of the new variable, while values 6 through 10 are the second category.

Click on the circle beside Range, LOWEST through value. The line below it turns white. In the line, enter the value that represents the cutoff for your category containing the lowest numbers (in the religiosity example, 5 is the cutoff for the 1 through 5 category). This indicates that the lowest values in your old variable, all the way up to the number you enter in the box, will be part of one category of the new variable.

The top of the New Value column has a place where the new value can be typed in. Remember that your new collapsed variable has only two values: 1 and 2. Enter 2 in this line. To some this may be counterintuitive because most would want to number the lowest values with a 1. It will be explained in a moment why you should use 2, but first let's finish coding. After entering a 2 at the top of the New Value column, click on Add to see the recode statement appear in the white box.

Click on the circle beside Range, value through HIGHEST. Enter the lowest value for the higher set of numbers you are collapsing. In the Religiosity example, 6 is the cutoff (or lowest number) for the numbers 6 through 10. By doing this, values 6 and higher will be recoded into one value in the new variable. This is what we want to do.

You probably know what to do next. Enter a 1 at the top of the New Value column. Then click Add to add this recode statement to the white box. For our Religiosity example, the dialog box looks like Figure 11.13.

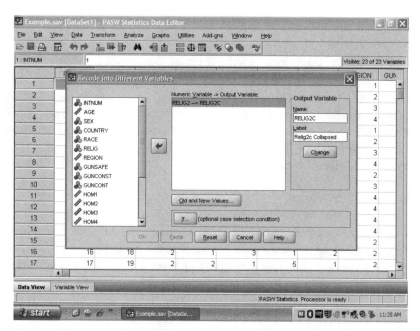

Figure 11.12. Recode into Different Variables Dialog Box with Completed Information for Collapsing Relig2.

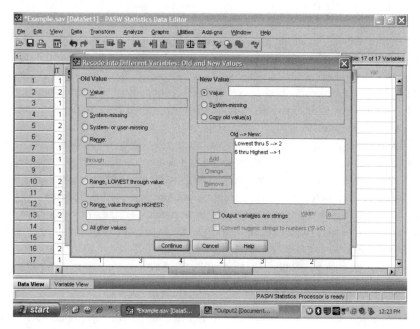

Figure 11.13. Recoded Information for Religiosity.

Clicking on Continue returns you to the recode dialog box. Click on OK to create your newly recoded variable.

Why recode lower values as a 2 and higher values as a 1 when recoding variables that differ by degree? Recall that your data will eventually be expressed in cross-tabulation tables. These tables are easiest to interpret if the values for continuous variables in the table are highest in the upper-left corner and lower as they spread down or across. SPSS always puts the values that start with a 1 in the upper-left corner. Thus, recoding higher values as a 1 ensures that they will be in that corner of the table. You'll see this as cross-tabulation tables are created in the next section of the book.

Defining Your New Variable

As you did before, click on the Data View tab in SPSS and scroll to the right side of the screen to see the new variable you created. Double-check to see if your recode statements are correct by eyeballing the data in the column. No value should be larger than 2 because we recoded the new variable only into values of 1 and 2. If this is correct, click on the Variable View tab to see the new variable listed at the bottom.

Define your variable by making changes in the necessary columns. Click on the Decimals column and either enter 0 or click on the Down arrow to reduce the number to zero. Next, click on the Values box in the row of your new variable. Click on the small light gray box that appears. In the dialog box that opens, type in a description or label for each value of the new variable. That is, enter a 1 in the value column and type a description of it in the label box. For the Religiosity example, I would enter something like "More Religious (6–10)." I include the actual values of the old variable in parentheses so I know exactly what the group is when examining the cross-tabulation tables. Do the same for the second value by replacing the 1 in the value box with a 2. Enter a new Label for this value. For Religiosity, I enter "Less Religious (1–5)."

As before, pay close attention to any directions your instructor may give you on how to deal with missing values. Any specific numbers identified for missing data are entered into the Missing column.

Think through which option to select from the drop-down menu in the Measurement column. Two of the three choices are relevant to variables that differ by degree and have been collapsed: ordinal and scale. Ordinal means there is some difference in degree between the attributes of the newly created variable (less or more of something, such as religiosity), but the difference is not precisely measured. Scale means that the difference between values is equivalent, as with degrees of temperature on a thermometer or the number of dollars someone earns every year.

For collapsed variables that differ by degree, the correct designation is most frequently ordinal. This is the case for the religiosity example. People in the first group we know are "more" religious than the other group, but we don't know by how much. Consequently, the variable is measured at the ordinal level. Because we are collapsing all variables into only two categories for this assignment, it is likely that the designation of your variables differing in kind will be ordinal. More than two attributes are typically required for a scale-level variable.

CHECKING YOUR WORK

The process of collapsing variables correctly is obviously important. If done wrong, all conclusions drawn from further analyses of your data could be completely incorrect. This would lead to embarrassment, incorrect conclusions drawn, and a lower grade for this assignment—not such dreadful outcomes, perhaps. Imagine, though, what will happen if a researcher gets it wrong. Other researchers, even politicians and policy makers reading the published article, would make erroneous conclusions and possibly pass legislation that is flawed or even harmful to many people.

This actually happened in 1985. At the time, the women's movement was drawing attention to the fact that divorce had a more negative impact on the economic situation of women than men. Hard data were needed. A formative study was carried out by Weitzman (1985), who demonstrated that women's economic well-being decreased a remarkable 70 percent after a divorce, while men's standard of living generally increased by about 30 percent. Custody of the children, limited involvement in the labor force, and lower earning power of women were thought to contribute to this discrepancy. As a result, the state of California and others modified their divorce laws in an attempt to compensate for this inequality. It is normally unusual for just one study to have as large a political impact as this one did, but it occurred nonetheless.

In 1996 a researcher named Richard Peterson (1996) gained access to Weitzman's original data and replicated the analysis. He found several errors in the dataset, including errors in recoding statements. By Peterson's analysis, women were still the losers in divorce, but their standard of living decreased only about 30 percent, not 70 percent, and men's standard of living increased about 10 percent, not 30 percent. The moral of the story, of course, is to double-check your work. Society puts a good deal of trust in researchers, and not all errors will be caught immediately in the peer review process. It is up to us as professionals to do all we can to get it right.

There are at least two ways you should check to see if the new variables you have created are accurate. The first way is to eyeball the column of data in your new variable in the data view of SPSS to see if any values larger than 2 appear in the column. The second is to run a frequency table on the new variable and compare the percentage of respondents in each attribute of the new variable to the percentages in the Cumulative Percentage column of the uncollapsed variable. In Figure 11.13, for example, 58.4 percent of all respondents showed up in categories 1 to 5. This percentage should be equal to the second category of the new variable (recall that values 1 to 5 were recoded as a 2, or "lower religiosity").

If either of these double-check methods detects an error, it is best to delete the new variable entirely and re-create it. You can delete a variable in the Data View by right-clicking (Control-click on a Mac) on the variable name at the top of the column and then hitting Delete. This will also erase all information in the Variable View. Repeat the steps above to re-create the variable, this time paying close attention to correctly typing in each recode statement so as to avoid making errors. It's clearly important to get it right.

SUMMARY

Producing frequency tables is the first step in data analysis; they report on the distribution of responses for single variables. You are now able to produce and interpret frequency tables on your own for a set of data; this is a marketable skill.

Variables often need to be transformed during data analysis, and this class project is no different. To simplify the cross-tabulation analysis to come, you have learned how to transform both discrete and continuous variables into just two attributes, and to determine whether the variables are measured at the nominal, ordinal, or interval level of measurement. Take a moment to appreciate the new skills you've acquired before moving on to the next chapter.

REVIEW QUESTIONS

1. Why are frequency tables of interest to you as a researcher?
2. What steps are necessary to produce frequency tables in SPSS?
3. How are frequency tables useful when collapsing variables?
4. What is the difference between a discrete variable and a continuous variable?
5. What principle(s) should be used in deciding how best to collapse variables?
6. What are the differences among nominal, ordinal, and interval level variables?
7. After collapsing a variable, what methods should be employed to make sure the recoding is accurate?

KEY TERMS

Continuous variables Variables that are infinitely divisible.
Discrete variables Variables with definite categories not easily further divided.

Interval variables Continuous data with hierarchical characteristics measured in equidistant intervals. SPSS substitutes the word *Scale* for interval level variables.

Law of large numbers The larger the sample, the more accurate the results or the less error there will be in representing the views or actions of the entire population.

Maximum variability When the same proportion of cases is represented within each attribute of a variable.

Nominal variables Variables measured at the nominal level of measurement, which contain discrete differences of kind.

Ordinal variables Variables measured at the ordinal level of measurement with attributes containing some kind of hierarchical difference. This can include more or less of something, or stronger versus weaker response.

12

Data Analysis 2

Creating Composite Variables and Cross-Tabs

The first half of this chapter demonstrates combining multiple items into a single score for a variable. If the interview schedule for your class includes more than one question or indicator to measure one variable, you can use SPSS to create a new variable that consists of a single score, representing all the items combined. A variable that combines multiple indicators is called a **composite variable**. Indices and scales are the most common types of composite variable.

The last half of this chapter shows how to compile your collapsed independent and dependent variables in the form of a cross-tabulation table. A properly constructed cross-tabulation table supplies the information necessary for you to see if there is support in the data for your class hypothesis.

INDICES AND SCALES

Indices and scales are the most common types of composite variable. An **index** is a series of several questions or indicators of a particular variable that are given equal weight as they are added together to create a composite. A **scale** has the same features as an index except that any particular indicator may be given a different weight by allowing responses that differ by degree rather than in kind. Typically, an index contains an either-or choice between two responses such as yes and no or agree and disagree. A scale also allows a respondent to indicate the degree to which she or he agrees or disagrees with a statement but offers an opportunity to indicate intensity. This may involve selecting a score on a scale from, say, 1 to 7, where 1 means strongly agree and 7 means strongly disagree.

It is not imperative that you understand the difference between indices and scales for this assignment. What is most important is that you understand how to combine multiple indicators to produce a single number or statistic that represents the variable you are attempting to measure.

CREATING AN INDEX FROM MULTIPLE ITEMS

Because concepts such as attitudes are often too complex to measure accurately with only one question, researchers may develop an index. An index consists of more than one measurement item. Each item taps an aspect of the concept, to give a fuller picture of the overall attitude of the respondent toward the concept.

Consider three items, for example. Interviewees respond to each statement by saying *yes* if they agree to it or *no* if they do not.

1. This country would be safer if more people owned guns.
   1 Yes 2 No
2. Americans have a constitutional right to bear arms.
   1 Yes 2 No
3. Passing gun control legislation will *increase* the crime rate.
   1 Yes 2 No

Can you tell the concept that these three items are attempting to measure? You are correct if you guessed attitude toward gun ownership. The first statement taps into the attitude regarding the safety of the country insofar as it is due to gun ownership. The second statement taps into whether one takes a literal interpretation of the U.S. Constitution, while the third specifically ties gun ownership to its perceived impact on the crime rate. Taken together, these three items generate a fuller picture of one's attitude toward gun ownership than only one item would.

The principle of index construction is to add together the responses of each interviewee on all the relevant items. Notice that, for each item, someone with a favorable attitude toward gun ownership will answer *yes*, while someone with an unfavorable attitude will respond *no*. To construct an index of favorable attitudes toward gun ownership, a researcher would simply have the computer count the number of times a yes shows up in these three statements. Notice that this then creates an index with a lowest possible score of zero (for someone who does not answer *yes* to any of the questions) to a high score of 3 (for someone who answers *yes* to every question).

It is important to note that we could just as well add up the number of times someone answers *no* instead of *yes*. This creates an index of unfavorable attitudes toward gun ownership. Again, this index could have a low score of zero (for someone who answered *yes* to all statements) and a high score of 3 (someone who answered *no* to all three statements). In this example, it does not matter what numerical code is assigned to the response. This is an important point to comprehend. Notice that the *no* response is precoded as 2 in the examples given here. This is irrelevant when using the Count command in SPSS; it simply *counts* the number of times the response occurs. It does *not* add up the numerical codes assigned to responses.

Using SPSS to Create an Index

In the dataset used in this example, the three items have the variable names Gunsafe, Gunconst, and Guncont. To create an index, we tell SPSS to count the number of times *yes* appears in each variable and deposit the total in a new variable that we will call Gunfav. (You can substitute the variable names from your own dataset that you wish to add together and create a new variable name on your own.)

With your master data file opened in SPSS, click on Transform, then Count Occurrences of Values Within Cases. A dialog box appears. Enter the name of the new variable as the Target Variable, and add more description of the variable in the Target Label box. In this example, Gunfav is the target variable, described in the Target Label box as Index of Favorable Attitudes Toward Gun Ownership. Highlight the variables from which your new variable will be computed and move them to the box on the right by clicking on the arrow between them. The dialog box will look similar to that depicted in Figure 12.1.

Next, click on Define Values to open another dialog box. In the Value box on the left, enter the code for the answer you wish SPSS to count. In this example, we desire to count the number of times the response *yes* appears in the three items. The *yes* has been coded as 1, so 1 is entered as the value for this example. Alternatively, the value 2 would be entered if we desire to count how many times *no* appears. Once you have entered the value, click Add to have the value show up in the right-hand column. Clicking Continue takes you back to the first dialog box, at which you click OK to execute the operation.

Shrink the output file that automatically pops up, and scroll to the right of the Data View screen. The last variable listed in your data file should be the new variable you have created. For Gunfav, only values between 0 and 3 should be listed.

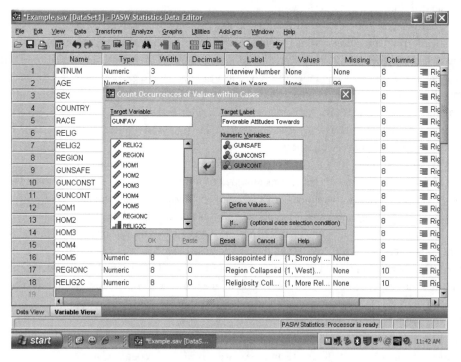

Figure 12.1. Count Command Dialog Box with Three Variables Selected and Information Completed for Target Variable and Target Label.

Next, be sure to define the new variable by clicking on the Variable View tab in the lower-left corner. Figure 12.2 depicts the new variable Gunfav in Variable View. Check to make sure that the values listed in each column in the Variable View are appropriate. For Gunfav, zero would be entered in the Decimals column. For the Values column, define labels for only the smallest and largest values of the index so that the direction of the index is obvious on any output produced. To do this, open the Value Labels dialog box by clicking on the correct row and column, and then on the gray square that appears within. Code 0 as Unfavorable and 3 as Favorable.

Enter one or more codes in the Missing column only if your dataset contains missing information. Finally, Ordinal is the correct choice for the Measure column. It may appear at first glance that an index is measured at the interval level of measurement, but the indeterminate meaning of counting the number of yes responses makes Ordinal the better designation.

Finally, request a frequency distribution from SPSS on your new variable so you can examine the distribution. A frequency distribution is also handy if you need to collapse the new variable into fewer categories. See the previous chapter for instructions on how to do this.

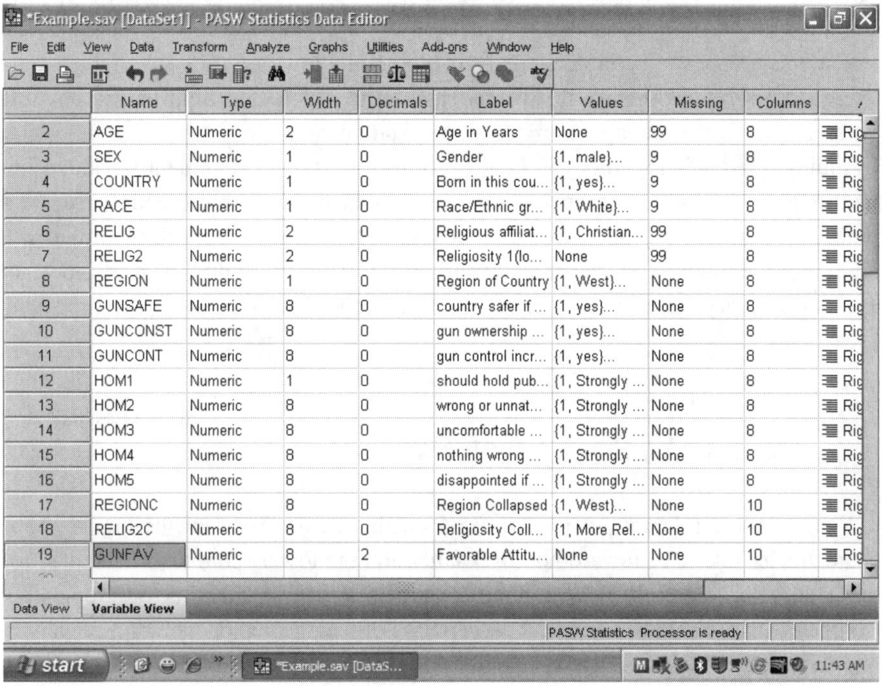

	Name	Type	Width	Decimals	Label	Values	Missing	Columns	
2	AGE	Numeric	2	0	Age in Years	None	99	8	Rig
3	SEX	Numeric	1	0	Gender	{1, male}...	9	8	Rig
4	COUNTRY	Numeric	1	0	Born in this cou...	{1, yes}...	9	8	Rig
5	RACE	Numeric	1	0	Race/Ethnic gr...	{1, White}...	9	8	Rig
6	RELIG	Numeric	2	0	Religious affiliat...	{1, Christian...	99	8	Rig
7	RELIG2	Numeric	2	0	Religiosity 1(lo...	None	99	8	Rig
8	REGION	Numeric	1	0	Region of Country	{1, West}...	None	8	Rig
9	GUNSAFE	Numeric	8	0	country safer if ...	{1, yes}...	None	8	Rig
10	GUNCONST	Numeric	8	0	gun ownership ...	{1, yes}...	None	8	Rig
11	GUNCONT	Numeric	8	0	gun control incr...	{1, yes}...	None	8	Rig
12	HOM1	Numeric	1	0	should hold pub...	{1, Strongly ...	None	8	Rig
13	HOM2	Numeric	8	0	wrong or unnat...	{1, Strongly ...	None	8	Rig
14	HOM3	Numeric	8	0	uncomfortable ...	{1, Strongly ...	None	8	Rig
15	HOM4	Numeric	8	0	nothing wrong ...	{1, Strongly ...	None	8	Rig
16	HOM5	Numeric	8	0	disappointed if ...	{1, Strongly ...	None	8	Rig
17	REGIONC	Numeric	8	0	Region Collapsed	{1, West}...	None	10	Rig
18	RELIG2C	Numeric	8	0	Religiosity Coll...	{1, More Rel...	None	10	Rig
19	GUNFAV	Numeric	8	2	Favorable Attitu...	None	None	10	Rig

Figure 12.2. Variable View Screen of Gunfav.

CREATING A SCALE FROM MULTIPLE ITEMS

Consider the statements in this example:

> For each of the next five statements, please say whether you strongly disagree, disagree, are neutral or undecided, agree, or strongly agree.

	SD	D	N/U	A	SA
A) Homosexuals should be allowed to hold public office.	1	2	3	4	5
B) There is something wrong or unnatural about homosexuality.	1	2	3	4	5
C) I would feel uncomfortable sitting next to a homosexual.	1	2	3	4	5
D) There is nothing wrong with having a homosexual as a teacher.	1	2	3	4	5
E) I would be disappointed if one of my children was a homosexual.	1	2	3	4	5

Notice that all five items in this example are statements that deal with the same topic of attitude toward homosexuality. For each item, respondents indicate the intensity of their feelings about the statement on a five-point scale, as opposed to indicating yes or no as per the example in the section above. Scores on each five-point scale can be added together to create a single statistic indicating the strength of one's attitude toward homosexuality. Scores in this composite variable range from a potential low of 5 (possible if a respondent answered *strongly disagree* to all five statements) to a potential high of 25 (possible if a respondent answered *strongly agree* to all five statements).

Adding all scores together can be done, but only if each statement is valued in the same direction. Say we want our scale to range in such a way that the higher the score, the more tolerant the attitude toward homosexuality. A lower score thus implies a less tolerant or more homophobic attitude toward homosexuality. To do this, it is important to first examine every statement to see if this is the case. Let's consider the first item in the scale:

	SD	D	N/U	A	SA
A) Homosexuals should be allowed to hold public office.	1	2	3	4	5

Would a more tolerant person score a 5 on this item? We want the higher score to indicate greater tolerance toward homosexuality and the lower score to indicate less tolerance. Does it? If you think about it, a more tolerant person would agree or strongly agree that homosexuals should be allowed to hold public office; the person wouldn't see anything wrong with it. Less tolerant persons would more likely disagree or strongly disagree with this. The statement is valued in the right direction.

Having approved the first item, let's move to the second:

	SD	D	N/U	A	SA
B) There is something wrong or unnatural about homosexuality.	1	2	3	4	5

Again, ask yourself if a tolerant person would agree or strongly agree with this state-ment. For this item it is unlikely; a more tolerant person would disagree with the notion that there is something wrong with homosexuality. This does not fit with the assumption of our overall scale that the higher the score the more tolerant a person is. Item B needs to be changed or **reverse coded**. Keep this in mind as we continue examining the remaining items in our scale.

	SD	D	N/U	A	SA
C) I would feel uncomfortable sitting next to a homosexual.	1	2	3	4	5
D) There is nothing wrong with having a homosexual as a teacher.	1	2	3	4	5
E) I would be disappointed if one of my children was a homosexual.	1	2	3	4	5

Are there any remaining statements with which a tolerant person would *disagree*? If so, we also need to mark them as needing reverse coding. Looking closely, we see that a tolerant person would likely disagree with items C and E but agree with D. A tolerant per-son wouldn't have a problem sitting next to a homosexual, and wouldn't have a problem if his child were homosexual because the person wouldn't see it as a bad thing. Less tolerant individuals would more often have the opposite feeling.

The Logic of Reverse Scoring

Examination of the items in our scale reveals that the scoring for items B, C, and E need to be reversed. If the scale or index for your class contains no items that are in need of reverse scoring, you may skip this section.

Each statement is treated as a separate variable in SPSS, so a frequency distribution can be produced on each item. Step one, then, is to produce frequency distributions for the items in your scale or index. Can you now produce frequency tables on these items on your own? In case you need a refresher: with your data file open in SPSS, click on the Analyze menu on the top of the screen. Select Descriptive Statistics from the drop-down menu and then Frequencies. In the dialog box, highlight the names of the variables in the box on the left for which you want frequency tables. Click on the arrow to move those variable names to the box on the right. Click OK.

SPSS opens the output file with the requested frequency tables. *Don't delete this output file until you have finished reverse coding your variables.* To ensure recoding accuracy, you'll want to compare these initial frequency distributions to new ones that you request after reverse coding is complete.

Reverse coding involves creating a new variable for each item to be recoded. In the new variable, a 5 will be recoded as a 1 while a 4 will be recoded as a 2. A 3 will remain unchanged, but a score of 2 in the old variable will now be a 4 in the new variable and 1 a 5. In this way we can change the coding of items so that the higher the score the more tolerant to homosexuality the response.

This makes sense if you think about it; the number a person is assigned is really just a symbol to indicate where the person falls on a continuum of emotions about homosexuality. For items B, C, and E, the ends of the continuum have been reversed. Instead of answering on a continuum that ranges from intolerance on the left to tolerance on the right, the continuum of scores for the items in the question actually have tolerant scores on the left and intolerant scores on the right. By reverse coding we are simply making the continuum the same for all items, while preserving the integrity of where each individual places himself on that continuum.

Using SPSS to Reverse Code

Return to the Data View in SPSS and click on Transform, then, Recode into Different Variables. Highlight the name of the first item you want to recode, and click on the arrow to move it to the box in the middle. Give the new variable a new name. Using the old variable name and adding "rev" is a simple way to indicate that the variable has been reverse coded. In the box marked Label, type out a description of the item with "reverse coded" added to remind yourself that this variable has been changed. Click Change.

Click on Old and New Values. For every value in the old variable, indicate, one at a time, what the value will be in the new variable. A 1 is entered in the Old Value box at the top and a 5 in the New Value box. Click Add to enter the recode statement in the box. Next, a 4 is entered in the Old Value box and a 2 is typed in the New Value box. Even though 3 will mean the same in both variables, enter a 3 in both the Old Value and New Value boxes and click Add so that SPSS knows for sure what to do with the value. Create similar statements for the remaining values in your variable. When finished, the Recode into Different Variables: Old and New Values dialog box will look similar to Figure 12.3.

Click Continue to return to the original dialog box, and then click OK to execute the command. SPSS creates a new variable named Hom2rev. As before, be sure to immediately eyeball the new column at the end of the Data View. There should be no new values in the data column that you did not create. In this example, all values should still be between 1 and 5. Further, values in the new Hom2rev variable can also be compared to the values of the original Hom2 variable. Every value in Hom2rev should be completely reversed from that in Hom2. That is, a 5 in the old variable should be recoded as a 1 for the same case number in the dataset. If this is not so, an error occurred in the recoding process. Delete the new variable if this is the case and repeat the process, being careful to avoid making errors.

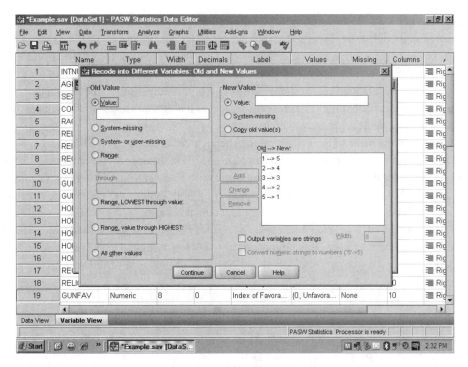

Figure 12.3. Completed Old and New Values Dialog Box for the Variable Hom2.

If the newly created variable passes these inspections, click on Variable View in the lower-left corner of the screen and define your new variable. Look to the earlier sections in this book on recoding a continuous variable if you need a reminder on how to do this. Once the variable has been correctly defined, you're ready to recode any other items you wish to change by repeating the process. In this example, Hom3 and Hom5 would also be reverse coded.

After you have finished reverse coding all desired items, produce frequency tables on the newly created variables. The percentages in the Valid Percentage column of the new variable should be the same as in the old variable, but in reverse order. Be sure that no new missing cases have been created in the process as well. If this happens, delete the variable in the dataset and repeat the process as described here, correcting any errors from before.

Creating the Scale with SPSS

Once all necessary items have been reverse coded, you are ready to combine all the items to create the new scale. With your dataset open, click on Transform, but this time click on Compute Variable from the drop-down menu. Enter a name for the new variable in the

Target Variable box. In this example, Homtol can be entered to stand for tolerance toward homosexuality. Click on Type & Label. Enter a fuller description of the variable in the Label box (such as "Tolerance toward homosexuality" as in our example). Choose Numeric if it is not already highlighted. Click Continue.

Because an interviewee's responses to the five items are simply added together, the recode statement (or Numeric Expression) involves listing the names of all variables we want to include in the scale, separated by a plus sign.

Highlight the name of the first variable to be included and click on the arrow to move it to the Numeric Expression box. Next, click on the + sign in the upper-left corner of the array of buttons under the box. A plus sign should show up to the right of the variable name in the Numeric Expression box. Follow this action by highlighting the name of the second variable in the list, clicking on the arrow key, and then clicking on the plus sign. Continue this process until all variable names to be added together are in the Numeric Expression box, separated by plus signs. It is not necessary to put a plus sign after the name of the last variable. Figure 12.4 depicts the completed Numeric Expression for the scale Homtol to be created.

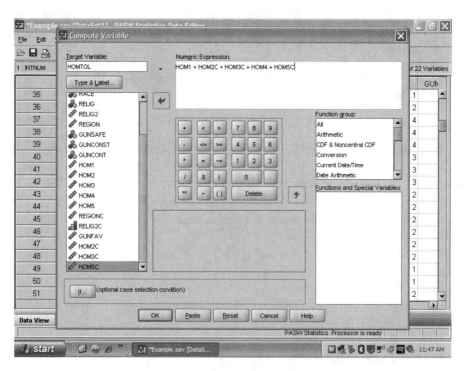

Figure 12.4. Completed Numeric Expression for Homtol Scale.

Double-check the statement in the Numeric Expression box to make sure it is correct. Did you select the names of the reverse coded variables instead of the old variables? Are any variable names included in the statement that should not be? Are the original names of the items selected for those that needed no reverse coding? Is every pair of variable names separated by a plus sign? Once you are sure that the statement is correct, click OK to create the new variable.

Guess what the next step is. Yes: the new variable needs to be examined in the Data View and then defined in the Variable View. First, eyeball the column of data for the new variable (Homtol in this case) in the Data View field to see if there are any values less than 5 or greater than 25, or if there are any unnecessary missing cases. Next, click on Variable View and define the new variable. As before, be sure the decimal place column is set to zero and a description of the variable is entered in the Label column. Be sure that Scale is selected in the Measure column. That's it! It is not necessary to enter any Values because the data are continuous.

Examining the New Scale

Now that your new composite variable has been created, request a frequency table on the variable from SPSS to see the results. You should be able to do this on your own at this point. (If you need a reminder, the steps are Analyze → Descriptive Statistics → Frequencies.) Highlight the variable name and click on the arrow key to move it to the white box. Then click OK to execute.

Examine the distribution of your newly created variable by noting the minimum and maximum values and the cutoff for maximum variability. Table 12.1 depicts the frequency distribution for the variable Homtol, which measures tolerance toward homosexuality. Although the values of the Homtol scale could range from a minimum of 5 to a maximum of 25, notice that there were no respondents who scored a 5, or even a 6. Two respondents ended up with the lowest score of 7. Only one respondent scored a 25 (a very tolerant person indeed). This distribution gives us a range of eighteen values on our scale.

The scale you create for your class project may have less variation than that of the Tolerance Toward Homosexuality variable in our example. This, again, is a place where a researcher must make a judgment call as to whether there is enough variation in the scale to warrant further analysis. As long as most (let's say 80 percent) of the cases are not clustered within two or three values, meaningful analysis should be possible. The less variation in the scale, of course, the closer it is to being a constant rather than a variable. This is why it is important to check the frequency distribution for good variation.

Collapsing the New Scale

Finally, notice the place in the Cumulative Percent column where approximately 50 percent of the cases fall above and below a particular value. It is important to record

Table 12.1. Frequency Distribution for Homtol: Tolerance Toward Homosexuality.

	Frequency	Percent	Valid Percent	Cumulative Percent
7	2	.8	.8	.8
8	4	1.5	1.5	2.3
9	4	1.5	1.5	3.8
10	15	5.7	5.7	9.5
11	20	7.6	7.6	17.2
12	20	7.6	7.6	24.8
13	15	5.7	5.7	30.5
14	30	11.5	11.5	42.0
15	27	10.3	10.3	52.3
16	49	18.7	18.7	71.0
17	26	9.9	9.9	80.9
18	23	8.8	8.8	89.7
19	6	2.3	2.3	92.0
20	9	3.4	3.4	95.4
21	6	2.3	2.3	97.7
22	5	1.9	1.9	99.6
25	1	.4	.4	100.0
Total	262	100.0	100.0	

this for the purposes of collapsing the scale into two categories for cross-tabulation analysis. For the data in Table 12.1, notice that 52.3 percent of the cases have a value of 15 or less on our scale. Unless a good theoretical reason exists for using another value, creating maximum variability based on the responses received is acceptable.

Now that you have checked for variation and noted the cutoff for maximum variability, use SPSS to collapse the composite variable into two categories. If you need a reminder on how to do this, refer to the section Collapsing Continuous Variables in Chapter Eleven.

Once you have transformed this variable into two categories and double-checked that no errors were committed during the process, sit back for a moment and enjoy the good feelings that come with mastering sophisticated tasks. You now know how to enter, clean, and transform data. Very few people in society know how to handle data in such a way.

Now that the tough stuff is finished, let's get to the real joy of discovery: testing our hypothesis to see if there is support for it in the data we collected.

CREATING CROSS-TABULATION TABLES

There is a diverse array of statistical methods used by sociologists and other social scientists to draw out the most nuanced of patterns in datasets both large and small. Cross-tabulation, the method of analysis used in this assignment, is one of the most basic methods of analysis in looking for relationships between variables. We use it here because (1) it is relatively simple to do and (2) it nicely illustrates the comparative nature of most science in a manner that is straightforward. Once you see the logic in cross-tabulation analysis, you'll be in a better position to decide for yourself whether the method of reasoning in science is generally credible.

The variables you will use in this analysis should now be transformed into new variables with only two attributes or categories. Note that variables can be collapsed into more than two attributes. Only two attributes have been created for each variable in this assignment to illustrate the analytical process without making it overly complicated.

PRODUCING TABLES TO TEST YOUR CLASS HYPOTHESIS

Recall your class hypothesis that you developed together with your instructor. Be sure you are able to identify the independent and dependent variables.

For purposes of illustration, the hypothesis tested here is that sex affects one's religiosity. Specifically, it will be determined whether more women identify themselves as religious than men. Incidentally, the theory or explanation as to why one would expect these two variables (sex and religiosity) to be related in this way is called the Comfort Hypothesis, which was developed by Glock, Ringer, and Babbie (1967). This theory predicts that groups who are less successful in mainstream society are likely to turn to religion to gain a sense of meaning and satisfaction in life. Because women as a group earn less than men on average, one would reasonably expect more women than men to be religious.

With your dataset opened in SPSS, click on Analyze, and then Descriptive Statistics. Choose Crosstabs. The Crosstabs dialog box opens. Notice that all variables are once again listed on the left side of the box. In the center are three boxes into which you can move variable names. The Row box is where your dependent variable must be moved. Click on the variable name for your dependent variable and then the arrow key beside the box labeled Row to move it. Next, highlight the name of your independent variable and move it into the box labeled Column. *Note*: be sure to select the variables that have been collapsed. If you choose the uncollapsed variables, you will end up with crosstab tables that contain many columns or rows. Do *not* move any variable into the box labeled Layer 1 of 1. Your dialog box should look similar to that in Figure 12.5.

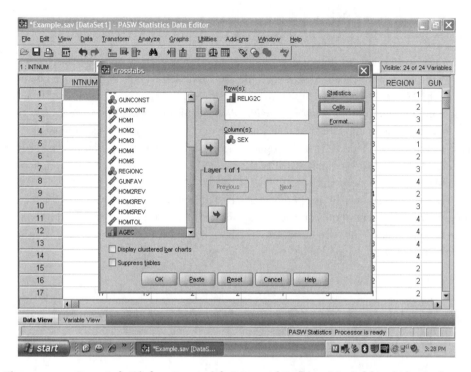

Figure 12.5. Crosstab Dialog Box with Sex and Relig2c Variables Selected.

Next, click on the gray box in the upper-right corner called Cells . . . and another dialog box opens. In the Percentages box, click on the small white box beside Column. A check mark should appear. This tells SPSS to calculate percentages in every cell so that they add up to 100 percent in columns—that is, in the direction of your independent variable. Don't make any other changes to the dialog box. It should look similar to that in Figure 12.6, except that your variable names will be in place of those used in this example.

Click Continue to close the box, and then OK to execute the command.

SPSS quickly computes the cross-tabulation table and places it in the output file, which opens automatically on your screen. Scroll down to the end of the output file to find the newly created crosstab table. If you've made the request correctly, you should see a table in the output file structured similarly to that in Table 12.2.

Table 12.2 shows a cross-tabulation table for the hypothesis stated earlier: that sex affects religiosity. Notice the independent variable is on the top of the table, and its two attributes, male and female, are represented in two columns. The dependent variable is expressed in the rows of the table, with its two attributes of more religious and less religious represented in two rows. Note as well that, along with raw numbers of people interviewed, percentages are calculated and included in each cell. These should add up to 100 percent in the columns. They will *not,* however, add up to 100 percent in the rows.

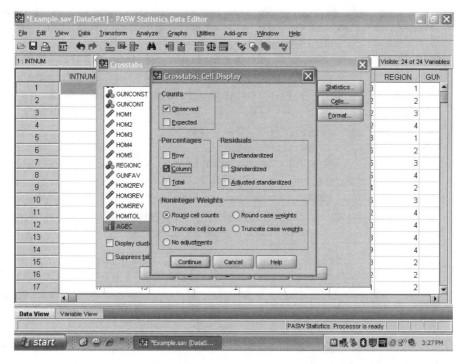

Figure 12.6. Column Selected in Crosstabs: Cell Display Dialog Box.

Table 12.2. Cross-Tabulation of Sex and Religiosity.

			Sex		
			1 Male	2 Female	Total
Relig2c (Religiosity Collapsed)	1 more religious	Count	41	68	109
		% within Sex	38.3%	43.9%	41.6%
	2 less religious	Count	66	87	153
		% within Sex	61.7%	56.1%	58.4%
	Total	Count	107	155	262
		% within Sex	100.0%	100.0%	100.0%

If your table does not have the independent variable on the top and dependent variable on the side, if one of the variables has more than two attributes listed, or if the percentages do not total 100 percent added down each column, you will need to repeat the steps above to create a correct table. Once you are sure that your table contains the right information, proceed to the next chapter for instructions on how to interpret the table.

SUMMARY

Measuring multidimensional concepts often involves combining indicators to create a composite measure. Indices and scales are two composite measures used frequently in social science research. This chapter has reviewed the steps necessary for creating simple indices and scales. Be aware that much more is involved in testing the reliability and validity of an index or scale before it is used in a "real" research project. A research methods textbook would familiarize you with these important steps.

Social scientists often construct cross-tabulation tables before attempting more complex analyses of data. Cross-tabulation analysis has been simplified for you in this project by collapsing variables into only two categories. Much information is lost in collapsing variables; however, the strongest relationships between two variables become more apparent. Now that you have created a table that presents your data intelligibly, you're ready to make interpretations.

REVIEW QUESTIONS

1. What is a composite measure? How are indices and scales related to composite measures?
2. How does an index differ from a scale?
3. What SPSS procedure was used in this chapter to create an index? What SPSS procedure was used to create a scale? What is the difference in how the two procedures create their end product?
4. Describe a correctly formatted cross-tabulation table. Which variable should be at the top of the table? the side? How should percentages be displayed in the table? For this assignment, how many attributes of each variable should be present?

KEY TERMS

Composite variable A variable comprising more than one indicator of a concept.

Index A series of several questions or indicators of a particular variable that are given equal weight when added to create a composite.

Reverse coded Reversing the scores on a particular scale item so that the values increase in the same manner as other indicators in the same scale.

Scale A series of several questions or indicators that may be given different weights, added to create a composite variable.

13

Interpreting Your Results

Cross-Tabulation Tables

LEARNING OBJECTIVES

- Learn how to interpret the results of a cross-tabulation table and observe if the data collected support your class hypothesis.
- Understand the process of introducing a third variable into the analysis and controlling its effects through table elaboration.
- Develop hypotheses as to how the control variable will affect the original relationship, and test the hypotheses using collected data.

At this point you have in your possession a cross-tabulation table depicting the relationship between your independent and dependent variables. Do the data in the table support your hypothesis? We review two important ways to tell: eyeballing the data, and calculating and interpreting an epsilon.

READING A CROSS-TABULATION TABLE

EYEBALLING THE DATA

Examine the data in Table 12.2 in the last chapter. The hypothesis tested in that table was that more women than men would report a high level of religiosity. Is this hypothesis supported? The way to tell is to compare the relative size of the *percentages* in a given *row*. Raw numbers should *not* be used; they cannot be meaningfully compared because the number of people in each column is not equivalent. For example, notice that 41 men identified themselves as being more religious, compared to 68 women who indicated the same. On the basis of these numbers, it would be tempting to conclude that far more women than men are religious. Notice, however, that the group sizes differ. The total at the bottom of the column for men indicates that 107 men were interviewed—a smaller total than the 155 women. How can you compare 41 out of 107 to 68 out of 155?

The answer, of course, is to calculate and compare percentages rather than raw numbers. Percentages essentially make the two groups the same size by expressing the proportion as a percentage out of 100. Examining the first row in the table, we find that 38.3 percent of men were identified as more religious as compared to 43.9 percent of women. Thus a greater proportion of women than men are indeed more religious, but the difference is not nearly as dramatic as if we had erroneously compared the raw numbers. This is why comparing percentages is the proper way to make sense of the table. In eyeballing the data in the table, we note that 43.9 percent of women and 38.3 percent of men were more religious. Conversely, 56.1 percent of women and 61.7 percent of men were less religious. Because 43.9 is larger than 38.3, we tentatively conclude that there is support for our hypothesis that more women than men are religious.

DESCRIBING GROUP-LEVEL TRENDS

Two important points need to be made here regarding the language used to describe results. First, although there is support for the hypothesis that more women than men are religious, it would be technically incorrect to state that women are more religious than men. Clearly, there are many men who are religious and many women who are not. The statement is a broad stereotype that does not acknowledge the diversity of responses with each sex; it leads people to think in overgeneralized, stereotypical terms. When describing your results, then, be sure to use qualifying language that acknowledges the diversity of responses while noting the trend in the data at the same time. The statement "more women than men are religious" accurately acknowledges the variety of responses.

Second, because these results deal with group-level data, it is important to avoid the temptation to describe results in individualistic terms. Suggesting that "on the basis of these data, a woman is more religious than a man" makes a stereotyping error similar to the issue just described. It implies that every individual woman is going to be more religious than every individual man—something known to be untrue. The percentages in the table describe *group*-level patterns, which may or may not be true for specific individuals.

Assuming that group-level patterns are true for all individuals is an error known as the **ecological fallacy**. Grouped data can be used to describe only group-level patterns. This takes some practice if you are used to thinking about individuals rather than groups, but using the correct language to describe the results will help you become a better student of human behavior. Be sure that your language reflects this when you describe your results in the paper for your class.

CALCULATING EPSILON

There is beauty, simplicity, and magic inherent in a single number known as a *statistic*. Imagine a dataset containing the views of hundreds, thousands, even millions of people. How is a human mind to comprehend all the complexity contained therein? How is it possible to compare, say, one group of thousands with another group? Though your mind can do some amazing things, it has its limits. Increasingly, human beings are harnessing technology by way of computers to assist in sifting through mountains of information.

Before computers, some humans created techniques for information simplification. As far as social science is concerned, this involves coming to terms with the complexity in a population and agreeing on a summary number or statistic that represents a meaningful characteristic of the overall population. Some of the most popular statistics—such as the mean, median, and mode—are called **measures of central tendency**. They give an overall estimate of the characteristic of the group. Calculating the mean age of a population, for example, identifies the average age for that group. On the one hand, huge amounts of information are lost in calculating summary statistics. On the other, statistics allow humans, with their finite minds, to grasp major group characteristics and make meaningful comparisons between groups. In short, statistics are your *friends*, and the process of data simplification and calculating statistics is your path to understanding. It's all about making reality comprehensible.

Eyeballing the data is a quick and easy way to see if a hypothesis is supported, but it is not precise enough for measuring the strength of association between two variables. Statistics offer us this level of precision and have the additional advantage of allowing relative comparisons to be made regarding the strength of relationships between variables. Epsilon is a simple statistic that can be used to estimate the strength of relationship between two variables. It is one of the most elementary statistics used in cross-tabulation analysis. If you can subtract one number from another, you can calculate an epsilon.

Epsilon is best interpreted when applied to 2×2 tables (containing two columns and two rows), but it can be used for 2×3, 3×2, and 3×3 tables *if* there appears to be a pattern in the data—that is, if percentages are highest in the upper-left and lower-right corners of the table or highest in the upper-right and lower-left corners.

To calculate epsilon in a 2×2 table, simply subtract the second *percentage* in a row from the first *percentage* in a row, or $\text{Cell}_a - \text{Cell}_b$ as depicted in Table 13.1.

Note that epsilon is calculated using the table *percentages* rather than the raw scores. Note also that epsilon is calculated on only *one* row. This is because in a 2×2 table $\text{Cell}_c - \text{Cell}_d$ results in the same value (except that the $+$ or $-$ sign changes). No new information is therefore gained by calculating epsilon on both rows of the table; one is sufficient. On a table larger than 2×2, epsilon is calculated by subtracting the value in the last cell in the first row from the value in the first cell in the first row.

Table 13.1. Structure of a Bivariate Cross-Tabulation Table.

	First Attribute of Independent Variable	Second Attribute of Independent Variable	Totals
First attribute of dependent variable	Cell_a	Cell_b	
Second attribute of dependent variable	Cell_c	Cell_d	
Totals			

Consider the data presented in Table 13.2, which test the hypothesis that the grade point averages (GPA) of women will be higher than those of men. Substituting the values in the table into the equation epsilon = $cell_a$ − $cell_b$,

$$38.6\% - 64.9\% = -26.3\%$$

Interpreting Epsilon

Epsilon may be interpreted as a measure of the strength of association between the independent and dependent variables. On a 2 × 2 table, epsilon can have a minimum value of zero, indicating no relationship at all between the variables, and a maximum value of ±100, indicating a perfect relationship between the independent and dependent variable.* The larger the epsilon, the stronger the relationship between two variables.

The sign (+ or −) is ignored in interpreting any specific measure of epsilon. This is because the sign is obviously a function of which attribute of the independent variable is listed first in the table, which is an arbitrary choice. In the example here, females could just as easily have been listed in the first column rather than males. It is important to always record the sign, however, especially in controlling for a third variable. The importance of this will become more apparent later in the chapter. If epsilon is a negative value in the original table but a positive value in one or both of the partial tables (created when controlling for a third variable), the researcher knows that the relationship has reversed itself from the original table. This is why it is important to always record the + or − sign along with the epsilon statistic.

Rules of Thumb in Interpreting Epsilon

Standards for measuring the magnitude of the effect of one variable on another in the social sciences are generally not as strict as they are in medical studies. This is because many factors

Table 13.2. Cross-Tabulation of Sex and Grade Point Average.

	Male	Female	Totals
High GPA	39 (38.6%)	74 (64.9%)	113 (52.6%)
Low GPA	62 (61.4%)	40 (35.1%)	102 (47.4%)
Totals	101 (100%)	114 (100%)	215 (100%)

*Given certain marginal distributions, the minimum and maximum values for epsilon may be slightly greater than 0 and less than ± 100 respectively, even on 2 × 2 tables (see Loether and McTavish, 1980). It is used here because its calculation is intuitive to most students otherwise unfamiliar with statistical analysis. Your instructor may substitute other nonparametric measures of association with a PRE interpretation.

can potentially cause a change in the dependent variable. In this example, sex is only one of a number of factors that influence one's GPA. Therefore if some change is noted in the dependent variable when comparing the attributes of only *one* independent variable, it is an indication that the independent variable is important in explaining some of the variation in the dependent variable. For our purposes, three categories are suggested for interpreting epsilon:

0 to 10 = weak relationship or none between the independent and dependent variables
11 to 20 = moderate relationship between the independent and dependent variables
21 or higher = strong relationship between the independent and dependent variables

APPLICATION TO SEX AND RELIGIOSITY

This information on how to calculate and interpret an epsilon can now be applied to the relationship between sex and religiosity presented in the last chapter. It is reproduced for you in Table 13.3 for convenience. Recall that the hypothesis tested was that women would be more religious than men. Subtracting the percentage in cell$_b$ from the percentage in cell$_a$ in Table 13.3 we see that $38.3 - 43.9 = -5.6$. Using the guidelines above to interpret epsilon, we note that the relationship between sex and religiosity is *weak*.

The results could be described this way:

Table 13.3 shows that 38.3 percent of males and 43.9 percent of females were more religious. Similarly, 56.1 percent of women and 61.7 percent of men were less religious. An epsilon of -5.6 percent ($38.3 - 43.9$) was calculated, indicating a weak relationship between the two variables.

Table 13.3. Cross-Tabulation of Sex and Religiosity.

			Sex		
			1 Male	2 Female	Total
Relig2c (Religiosity collapsed)	1 more religious	Count	41	68	109
		% within Sex	38.3%	43.9%	41.6%
	2 less religious	Count	66	87	153
		% within Sex	61.7%	56.1%	58.4%
	Total	Count	107	155	262
		% within Sex	100.0%	100.0%	100.0%

FALSIFICATION

In science, there is a real possibility that the data collected will *not* supply evidence supporting our hypothesis. If your epsilon is close to zero, the data give little evidence of a relationship between your independent and dependent variables. Ultimately, this means that the theory you used to explain the possible relationship between your variables is not supported.

It is also possible that the data you collected show evidence that the relationship is in the opposite direction from what you hypothesized. In this case, the epsilon may be fairly large but the size of the percentages in the cells are opposite of what was anticipated. In the earlier example, this would mean that more men were found to be religious than women, contrary to what was hypothesized.

How does a researcher deal with results such as these? There are two possibilities. The first is to accept the data as they are and conclude that, at least as far as the collected data are concerned, there is no support for the hypothesis. This can be difficult at times because we all hold beliefs we regard as being true. The nature of doing science, however, is such that one has to be mentally prepared for the possibility of a favorite theory or hypothesis not being supported and instead falsified.

Unlike accepting the results at face value, a second possible response to contradictory data is to conclude that a *methodological* error was committed. This can be a legitimate reaction to data of this type, especially if there is reason to suspect the study wasn't carried out as carefully as it could have been or if the results collected are different from those of other studies consulted in the review of literature. Scientists are human, though, and there are times when subjective bias influences how the results are interpreted. Rather than conclude that our favorite beliefs are wrong, we may be tempted to conclude we did something wrong in the experiment.

You may recall an earlier mention of androcentric bias (in Chapter Six). In *The Mismeasure of Woman*, Tavris (1992) notes that hundreds of studies conducted by scientists have tested for differences between men and women and failed to find evidence for what they were examining. Rather than concluding there are no differences between men and women, many of the scientists conclude they must have done something wrong methodologically. It is not easy to admit that our favorite beliefs may be incorrect.

Ultimately, the way to sort this out is through more testing and peer review. As more studies are done on the same hypothesis, a wealth of findings are compiled into a body of empirical literature. Data collected in most of the studies usually lead authors to similar conclusions. Therefore, comparing one's study to what most others have found on the topic is one way to test whether the results are typical or unusual. Results different from those in most other studies are often assumed to be the result of a methodological error.

Peer review is a second method of testing results. As other scientists read over a description of someone's research, they are in a better position to point out potential flaws in the thinking of a particular scientist who might try to interpret the data a little more in favor of a favorite theory. Other scientists routinely point out these logical flaws and help to improve how the results are interpreted.

CONTROLLING FOR A THIRD VARIABLE

At this point you've had an opportunity to test your hypothesis against the data you collected. Your hypothesis involved only *two* variables. During the process, you may have thought, "Testing two variables is all well and good, but there are many other possible variables that we haven't even considered that could influence this relationship as well." If you've thought something similar, you have a good scientific mind and you've anticipated some of what we will do in this section.

Science, a way of coming to know things through the scientific method, is an ongoing and growing process. Conclusions reached in a field of knowledge are always open for reexamination and retesting, instead of coming to a definitive conclusion and never considering the information again. Scientific knowledge grows through theory development, testing of those ideas, reconsidering the theory in light of the findings, perhaps revising the theory, and moving on to test new or revised ideas. In this way, what is known by human beings continues to grow, and we can accomplish what earlier generations didn't think was possible. The last thing to accomplish in this class project, then, is to examine the results, and then form and test a new hypothesis.

FROM THEORIZING TO TESTING AND BACK TO THEORIZING

Consider the hypothesis tested in the last chapter. It was hypothesized that more women would be religious than men because of the comfort hypothesis (groups of people who are generally less successful in society are more likely to turn to religion for satisfaction and meaning than those who are more successful). In testing this hypothesis, weak evidence was found to support it. On reflection, then, it is important to acknowledge that the data contain little evidence that sex is a meaningful predictor of religiosity.

However, consider the population on which this hypothesis was tested. The comfort hypothesis might be more applicable to people who have been in the workforce for some time and have realized greater or lesser success, rather than college students. The data for Table 13.3 came only from college students, where one might expect the relationship between sex and religiosity to be weak. College students have yet to establish themselves in their careers and either realize or fail to realize their dreams. Women today make up more than 50 percent of college students and are very successful as undergraduates.

Using the same data on college students, then, one can ask if anything else might influence this relationship. If the reasoning about the comfort hypothesis is correct, one would expect the relationship between sex and religiosity to be stronger for older college students (especially nontraditional students, those who have spent some time in the workforce) than it would be for younger, more traditional college students who entered college soon after high school. This is because older women would presumably have experienced less success in the workforce than men and have then turned to religion for satisfaction and meaning. This would not necessarily be the case for younger women, however, who would still be more optimistic that they will achieve a level of success comparable to their male counterparts.

Does this line of reasoning make sense to you? Reflecting on the findings of a study, in light of what it says about a theory or hypothesis, and then revising or elaborating the theory is an important part of the ongoing nature of science. The previous paragraph illustrates how a researcher might reflect on the results of a study and derive a new hypothesis to be tested as a result. Age was identified as a variable that might affect the original relationship. It would be interesting to see how age influences the *relationship* between sex and religiosity.

You can do the same kind of thinking with the variables you have been using in your class project. In light of the results you've examined with your class data, is there another variable you think might affect the relationship between your class's independent and dependent variables? Notice that you are *not* being asked to identify another variable that would affect your dependent variable or your independent variable *alone*, but rather a variable that affects the *relationship* between them. This kind of variable is typically referred to as a **control variable**.

Put another way, think of a sociological variable and divide it in your head into two attributes, such as education (high and low) and social class (more affluent, less affluent). Now ask yourself, "Would I expect the strength of the relationship between our independent and dependent variables to be the same for both attributes, or different?" In this example, it was hypothesized that the relationship between sex and religiosity would be stronger for older people but weaker for younger people. Put another way, you are really attempting to predict the value of epsilon of a cross-tabulation table containing your independent and dependent variables, but containing only one attribute of the control variable you identified.

Table Elaboration

Let's use the example of sex and religiosity to illustrate this. It was hypothesized that the control variable Age would affect the relationship between sex and religiosity in specific ways. An epsilon of -5.6 was calculated on the original table. To test whether the control variable has any effect on the original relationship, SPSS will be used to create two separate tables. One depicts the relationship between sex and religiosity, but for younger people only. The second table also depicts the relationship between sex and religiosity, but for older people alone.

The process of controlling for a third variable in this manner is called **table elaboration**. The original table containing only the independent and dependent variables is called the **zero-order table**, while the two new tables including attributes of the control variable are called the **partial-order tables** or the **partials**.

The effect of a control variable can be tested through table elaboration because of its inherent logic. If the control variable has no effect on the original relationship, the epsilons in both partial tables will be close or equal to the epsilon in the zero-order table. The greater the difference between an epsilon in one or both of the partial-order tables and the epsilon in the zero-order table, the greater the effect of the control variable on the original relationship.

Table 13.4 shows how two partial-order cross-tabulation tables are depicted in SPSS. No data have been entered in this table so you can take a moment to consider how the data are arranged before examining the results. Notice the independent variable, Sex, is at the top of the table. On the left the two attributes of the dependent variable are included twice, once for older people and the second time for younger people. Arranging tables in this way is essentially the same as placing one bivariate table on top of another, facilitating comparisons. The top table includes the original hypothesis, but only for older people. The bottom table also displays information testing the original hypothesis, but only for younger people.

Table 13.4. Empty Cross-Tabulation Table for Sex and Religiosity, Controlling for Age.

Agec				Sex		
---	---	---	---	1 Male	2 Female	Total
1 older (21–42)	Relig2c (Religiosity Collapsed)	1 more religious	Count % within Sex			
		2 less religious	Count % within Sex			
		Total	Count % within Sex			
2 younger (17–20)	Relig2c (Religiosity Collapsed)	1 more religious	Count % within Sex			
		2 less religious	Count % within Sex			
		Total	Count % within Sex			

Comparing the percentage values across rows again tests for the presence of a relationship between the independent and dependent variables. For Table 13.4, we will compare the percentages in two rows rather than one. Comparing the percentages across each of the "more religious" rows in the table gives us an idea of the magnitude or strength of the relationship for each attribute of the control variable. Note too that an epsilon will be calculated in each "more religious" row. This will tell us exactly how strongly the independent and dependent variables are associated for each attribute of age.

Developing and Recording Hypotheses for Partial-Order Tables

Do you expect any differences in the epsilons compared to what was calculated in the original relationship? We made predictions earlier for what would happen in each of the partial-order tables. That is, the strength of the relationship between the independent and dependent variables (as measured by epsilon) would be stronger for older people but weaker for younger people. Do you hypothesize the same thing, or does your reasoning lead you to making another hypothesis?

Before examining the data, take a moment to create a hypothesis for each of the tables included in Table 13.4. That is, do you think the relationship between sex and religiosity would be any different from that in Table 13.3 if we included only "older" college students (age 21 and over) in it? Is there anything inherently different about the way sex and religiosity interact among older people that would cause you to suggest the relationship changes? What about for younger people? Would you expect a different relationship between sex and religiosity for them? If you really cannot think why the results would be any different from those in Table 13.3, write down that you expect no real change in the relationship. In other words, you believe age will have no effect on the relationship between sex and religiosity.

Do record your guesses. The human mind is a wonderful instrument, but it is not perfect. If a prediction is not made before examining the data, one's mind will quickly make sense of the data *after* it is viewed. This makes it feel as though one would have made the correct guess anyway. But examining data contradicting one's hypothesis is a wonderful teachable moment, helping one question assumptions and form better theories that stand up to empirical scrutiny. Don't cheat yourself; write down your guesses and then allow the data to inform your thinking. Remember, falsification is a critical way in which scientific inquiry transcends ordinary human inquiry.

ANALYZING PARTIAL-ORDER TABLES

With your written hypotheses in hand, examine the data in Table 13.5. As before, the two ways to tell if either of your hypotheses is correct are to first eyeball the data and then calculate an epsilon.

Table 13.5. Cross-Tabulation of Sex and Religiosity, Controlling for Age.

Agec				Sex		
				1 Male	2 Female	Total
1 older (21–42)	Relig2c (Religiosity Collapsed)	1 more religious	Count	16	37	53
			% within Sex	32.0%	51.4%	43.4%
		2 less religious	Count	34	35	69
			% within Sex	68.0%	48.6%	56.6%
		Total	Count	50	72	122
			% within Sex	100.0%	100.0%	100.0%
2 younger (17–20)	Relig2c (Religiosity Collapsed)	1 more religious	Count	25	31	56
			% within Sex	43.9%	37.3%	40.0%
		2 less religious	Count	32	52	84
			% within Sex	56.1%	62.7%	60.0%
		Total	Count	57	83	140
			% within Sex	100.0%	100.0%	100.0%

The Partial-Order Table for Older Students

Let's first examine the data for the older age group, presented in Table 13.5. It was earlier hypothesized that the difference in religiosity between men and women would be even larger than the original relationship in Table 13.3, because one would expect more women than men to turn to religion after being denied success in the workforce. As a group, fewer men would exhibit a sense of religiosity because they experience more success in the workforce.

Comparing the percentages across the More Religious row in the table for the older age group, it is obvious this hypothesis is supported. Thirty-two percent of males were identified as being more religious, compared to 51.4 percent of females.

This relationship appears to be stronger than the −5.6 epsilon calculated for Table 13.3, but an epsilon must be calculated to measure this precisely. Accordingly, epsilon equals cell_a minus cell_b, or 32.0 −51.4 = −19.4. This certainly confirms the hypothesis that the relationship between sex and religiosity is *stronger* for older people, because −19.4 is greater than the epsilon of −5.6 (remember that the absolute value of epsilon is considered). An epsilon of −19.4 indicates a moderate to moderately strong relationship between the two variables, quite a change from Table 13.3. It appears, then, that sex is indeed an important predictor of religiosity *for older people.*

Recall the absolute value of epsilon is what is actually measured. As a result, the closer epsilon is to ± 100, the stronger the relationship. However, the plus or minus sign is always recorded so that the direction of the relationship is indicated and so that epsilons between tables can be compared. A change in sign in epsilon from one table to another indicates a change in the direction of the relationship. A relationship where the largest percentage is in cell$_a$ will have a positive epsilon, whereas a relationship where the largest percentage is in cell$_b$ will have a negative epsilon.

The Partial-Order Table for Younger Students

Let's examine the data for younger people, displayed in the bottom half of Table 13.5. What do you observe in eyeballing the data? You should be comparing the two percentages for men and women in the row for More Religious people. It is apparent from the table that 43.9 percent of younger men and 37.3 percent of younger women identify themselves as more religious. Without calculating an epsilon just yet, one can quickly surmise that the difference between these two percentages is roughly 6 percent, which is pretty close to the epsilon in Table 13.3.

However, these results are different from our original results in an important way: the relationship is reversed. Calculating an epsilon makes this more apparent. Subtracting cell$_b$ from cell$_a$, or 43.9 − 37.3, we get an epsilon of + 6.6 as the result. Although this number is not that different from the epsilon of −5.6 in the zero-order table, notice that the sign is reversed. *This means that, for younger people, more men than women identify themselves as being religious.*

Despite this interesting finding, it is also important to note that the strength of the relationship, as measured by an epsilon of + 6.6, is still weak. Reflecting on the hypothesis for this table, we find that it appears the data do not support the idea of the difference in religiosity between men and women being smaller than the epsilon for the zero-order table. This is because the absolute value of epsilon, 6.6, is larger than the 5.6 realized in the original relationship.

CONSIDERING THE IMPACT OF THE CONTROL VARIABLE

Once this descriptive analysis has been performed, sit back for a moment to reflect on the overall impact that age has on the relationship between sex and religiosity. The data clearly demonstrated that, for the older people in the dataset, sex is an important predictor of religiosity. The proportion of older women who are religious is larger than for older men. For younger people, however, the relationship is not so strong and, according to these data, not as straightforward as one would imagine. A greater proportion of younger men than women indicated being religious, though there was a relatively small difference.

Our theory, the comfort hypothesis, did anticipate the differences between older men and women, but it cannot explain the differences between younger men and women. Because the differences are so small, it could easily be the case that these results were realized by chance. On the other hand, one might consider how to otherwise explain these interesting but subtle differences. Could it be that younger men are slightly more spiritual or idealistic than younger women? Conversely, is it possible that the pressure on young women to prove themselves might lead more of them to be less concerned with spirituality than is the case with young men? Either is a plausible explanation. Can you think of any other explanations for these results?

It is important to note here that developing potential explanations after the data have been gathered is a process known as **ex post facto hypothesizing**. This means, essentially, guessing after the fact. We have no evidence to support whatever explanation we eventually adopt for why a larger percentage of younger men are religious than younger women. It is merely a guess or informed interpretation. It is not science, in that our ideas have not been empirically tested. To test our newly developed explanation, another study would have to be designed in a way that could falsify the idea. This nicely illustrates the process of scientific thinking: theorizing, testing, revising, developing new theories, and testing once again.

CONTROLLING FOR A THIRD VARIABLE USING SPSS

You may skip this section if your instructor has supplied cross-tab tables for you to control for a third variable. If she or he wants you to produce tables on your own, you'll want to pay careful attention to the directions in this section.

By now, you should be familiar with the logic of controlling for a third variable. By examining a relationship in two attributes of the control variable, one can discern if the third variable has any mediating effect on the original relationship. It is your turn to produce your own partial-order tables and analyze the results.

STEP ONE: COLLAPSING THE CONTROL VARIABLE INTO TWO ATTRIBUTES

Your instructor will likely identify for you the control variable that should be used for analysis by your class. If your control variable has more than two attributes, it will be necessary to first collapse the variable into two attributes before attempting your analyses. Refer to Chapter Eleven if you need to refresh your memory on how to collapse a variable into two categories.

STEP TWO: PRODUCING CROSS-TAB TABLES

With your dataset open in SPSS, click on Analyze from the menus along the top of the screen. Choose Descriptive Statistics, then Crosstabs to open the cross-tab dialog box. Your dependent and independent variables may already be listed in the row and column boxes respectively. If other variable names are listed in these boxes, remove them by highlighting them and then clicking on the reverse arrow to move them back to the large list of variables.

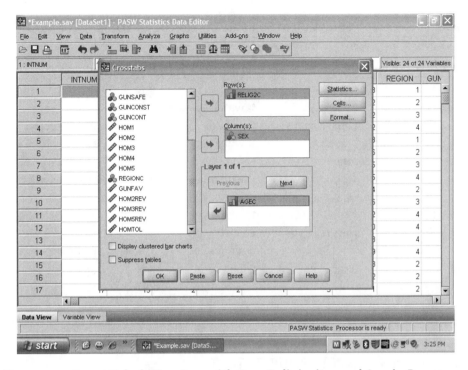

Figure 13.1. Cross-Tabulation Box with Sex, Religiosity, and Age in Boxes.

Choose the name of your collapsed dependent variable from the list on the left-hand side of the box and move it to the box labeled Row(s) variable. It is important to identify your dependent variable as the row variable.

Place the name of your collapsed independent variable in the box labeled Column(s) in the same manner. Finally, move the name of your collapsed control variable to the box labeled Layer 1 of 1. Each of the three boxes in this dialogue box should now have one variable listed in it, as in Figure 13.1. *Before* you click on OK, click on the Cells button to open another dialog box. Make sure that a check mark appears beside the Column label in the Percentages box. Click on Continue once this is completed, and then OK in the main dialog box.

Voila! SPSS produces the table for you and automatically opens the output file so you can view it. If you've followed the instructions carefully, your output should look like that shown in Table 13.6. That is, two tables, each with your independent variable on top and dependent variable on the side, should be stacked on top of one another. One of the tables should present the analysis of the first attribute of your control variable, while the second table should present the analysis of the second control variable attribute. If your table doesn't look like Table 13.6, close the output file, repeat the steps, and correct any errors you may have made in requesting the output.

Table 13.6. Cross-Tabulation of Sex and Religiosity, Controlling for Age.

Agec (Age Collapsed)				Sex		
				1 Male	2 Female	Total
1	Relig2c (Religiosity Collapsed)	1 more religious	Count	16	37	53
			% within Sex	32.0%	51.4%	43.4%
		2 less religious	Count	34	35	69
			% within Sex	68.0%	48.6%	56.6%
		Total	Count	50	72	122
			% within Sex	100.0%	100.0%	100.0%
2	Relig2c (Religiosity Collapsed)	1 more religious	Count	25	31	56
			% within Sex	43.9%	37.3%	40.0%
		2 less religious	Count	32	52	84
			% within Sex	56.1%	62.7%	60.0%
		Total	Count	57	83	140
			% within Sex	100.0%	100.0%	100.0%

STEP THREE: INTERPRET YOUR OUTPUT

For assistance in making sense of the tables you've created while controlling for a third variable, refer to the discussion earlier in this chapter. Your analysis involves eyeballing the data in each of the new tables and comparing them—*not* to each other as much as to the table produced earlier depicting the *original* relationship between your independent and dependent variables. You'll want to know whether the strength of the relationship in each of the two partial-order tables changed from that in the original table.

The best way to make this comparison is by using the epsilon statistic, which you will need to calculate for each table. If the control variable is unimportant, the epsilon for each of the partial-order tables will be very close to the epsilon in your zero-order table. The greater the difference in epsilon in either or both of the partial-order tables, the more important the control variable is in qualifying the relationship between your independent and dependent variables.

SUMMARY

Correctly interpreting cross-tabulation results is an acquired skill. It may come more easily to some than to others, but learning to eyeball the data, calculate and interpret an epsilon, and draw a conclusion regarding a hypothesis is now something you are able to do. There is no shame in creating a hypothesis not supported by collected data, because *all* information is valuable in and of itself. Noting a lack of support for certain hypotheses leads us to consider other plausible relations between concepts that might better fit reality. Of course, all this depends ultimately on the validity and reliability of the data.

The logic and process of controlling for a third variable puts us even closer to modeling causal processes in the world, by developing complex theories that better match the complex social world in which we exist. This analysis is somewhat limited by the fact that variables were collapsed into only two categories. Even so, analyses of this sort can be revealing.

Perhaps your analysis of the data you and your classmates collected elicited some interesting results. Because you collected the data and know what kinds of people were interviewed to gather this information, you are in a unique position to decide for yourself whether or not these results are trustworthy. In scientific terms the more valid and reliable the data, the more trustworthy the results.

Statistics such as percentages and epsilons are used to add precision to analyses. Social scientists understand that statistics are at best an approximate indicator of whatever it is one is attempting to measure. Creating standardized yet approximate measures of human behavior, though, is often better than simply relying on one's own intuition or impressions of group trends. Personal impressions can be less accurate than percentages or statistics. This point is no doubt illustrated for you if there is a difference between the impressions you derived about your hypothesis after you performed the interviews and saw the overall results for the class. These are two different ways of knowing. Is one better than the other? You can now see how information collected from an entire group is sometimes different from the informal impressions we hold.

This chapter concludes the statistical analysis needed to complete this assignment. Take a moment to congratulate yourself for carefully proceeding through this part of the project and being able to produce tables and analyze statistical results. There are few people in the world who are comfortable with or have enough training to develop these kinds of skills. You are the better for it, since you'll no doubt apply this knowledge in other classes. It could even help you become a better, more logical thinker in the long run. That's worth something, yes?

REVIEW QUESTIONS

1. What two methods are used in cross-tabulation to determine if there is a relationship between two variables?
2. How is the epsilon statistic interpreted?
3. What is the difference between zero-order tables and partial-order tables?
4. How can a researcher tell if a control variable has an effect on the relationship between independent and dependent variables?

KEY TERMS

Control variable A third variable examined to see how its presence influences the relationship between the independent and dependent variables.

Ecological fallacy Assuming that patterns observed at the group level are also true at the individual level.

Ex post facto hypothesizing Guessing after the fact, or creating one or more plausible explanations of why two variables are correlated.

Measures of central tendency Statistics giving an overall measure of a group characteristic, such as the mean, median, and mode.

Partial-order tables Tables controlling for a third variable, produced during table elaboration. Called **partials** for short.

Table elaboration The process of controlling for variables other than the independent and dependent variables through examination of cross-tabulation tables derived from the original relationship.

Zero-order table A cross-tabulation table depicting the interrelation of independent and dependent variables.

14

Writing Up Your Assignment

LEARNING OBJECTIVES

- Understand why excellence in this project is a goal worth pursuing.
- Think through the questions posed to help you articulate your understanding of the process of social science.
- Familiarize yourself with formatting expectations at the undergraduate level.
- Contextualize the knowledge gained in this class project in the human pursuit of creating a better world.

With your data analysis complete, you're now in a position to demonstrate what you have learned through the project. To conclude this assignment, you will answer questions to indicate your grasp of the logic and process of social science as described in this book. The goal of this project has been to give you some personal experience in conducting social scientific research and the joy that can be experienced through discovering something new. You created a hypothesis and collected and interpreted data in an effort to test the validity of your hypothesis. By now your understanding of the research process should be greater than what it was before you started this project. You've learned how to interpret cross-tab tables and control for a third variable. Now is your chance to demonstrate what you've learned in your write-up.

Logic, clarity, precision, and brevity are the hallmarks of good scientific writing. This chapter gives you an opportunity to hone these skills. Describing your experiences is not difficult, but demands your focus. *Every sentence* is important in this assignment. Your task is to communicate to the reader that, without any doubt, you know exactly what you are talking about. As you write, assume that the reader has had no prior exposure to the assignment or course material. In other words, conceive of an audience for your paper that consists of other students rather than your instructor. This way you'll be more careful in describing your ideas than if you were writing for someone teaching this course.

DOING IT RIGHT THE FIRST TIME

If you are a typical college student, there are no doubt other things in your life distracting you from doing an excellent job on this assignment. First-year college students are particularly prone to distraction because they are dealing with other issues, such as homesickness, setting boundaries for their own behavior, and struggling to stay on top of increased responsibilities. As a result, assignments are sometimes produced at the last minute, without paying attention to detail and hoping for the best. Given the work you've done to this point, it would be disappointing to get a failing grade on an important project such as this one.

There is good reason to dedicate some serious time and effort to your write-up. Part of the reason many instructors engage in teaching is because it is exciting to be a part of the process that helps people learn and discover new things. When a student does poorly, an instructor may feel he or she has failed as well. Therefore both students and instructors have a vested interest in seeing you do well. Put forth a good effort and produce an excellent write-up.

Keeping these points in mind should help motivate you to take the time necessary to do an excellent job. There is no make-up assignment if you miss this one. In my own classes, not handing in the assignment results in a failing grade for the course. Check your syllabus to see if your instructor has the same policy. Similarly, don't count on extra credit opportunities to replace a poor grade. Opportunities for extra credit may not exist, or be severely limited in the number of extra points one can earn. This is just like many things in life. Do it right the first time.

Hand the paper in on time. Get it done well ahead of the due date so you can make up any printer problems, software glitches, viruses, or other unforeseen setbacks. School is preparation for real life. In the work world, a customer doesn't care about why you didn't get his project finished on time. You lose the contract, the job, or a paycheck. Get your paper finished ahead of schedule to allow time for any last-minute emergencies, and keep a back-up copy of your paper.

Excellence in both *content* and *presentation* is your goal. This is college; nowhere else will the academic standards be higher to assess your work. Make the effort. Besides being rewarded by way of grades, excellence is its own reward. It raises your self-esteem and opens new opportunities for scholarships and better jobs.

Invite others to give you *feedback* on your paper before turning it in. Your instructor may arrange for feedback from another student on the first due date. Many colleges and universities have writing centers that give additional assistance if asked. See your instructor during office hours to clarify any questions you have as you work on the assignment. A face-to-face dialogue is superior in many ways to other methods of communication. In large classes, it also helps the instructor get to know who you are and impresses him or her that you cared enough about the assignment to seek assistance.

Your assignment simply involves answering several questions about the data collection project in which you have engaged this semester. Pay attention to detail and answer the questions fully but without being overly verbose. Tips on good scientific writing are included later in this chapter. Everything is here to help you do an outstanding job. Your effort will dictate your final grade.

HINTS ON ANSWERING QUESTIONS

The questions you need to address in your paper are presented in Box 14.1. To ensure you have done everything you need to do well, let's review the questions (referring to them as found in the box).

1. THEORIZING

Describe the results of the three empirical studies (more if so instructed) you located while doing your literature review. You'll want to describe the major variables and research question, data collection method, the population and sample, and the major findings. After discussing each article in turn, conclude this section by identifying one or more gaps in knowledge about the subject on which your class research project can shed light.

You should by now be familiar with recognizing the two variables in your class project: your independent and dependent variables. Review the information in Chapter Three if you need to refresh your knowledge about thinking causally, or how to specify how one variable is going to affect the other. This is the place where you will want to record the guess you made at the beginning of the assignment as to how you thought one variable would affect the other. Remember, you do not lose any marks for making a guess that turns out to be unsupported by the data.

Chapter Four also contains information related to theorizing. Recall that a theory is simply an explanation of why it is suspected that two variables are related causally. Your challenge here is to (1) adequately describe the theory and (2) connect the theory such that it provides a logical explanation for the hypothesis adopted by the class. If you need an example of this, refer to the explanation in the last chapter where the comfort hypothesis was used to explain the hypothesized relationship between sex and religiosity. Three major sociological theories are structural functionalist, conflict, and symbolic interactionist theory. Use one to explain the prediction you make for your hypothesis.

2. INTERPRETING DATA

Information relevant to this question can be found in Chapter Thirteen. Describe the numbers in the table that you take as evidence of there being a relationship (or not) between the independent and dependent variables in the way you originally hypothesized. After doing this, calculate an epsilon and interpret it. That is, what does the epsilon tell you about the relationship and its strength? Be very clear.

3. MORE THEORIZING

Be sure you understand the process of controlling for a third variable before attempting to answer this question because it is difficult to fake what you do not know. Chapter Thirteen contains a description of the logic of controlling for a third variable. If you are still unsure after reading it, consult your instructor.

BOX 14.1 THE ASSIGNMENT

Number your answers to the questions below in your paper, but answer in essay style (complete sentences and paragraphs, not point form). Answer each question fully. You will need to consult the SPSS tables to complete this assignment.

1. *Theorizing* Introduce the topic of study, and describe your literature review as instructed in Chapter Two. State the hypothesis you are testing in this research and identify the independent and dependent variables. Be sure to *specify* how you think one variable is going to affect the other. In a paragraph, describe a sociological theory that you feel explains *why* you think the two variables are related. Be sure to include a parenthetical citation with page number(s) as to where you found your description of the theory.

2. *Interpreting data* What can you conclude from the zero-order table showing the cross-tabulated results of your independent and dependent variables? In other words, do the data support or disconfirm your hypothesis? How do you know? Remember: describe the statistics, and calculate and interpret an epsilon.

3. *More theorizing* Identify the *control* variable, and specify how you think it will affect the *original relationship*. In other words, for each attribute of the control variable, do you think the strength of the relationship between the original two variables will increase, decrease, or stay the same? Take a guess for each attribute of the control variable, and give reasons for your estimations.

4. *Interpreting data* What can you conclude from your first partial-order table? Do the data support or disconfirm your guess? How do you know? Remember: describe the statistics, and calculate and interpret an epsilon.

5. *Interpreting data* What can you conclude from your second partial-order table? Do the data support or disconfirm your guess? How do you know? Remember: describe the statistics, and calculate and interpret an epsilon.

6. *Reflecting on method* From your experience of interviewing, (1) do you feel that interviews are a good way to gather information? Explain your answer. (2) What advantages and disadvantages of interview research are described by at least one other author? (3) If you could *not* use the interview method, what other method would you use to study our hypothesis? What would be the advantage of using this other method over interviews? Explain fully.

7. *Reflecting on sampling* From a scientific point of view, are these results generalizable to more than just the people we gathered information from? If yes, what is it about the study that makes these results generalizable to a larger group of people? If not, how could the data have been collected so as to increase the likelihood of representing the views of, say, all students at your educational institution?

Your answer should contain two components. First, include a description of your hypothesis for the first partial-order table. Predict what you think will happen to epsilon compared to the zero-order table, and offer an explanation for your hypothesis. Your explanation here is your theory. For the purposes of this assignment, it is not necessary to connect your explanation to a formal theory as you did in question one.

The second part of your response should include a description of your hypothesis for the second partial-order table. Predict what will happen to epsilon compared to the zero-order table, and offer an explanation for your hypothesis. Be sure to avoid discussing any data other than that found in the zero-order table. Your response to question three should contain a description of your thinking after you saw the results of the zero-order table alone.

Focus your hypotheses and explanations on your independent and dependent variables. You are still looking at differences between categories of the independent variable as you did in the original relationship. The only thing that has changed in the partial-order tables is the group in which the hypothesis is being tested. In the example in the preceding chapter, the hypothesis that sex and religiosity were related was still tested in the partial-order tables. The first partial table tested it on older people. The second partial table tested it on younger people.

4 AND 5. INTERPRETING DATA

The information you need to supply in questions four and five is identical to that provided in question two. The only difference is that you are examining the results of different tables in each question. Do not attempt to take any shortcuts in your answers. Furnish all the information asked of you.

6. REFLECTING ON METHOD

Your response to this question should be organized into at least three paragraphs. First, *your* opinion is needed regarding interviewing as a data collection tool. How valid and reliable do you feel interviewing is? Your opinion is asked for because you now have some training and experience in this data collection method. Explain your answer fully, and feel free to give examples from your experience. It is fine to write in first person here.

Once you have shared your opinion, you can begin a new paragraph in which you will share information about what the author of another book describes as the advantages and disadvantages of interviewing. You may be able to use another text for this class if one has been assigned to you. If you have no other textbook, refer to Chapter Five for information on interviewing. Be sure to include a parenthetical citation.

Finally, in a third paragraph you should reflect on what other data gathering method you personally would use if interviews were not employed. Refer to Chapter Five for ideas. This question is designed to have you think about the advantages and disadvantages inherent in any data gathering method. You are asked for your informed opinion, so share it.

7. REFLECTING ON SAMPLING

In social science, the ability to generalize the findings of a study is based on the sampling method used in the study. You'll find information in your course textbook and this book. Chapter Six describes the kind of sample that allows you to generalize beyond the subjects from whom you gathered information. Decide if a sample was used in this class assignment that allows generalization beyond the people from whom information was collected. Because you will be describing information about sampling that you gathered from another source, be sure to document the source(s) with a parenthetical citation.

FORMATTING YOUR PAPER

In addition to giving thoughtful responses to the questions above, a correctly formatted paper with proper grammar and spelling implies a certain amount of respect for the reader. You care enough about the project and the reader to do all you can to make your ideas as accessible as possible. This can have only a positive impact on your grade. More important, paying attention to detail can be habit-forming. This influences your own character in a way that can pay off in the future. People like working with those they know they can trust to do an excellent job. Many grant applications are rejected simply because the researcher failed to pay attention to detail and fill out the application as instructed.

FORMAT

Unless directed otherwise, double-space your paper, use one-inch margins, and do not exceed five typed pages in length. Attach a separate title page with your name, class, section number, professor's name, and date you handed in the assignment.

SUBMISSION

Follow your instructor's directions regarding submission of your paper, because some instructors want papers turned in electronically. If you are handing in a paper copy, staple the pages together in the upper-left corner. Do not use a report cover; they look great but are slippery in a stack of other papers. Most plastic report covers don't let the papers lie flat when they are opened.

SOURCES

Reference the sources of any specific information you use by placing in parentheses the author's last name, the year of publication, and the page number(s). For example: (Ritzer, 1996:132). Give the full citation of the publication in a bibliography on a separate, titled page at the end of the paper (Ritzer, George. 1996. *The McDonaldization of Society,* *rev. ed.* Thousand Oaks, CA: Pine Forge Press). Readers of scientific articles often want to be able to look up information you cite. Furnish enough detail that they can easily do so.

WRITING TIPS

Some writing errors are common in undergraduate papers. Most instructors in the social sciences are primarily interested in the content of a paper, but a certain level of quality writing is expected of college students. Falling below these expectations can hurt your grade. For many, writing a scientifically oriented paper is a new experience. The standards, conventions, and style of writing are different from those of, say, a creative essay. It is important to aim for excellence and avoid mediocrity.

Here is a list of writing tips to assist you as you prepare your paper for submission to your instructor. Your paper will stand out if you follow these simple tips:

- Indent your paragraphs.
- Make sure every sentence contains a complete thought. For example, the statement "Although older students were more likely than younger students to be married" is a sentence fragment.
- Avoid long sentences, separated with many commas. Turn them into several sentences instead.
- Avoid use of contractions. For example, use "do not" instead of "don't."
- Use "than" instead of "then" when appropriate ("Ten is more *than* five").
- "Society's" means one society owning something. "Societies" means more than one society.
- "alot" is not a word; "a lot" is correct.
- The word "data" is plural. Its singular form is "datum." Use plural qualifiers when using the word *data*, as in "The data *are* presented in Table 1."
- "Would of" is often used but is incorrect. "Would have" is correct ("The data would have supported the hypothesis if the value of epsilon had been higher").
- "Woman" refers to one woman (singular); "women" refers to more than one.
- Identify compound words: "can not" should be "cannot," "where as" should be "whereas." Consult a good dictionary for other potential compound words, because context will determine when words like "can not" and "in to" should become "cannot" or "into" and when they should not.
- Always complete "more . . . than" statements. Here's a bad example: "More men had favorable attitudes toward drug use." More than what, or whom? Complete the thought. It might read, for instance, "More men than women had favorable attitudes toward drug use."

- There are *no* spaces between a sentence and its period, between a phrase and its comma, or between a phrase and a semicolon or full colon. There are no spaces between parentheses and their contents, or between quotation marks and their contents.
- There *are* spaces after periods and colons, after commas, and before and after parentheses.
- A suggestion: use inclusive language such as "she or he" rather than just "he," and "humankind" rather than "mankind." Some people feel offended by exclusive language. No one feels offended when inclusive language is used.
- Limit use of first person (use of "I," "me," "my," and "mine"). Many scientific journals are more willing to accept this style of writing today than in years previous, but the dominant style is still to write in third person. Of course, use first person when appropriate, such as giving your opinion in question 6 of your assignment (see Box 14.1).
- Use active verbs in place of passive verbs. The passive voice is boring and sounds descriptive, as in: "Data were collected by having an interviewer examine responses that were made by students to a series of questions." Active verbs are more exciting: "Students shared their opinions with interviewers who asked similar questions of all respondents."

A good way to make use of this list is to read it over before you begin writing your assignment, doing your best to keep the points in mind as you write. Review the list again after you have completed your first draft, and make additional corrections if necessary.

SUMMARY

Making discoveries is part of the process of social science, but discoveries can remain hidden or uninteresting unless their importance is clearly communicated to others. The questions posed to you in the assignment in this chapter give you an opportunity to clearly communicate that you understand the logic inherent in the process, the discoveries made through data collection and analysis, the method of interviews, and the importance of sampling. Finally, writing tips are offered so you can convey your ideas at a level expected of undergraduate college students. You have everything you need to produce an excellent paper. Don't settle for anything less; your education is an endeavor that will have lifelong benefits.

Human beings are naturally curious creatures. Discovery is intrinsically satisfying. It gives us a great deal of satisfaction to learn, to know, to grow, to become. As a teacher, I constantly make use of this natural inquisitiveness to stimulate interest in a particular field. You may feel your interests lie elsewhere than in sociology. Fair enough. Are you interested, though, in knowing whether or not human beings are capable of eliminating or reducing the amount of killing of other humans that takes place in the world? Sociology has something to contribute to our knowledge of what causes, and what can reduce, killing, among many other social maladies; these are dynamics that affect your life. The trick is to ask the right question, one that leads us as human beings into the process of discovering solutions.

Having you take part in adoption of your class hypothesis was part of this endeavor, as was giving you an opportunity to individually articulate your own theory for why you suspect the hypothesis to be true. *You* personally collected data that informed your hypothesis. *You discovered* whether or not there was support for the hypothesis. No doubt this stimulated new questions or assumptions, as well as ideas on how to collect better data. In other words, you have become a student of human behavior. *You* have discovered the social scientist inside you.

THE LARGER BENEFITS OF SOCIAL SCIENCE

Aside from the joy derived from answering questions for oneself, discovery often benefits other people. Can you list the names of scientists, living or dead, who have made new discoveries that ultimately had an impact on the quality of life of human beings? No doubt you are familiar with some of the more famous: Einstein, Freud, Darwin, and perhaps even Copernicus or Galileo. Lesser known are the equally important endeavors of women and minorities who broadened our knowledge, such as Marie Curie and her discovery of radioactivity and Florence Nightingale and her studies in epidemiology. Garrett Morgan invented the gas mask and the traffic signal. Daniel Hale Williams performed the first successful open heart surgery in the United States. Both Morgan and Williams were African Americans who made important contributions to the betterment of humankind.

Social scientists are in a unique position in society. Many use the scientific method to discover connections, relationships, and processes that pertain to various aspects of human social life. Their names are less well known, but their discoveries are equally exciting, important, and extremely influential. Friedrich Winslow Taylor developed a method in the 1930s, known as scientific management, that greatly increased productivity in industrial organizations. John Maynard Keynes's ideas on economics had an enormous impact on how modern societies developed after World War II. Bronislaw Malinowski's insights into the function of magic and religion, based on his observations of the Trobriand Islanders, still produce greater understanding of these processes in modern societies. George Gallup, a statistician by training, developed a method of polling Americans to reveal remarkably accurate portraits of attitudes and voting behavior in the 1960s; his methods are still used today. Sociologist William Julius Wilson has clearly documented the correlation between economic decline and increasing racism. Understanding of such processes allows us to make better choices, create better policies, and ultimately produce a better world.

My own findings on research I conducted on child day care in the early 1990s resulted in policy changes in government. I gained a great deal of personal satisfaction, knowing that the information I collected ultimately acted as a catalyst to improve the lives of many young children. What a humbling experience to have contributed to the great body of knowledge that is available to all humankind. To be a scientist, natural or social, is to be motivated by the knowledge that one's work has implications for others. It is why people will spend months living with gorillas, or counting cells through a microscope, or going door-to-door asking questions of others, risking insult, rejection, and ridicule.

If discovering things for yourself that may also benefit others excites you, you may be a sociologist in the making. Sociology is the science of society. Imagine discovering a better way to live. You now know how to do it.

REVIEW QUESTIONS

1. What is involved in producing an excellent final paper for this project?
2. How do the questions posed in the final assignment help affirm the stages of the social scientific enterprise?
3. If you were an instructor, would you assign a higher grade to papers that meet formatting expectations for college work? Why or why not?
4. Now that you've taken part in a social science data collection project, how important do you feel knowledge is that is gained through social science? What purpose(s) does it serve for human beings?

GLOSSARY

Androcentric Male-centered.

Behaviors Actions exhibited by units under study. Behaviors can be carried out by individuals or larger social units such as organizations.

Beliefs Values or attitudes held by individuals that take on a social component when collectively shared and reinforced by a group.

Causal model A model inherent in the scientific method; the belief that the world is ordered in terms of cause and effect.

Causation When a change in an independent variable *causes* a change in the dependent variable.

Closed-ended questions Questions in an interview or survey with a predetermined and limited number of possible responses.

Codebook A document separate from an interview, listing all variables measured in the study, the question or questions asked to measure the variable, and a number assigned to every possible response to every question.

Composite variable A variable comprising more than one indicator of a concept.

Constant An aspect of social life that has no change or variation within a given context. For example, if everyone in a group is twenty years of age, then age is a constant in that it does not vary in the group.

Constructs Individual perceptions and assumptions regarding how the world is ordered.

Contingency questions Questions determining whether or not other questions in a survey or interview will be asked of the interviewee.

Continuous variables Variables that are infinitely divisible.

Control variable A third variable examined to see how its presence influences the relationship between the independent and dependent variables.

Correlation An observed covariation between two variables; as one (the independent variable) changes, a change in the second variable (the dependent variable) is also observed.

Covary Two variables that change together. When one variable changes at a rate consistent with another, they are said to covary.

Data cleaning Identifying and correcting errors made during the data entry process.

Dependent variable The variable in a causal hypothesis believed to be affected by the influence of another variable identified as the independent variable.

Deportment How a person presents himself or herself to others.

Discrete variables Variables with definite categories not easily further divided.

Ecological fallacy Assuming that patterns observed at the group level are also true at the individual level.

Ego involvement An error of human inquiry in which data are interpreted in a biased manner that affirms one's pet theories or ideas.

Empathy The ability to understand another's decisions and feelings.

Empirical articles Those reporting the results of research involving new data being collected about a topic.

Empiricism The practice of testing beliefs, ideas, and theories through sensory input or observations of the world as opposed to intuition, faith, or logic alone.

Ex post facto hypothesizing Guessing after the fact, or creating one or more plausible explanations of why two variables are correlated.

Falsification Before a study is undertaken, the practice of identifying the kind of information collected that would be interpreted as negating or failing to support a hypothesis.

Hypothesis A supposed relationship between two or more variables.

Ideology A vision of society or a set of beliefs that have the consequence, if believed, of benefiting one group in society at the expense of another.

Idiographic mode of explanation An attempt to uncover all the richness and detail of a particular situation to understand its uniqueness.

Illogical reasoning Deducing something such that one thought or idea does not meaningfully follow from the other; it is nonsensical.

Independent variable The variable in a causal hypothesis believed to exert an influence on another variable identified as the dependent variable.

Index A series of several questions or indicators of a particular variable that are given equal weight when added to create a composite.

Indicator The actual question or item used to measure a variable.

Institutional review board A board at a research institution, consisting of experienced social researchers, that protects human rights by reviewing research proposals before they are carried out.

Intelligence quotient A score on a test by the same name, taken to be a valid and reliable indicator of an individual's overall intelligence.

Interval variables Continuous data with hierarchical characteristics measured in equidistant intervals. SPSS substitutes the word *Scale* for interval level variables.

Interview schedule The complete list of questions and instructions constituting the content of an interview.

Law of large numbers The larger the sample, the more accurate the results, or the less error there will be in representing the views or actions of the entire population.

Longitudinal study A study that involves repeated measures over an extended period of time.

Maximum variability When the same proportion of cases is represented within each attribute of a variable.

Measurement error Variation in data caused by mistakes made in the data collection process.

Measurement validity Exists when an indicator measures what it is intended to measure.

Measures of central tendency Statistics giving an overall measure of a group characteristic, such as the mean, median, and mode.

Mechanical solidarity Social solidarity created through a sense of face-to-face relationships and kinship ties that, according to Durkheim, is typically found in traditional societies.

Meticulous rituals of surveillance Daily activities in which we are asked by store personnel, online sites, and the like to reveal personal information about ourselves.

Missing data Information that was not collected on one or more interview schedule items during the interview process, because of refusal or failure to answer or interviewer error.

Negativistic logic An assumption of the scientific method whereby every statement is assumed to be false until incontrovertible proof renders the negative position untenable.

Nominal definition A specific definition of a concept that the researcher will use for the purposes of the study.

Nominal variables Variables measured at the nominal level of measurement, which contain discrete differences of kind.

Nomothetic mode of explanation An attempt to identify the major explanations for a particular phenomenon, to articulate possible commonalities with similar situations.

Nonempirical articles Articles doing something other than reporting the findings from data collection. Such articles offer something else to the scientific enterprise, such as exploring or applying new theories.

Nonrational Aspects of life that have not been examined through the use of logic.

One-shot case study A study that involves collecting data at one point in time only.

Open-ended questions Questions asked of an interviewee with no predetermined responses or categories created.

Operational definition The actual manner in which a variable is measured. In survey research, this often takes the form of a specific question or set of questions.

Operationalization The process of deciding exactly how a variable will be measured.

Ordinal variables Variables measured at the ordinal level of measurement, with attributes containing some kind of hierarchical difference. This can include more or less of something, or stronger versus weaker response.

Organic solidarity Social solidarity created through the realization that various parts of society are interdependent for survival and success. According to Durkheim, organic solidarity is typical in modern societies.

Parsimonious A state of a particular model of human behavior in which almost all the variation is accounted for or explained by the independent variables identified in the model.

Partial-order tables Tables controlling for a third variable, produced during table elaboration. Called **partials** for short.

Population A group that is the focus of an investigation.

Positivistic logic A process of inquiry involving first adopting certain beliefs or perspectives and then gathering supporting information.

Precoding The process of identifying numerical values or codes directly on the interview schedule so as to facilitate data entry.

Primary sources Articles reporting on the original collection or analysis of data. In the humanities, primary sources are actual historical artifacts such as a letter or journal.

Privacy Freedom from intrusion into one's own life or activities.

Probing A practice in interviews where the interviewer prompts the interviewee to share additional information.

Quantification The process of assigning numbers to collected information so as to facilitate computer data entry and analysis.

Randomization In sampling, randomization refers to the principle of every unit of the population having an equal chance of being included in the sample.

Rapport The feeling of trust and comfort the interviewee has toward the interviewer.

Reactive A situation in social research where the information being gathered may be changed simply because of the data collection method.

Reliability The extent to which a measure produces the same results in repeated trials of measuring the same thing.

Research monograph A book describing the results of an original research project.

Reverse coded Reversing the scores on a particular scale item so that the values increase in the same manner as other indicators in the same scale.

Sample of convenience A sample generated simply by gathering information from units most easily accessed by the researcher.

Sampling Learning about a population by studying a subset of its units.

Scale A series of several questions or indicators that may be given different weights added to create a composite variable.

Secondary sources Sources describing a primary source or attempting to make sense of it in some fashion.

Self-fulfilling prophecy A process in which the expectations of others so affect an individual that the person becomes what others expect.

Social problem A characteristic of society generally defined as something that should be reduced or eliminated because of its negative impact.

Social Science Citation Index A resource combing through hundreds of social science journals and organizing them by subject, author, and cited references.

Sociological imagination A way of thinking about the world that sees personal problems as the result of public issues.

Sociological problem A puzzle regarding human social behavior needing to be solved. Answers to sociological problems are typically generalizable to more than one social situation.

SPSS A proprietary statistical software package.

Spurious correlation A correlation between two variables caused by the effect of a third variable.

Table elaboration The process of controlling for variables other than the independent and dependent variables through examination of cross-tabulation tables derived from the original relationship.

Tautologies Statements that are true by definition and thus cannot be disproved.

Unit of analysis The entity or "thing" whose behavior the researcher is interested in studying. Individuals, groups, organizations, and countries are examples of units of analysis.

Validity The accuracy of a study or measure.

Variable A concept defined such that it can be measured and has various possible values.

Variation A feature of life that differs among individuals or groups. For example, if the ages of individuals in a group range widely between twenty and sixty years, the feature of age for that group exhibits variation.

Zero-order table A cross-tabulation table depicting the interrelation of independent and dependent variables.

BIBLIOGRAPHY

American Sociological Association. "Sociology and General Education, " *ASA Task Force Report to Council.* Washington, D.C.: American Sociological Association, July 15, 2006. Retrieved May 26, 2009, from http://www.asanet.org/galleries/Governance/General%20Education%20Council%20Rep ort%207-15-2006.pdf.

Annas, G. J., and Grodin, M. A. *The Nazi Doctors and the Nuremberg Code.* New York: Oxford University Press, 1992.

Asch, S. E. "Studies of Independence and Conformity: A Minority of One Against a Unanimous Majority." *Psychological Monographs*, 1956, *70*, (9).

Babbie, E. *The Practice of Social Research, 12th ed.* Belmont, Calif.: Wadsworth, 2007.

Bain, K. *What the Best Teachers Do.* Cambridge, Mass.: Harvard University Press, 2004.

Balko, R. "Criminalization Doesn't Curb Drug Use." *Capitalism*, 2004. Retrieved April 27, 2009, from http://www.capmag.com/article.asp?ID=3435.

Bamshad, M. J., and Olson, S. T. "Does Race Exist?" *Scientific American*, Dec. 2003, pp. 113.

Boyer, E. *Scholarship Reconsidered.* San Francisco: Jossey-Bass, 1997.

Brookfield, S. *Becoming a Critically Reflective Teacher.* San Francisco: Jossey-Bass, 1995.

Brotherton, D. "Old Heads Tell Their Stories." *Free Inquiry in Creative Sociology*, 2000, *28*, (1), 41–56.

Campbell, D. T., and Stanley, J. C. *Experimental and Quasi-Experimental Designs for Research.* Chicago: Rand McNally, 1966.

Cantor, J., Alfonso, H., and Zillmann, D. "The Persuasive Effectiveness of the Peer Appeal and a Communicator's First Hand Experience." *Communication Research*, 1976, *3*, 203–310.

Chan, J. "When Does Retrieval Induce Forgetting and When Does It Induce Facilitation? Implications for Retrieval Inhibition, Testing Effect, and Text Processing." *Journal of Memory and Language*, 2009, *61*(2), 153–170.

Cicognani, E., and others. "Social Participation, Sense of Community and Social Well Being: A Study on American, Italian and Iranian University Students." *Social Indicators Research*, Oct. 2008, *89*(1), 97–112.

Collins, R. *Sociological Insight: An Introduction to Nonobvious Sociology.* New York: Oxford, 1992.

Comte, A. *The Positive Philosophy.* (F. Ferre, ed.). Indianapolis, Ind.: Hackett, 1988.

Cook, K. S., and Whitmeyer, J. M. "Two Approaches to Social Structure: Exchange Theory and Network Analysis." *Annual Review of Sociology*, 1992, *18*, 109–127. http://arjournals.annualreviews .org/doi/abs/10.1146/annurev.so.18.080192.000545. Retrieved Oct. 20, 2009.

Corona, R., Gonzalez, T., Cohen, R., Edwards, C., and Edmonds, T. "Richmond Latino Needs Assessment: A Community-University Partnership to Identify Health Concerns and Service *Needs* for Latino Youth." *Journal of Community Health,* June 2009, *34*(3), pp. 195–201. DOI: 10.1007/s10900-008–9140–6 (*AN 37143276*). Retrieved Oct. 20, 2009.

Darwin, C. *The Origin of Species.* New York: Gramercy, 1859/1979.

Durkheim, E., and Lukes, S. (eds.). Trans. by W. D. Halls. *The Rules of the Sociological Method.* New York: Macmillan, 1982.

Fink, L. D. *Creating Significant Learning Experiences.* San Francisco: Jossey-Bass, 2003.

Finkel, D. *Teaching with Your Mouth Shut.* Portsmouth, N.H.: Boynton/Cook, 2000.

Friesen, B. K. "Powerlessness in Adolescence: Exploiting Heavy Metal Listeners." In C. R. Saunders (ed.), *Marginal Conventions: Popular Culture, Mass Media and Social Deviance.* Bowling Green, Ohio: Bowling Green University Press, 1990.

Friesen, B. K., and Epstein. J. S. "Rock 'n' Roll Ain't Noise Pollution: Artistic Conventions and Tensions in the Major Sub-Genres of Heavy Metal Music." *Popular Music and Society*, 1994, *18*(3), 1–18.

Gilligan, C. *In a Different Voice.* Cambridge, Mass.: Harvard University Press, 1982.

Glock, C. Y., Ringer, B. B., and Babbie, E. R. *To Comfort and to Challenge: A Dilemma of the Contemporary Church.* University of California Press: Berkeley and Los Angeles, 1967.

Goldenberg, S. *Thinking Sociologically.* Belmont, Calif.: Wadsworth, 1987.

Humphreys, L. *Tearoom Trade.* London: Duckworth, 1970.

Kellehear, A. "Dying as a Social Relationship: A Sociological Review of Debates on the Determination of Death." *Social Science & Medicine*, April 2008, *66*(7), 1533–1544. http://www.sciencedirect.com/science, Doi: 10.1016/j.socscimed.2007.12.023. Retrieved Oct. 20, 2009.

Loether, H., and McTavish, D. *Descriptive and Inferential Statistics: An Introduction.* Boston: Allyn & Bacon, 1980.

Marx, K. *Capital: Volume 1: A Critique of Political Economy.* (B. Fowkes, trans.). New York: Penguin, 1992.

McFarland, S. 1996. "Keeping the Faith: The Roles of Selective Exposure and Avoidance in Maintaining Religious Beliefs." In *Religion & Mass Media.* Thousand Oaks, Calif.: Sage, 1996.

McKeachie, W. *McKeachie's Teaching Tips.* Belmont, Calif.: Wadsworth, 2005.

McKinney, K. *Enhancing Learning Through the Scholarship of Teaching and Learning: The Challenges and Joys of Juggling.* San Francisco: Jossey-Bass, 2007.

Merton, R. K. *Social Theory and Social Structure.* Toronto, Canada: Collier-Macmillan, 1968.

Milgram, S. "Behavioral Study of Obedience." *Journal of Abnormal and Social Psychology*, 1963, *67*, 371–378.

Mills, C. W. *The Sociological Imagination.* New York: Grove Press, 1959.

Morsink, J. *The Universal Declaration of Human Rights.* Philadelphia: University of Pennsylvania Press, 1999.

Peterson, R. R. "A Re-Evaluation of the Economic Consequences of Divorce." *American Sociological Review,* June 1996, *61*, 528–536.

Ragin, C. *Constructing Social Research.* Thousand Oaks, Calif.: Pine Forge, 1994.

Reverby, S. *Tuskegee's Truths: Rethinking the Tuskegee Syphilis Study.* Chapel Hill: University of North Carolina Press, 2000.

Rosenhan, D. L. "On Being Sane in Insane Places." *Science*, Jan. 1973, *179*, 250–258.

Rothenberg, P. (ed.). *White Privilege: Essential Readings on the Other Side of Racism, 3rd ed.* New York: Worth, 2008.

Sjoberg, G., and Nett, R. *A Methodology for Social Research.* New York: Harper & Row, 1968.

Stack, S., and Gundlach, J. "The Effect of Country Music on Suicide." *Social Forces*, 1992, *71*, 211–218.

Staples, W. G. *The Culture of Surveillance.* New York : St. Martin's Press, 1997.

Tavris, C.. *The Mismeasure of Woman.* New York: Touchstone, 1992.

U.S. Census. *Earnings by Occupation and Education, Table 1.* Decennial Census, 2005. Retrieved July 26, 2009, from http://www.census.gov/hhes/www/income/earnings/call1usboth.html.

Webb, E. J., Campbell, D. T., Schwartz, R. D., and Sechrest, L. *Unobtrusive Measures: Non-Reactive Research in the Social Sciences*. Chicago: Rand McNally, 1966.

Weitzman, L. J. *The Divorce Revolution: The Unexpected Social and Economic Consequences for Women and Children in America.* New York: Free Press, 1985.

Weimar, M. *Learner-Centered Teaching.* San Francisco: Jossey-Bass, 2002.

Yunus, M. *Banker to the Poor: Micro-Lending and the Battle Against World Poverty.* New York: PublicAffairs, 2003.

Zelditch, M. Jr. "Can You Really Study an Army in the Laboratory?" In A. Etzioni (ed.), *A Sociological Reader on Complex Organizations*. New York: Holt, 1969.

INDEX